HAMLET

Dear ~~Roberto~~

Have fun with it!

Ben

27/3/96

THEORY IN PRACTICE SERIES

General Editor: Nigel Wood, School of English, University of Birmingham

Associate Editors: Tony Davies and Barbara Rasmussen, University of Birmingham

Titles:
Antony and Cleopatra
Don Juan
Hamlet
Henry IV
Mansfield Park
Measure for Measure
The Merchant of Venice
A Passage to India
The Prelude
The Tempest
The Waste Land

HAMLET

EDITED BY
PETER J. SMITH AND
NIGEL WOOD

OPEN UNIVERSITY PRESS
BUCKINGHAM · PHILADELPHIA

Open University Press
Celtic Court
22 Ballmoor
Buckingham
MK18 1XW

and
1900 Frost Road, Suite 101
Bristol, PA 19007, USA

First Published 1996

A catalogue record of this book is available from the British Library

ISBN 0 335 19235 1 (pb)

Library of Congress Cataloging-in-Publication Data

Hamlet / edited by Peter J. Smith and Nigel Wood [and] Mark
    Thornton Burnett.
        p.   cm. — (Theory in practice series)
    Includes bibliographical references and index.
    ISBN 0-335-19235-1 (pbk.)
    1. Shakespeare, William, 1564–1616. Hamlet. 2. Denmark — In
literature. 3. Princes in literature. 4. Tragedy. I. Smith, Peter J.,
1964– . II. Wood, Nigel, 1953– . III. Burnett, Mark Thornton.
IV. Series.
PR2807.H26238   1996
822.3'3 — dc20   95-31559
                                                                      CIP

Typeset by Colset Pte Ltd, Singapore
Printed in Great Britain by St Edmundsbury Press,
Bury St Edmunds, Suffolk

Contents

The Editors and Contributors   vii
Editors' Preface   ix
How to Use this Book   xi
A Note on the Texts Used   xiii

Introduction   1
PETER J. SMITH

1   'For they are actions that a man might play': Hamlet
    as Trickster   24
    MARK THORNTON BURNETT

2   *Hamlet*: Text in Performance   55
    PETER HOLLAND

3   Explaining Woman's Frailty: Feminist Readings of
    Gertrude   83
    SHARON OUDITT

4   'Vnfolde your selfe': Jacques Lacan and the
    Psychoanalytic Reading of *Hamlet*   108
    NIGEL WHEALE

Endpìece   133
NIGEL WOOD

Notes	138
References	145
Further Reading	154
Index	158

The Editors and Contributors

MARK THORNTON BURNETT teaches in the School of English at The Queen's University of Belfast. He has published numerous essays on English Renaissance drama and culture, in books, anthologies and such journals as *Cahiers Elisabéthains*, *Connotations*, *Criticism*, *Emblematica*, *English Literary Renaissance*, *Parergon*, *The Review of English Studies*, *Studia Neophilologica*, *Studies in Philology* and *The Yearbook of English Studies*. He is the co-editor of *New Essays on 'Hamlet'* (1994) and has recently completed a study of master–servant relations in English Renaissance culture. His current project is a new edition of Marlowe's complete plays for Everyman Paperbacks.

PETER HOLLAND is University Lecturer in Drama in the English Faculty at Cambridge, the post previously held by Raymond Williams. He has written and edited many books and articles on theatre analysis and Shakespeare in performance and has recently edited *A Midsummer Night's Dream* in the Oxford Shakespeare (1994). He has reviewed the year's Shakespeare productions in England for *Shakespeare Survey* since 1990.

SHARON OUDITT is a lecturer in English at Nottingham Trent University and teaches broadly in the fields of English literature and Women's Studies. She is the author of *Fighting Forces, Writing Women: Identity and Ideology in the First World War* (1993) and of other articles and reviews on women's writing and feminist theory. She is presently working on a second book on women's war writing.

NIGEL WHEALE teaches English with Text and Image Studies at Anglia Polytechnic University, Cambridge. His recent publications include *Shakespeare in the Changing Curriculum* (1991) co-edited with Lesley Aers, and *The Postmodern Arts: An Introduction* (1995). He contributed two chapters to *Poets on Writing: Great Britain 1970–1991*, edited by Denise Riley (1992), and entries for *Cultural Icons* edited by James Park (1991) and the *Oxford Companion to Twentieth-Century Poetry in English* edited by Ian Hamilton (1994). His latest collection of poetry is *Phrasing the Light* (1994).

PETER J. SMITH is lecturer in the Department of English and Media Studies at the Nottingham Trent University. He is the author of *Social Shakespeare: Aspects of Renaissance Dramaturgy and Contemporary Society* (1995). He has edited Marlowe's *Jew of Malta* (1994) and is associate editor of the international journal of renaissance studies, *Cahiers Elisabéthains*. He is currently working on scatology in the early modern period.

NIGEL WOOD is senior lecturer in English at the University of Birmingham. He is the author of a study of Jonathan Swift (1986), and of several essays on literary theory, has co-edited essays on John Gay (1989), edited a selection from Frances Burney's diaries and journals (1990), and is general editor of the *Theory in Practice* series. To date he has edited the volumes on *Don Juan*, *The Prelude*, *Mansfield Park* (all 1993), *The Tempest*, *Henry IV, Parts One and Two*, *Measure for Measure* and *The Merchant of Venice* (all 1995), and co-edited (with Tony Davies) the volumes on *A Passage to India* and *The Waste Land* (both 1994).

Editors' Preface

The object of this series is to help bridge the divide between the understanding of theory and the interpretation of individual texts. Students are therefore introduced to theory in practice. Although contemporary critical theory is now taught in many colleges and universities, it is often separated from the day-to-day consideration of literary texts that is the staple ingredient of most tuition in English. A thorough dialogue between theoretical and literary texts is thus avoided.

Each of these specially commissioned volumes of essays seeks by contrast to involve students of literature in the questions and debates that emerge when a variety of theoretical perspectives are brought to bear on a selection of 'canonical' literary texts. Contributors were not asked to provide a comprehensive survey of the arguments involved in a particular theoretical position, but rather to discuss in detail the implications for interpretation found in particular essays or studies, and then, taking these into account, to offer a reading of the literary text.

This rubric was designed to avoid two major difficulties which commonly arise in the interaction between literary and theoretical texts: the temptation to treat a theory as a bloc of formulaic rules that could be brought to bear on any text with roughly predictable results; and the circular argument that texts are constructed as such merely by the theoretical perspective from which we choose to regard them. The former usually leads to studies that are really just footnotes to the adopted theorists, whereas the latter is effortlessly self-fulfilling.

It would be disingenuous to claim that our interests in the teaching of theory were somehow neutral and not open to debate. The idea for this series arose from the teaching of theory in relation to specific texts. It is inevitable, however, that the practice of theory poses significant questions as to just what 'texts' might be and where the dividing lines between text and context may be drawn. Our hope is that this series will provide a forum for debate on just such issues as these which are continually posed when students of literature try to engage with theory in practice.

Tony Davies
Barbara Rasmussen
Nigel Wood

How to Use
this Book

Each of these essays is composed of a theoretical and a practical element. Contributors were asked to identify the main features of their perspective on the text (exemplified by a single theoretical essay or book) and then to illustrate their own attempts to put this into practice.

We realize that many readers new to recent theory will find its specific vocabulary and leading concepts strange and difficult to relate to current critical traditions in most English courses.

The format of this book has been designed to help if this is your situation, and we would advise the following:

(i) Before reading the essays, glance at the editor's introduction where the literary text's critical history is discussed, and

(ii) also at the prefatory information immediately before the essays, where the editor attempts to supply a context for the adopted theoretical position.

(iii) If you would like to develop your reading in any of these areas, turn to the annotated further reading section at the end of the volume, where you will find brief descriptions of those texts that each contributor has considered of more advanced interest. There are also full citations of the texts to which the contributors have referred in the references. It is also possible that more local information will be contained in notes to the essays.

(iv) The contributors have often regarded the chosen theoretical texts as points of departure and it is also in the nature of theoretical discussion to apply and test ideas on a variety of texts. Turn, therefore, to question and answer sections that follow each essay which are designed to allow contributors to comment and expand on their views in more general terms.

A Note on
the Texts Used

Quotations from *Hamlet* are taken from the Oxford University Press volume edited G.R. Hibbard (1987).

In addition, the following Shakespeare editions have been consulted:

Julius Caesar	ed. Marvin Spevack (Cambridge, 1988)
Love's Labour's Lost	ed. G.R. Hibbard (Oxford, 1990)
The Tragedy of Macbeth	ed. Nicholas Brooke (Oxford, 1990)
The Merry Wives of Windsor	ed. T.W. Craik (Oxford, 1990)

Introduction

PETER J. SMITH

[W]hen the wind is southerly, I know a hawk from a handsaw.
(II.ii.373–4)

Hamlet is both the most discussed play in world literature and the least explained. Its complexity and intensity have often compelled its critics to acknowledge their resignation or bewilderment. For example, *Hamlet*'s currently most unfashionable yet abidingly perceptive commentator remarks that 'the text admits of no sure interpretation' and, having tried to explain both Hamlet's delay and his silence, is forced to conclude despondently: 'This paragraph states my view imperfectly' (Bradley 1974: 128). Wilson (1935: 229) ascribes this difficulty to the playwright's evasive design: 'we were never intended to reach the heart of the mystery. That it has a heart is an illusion; the mystery itself is an illusion; Hamlet is an illusion'. For T.S. Eliot (1951: 143–4) 'the play is most certainly an artistic failure . . . [it] is puzzling, and disquieting as is none of the others. . . . [But the] grounds of *Hamlet*'s failure are not immediately obvious'.[1] Nor might we be entitled to consider this uncertainty the feature of a critically unsophisticated past. G.R. Hibbard, who edited the play as recently as 1987, is similarly nonplussed: Shakespeare's tragedy 'means something, even though, or perhaps because, that "something" admits of no ready or simple definition' (Hibbard 1987: 29); and Rosenberg (1992: 294) concludes his mammoth study of the play in performance (which is just short of a thousand pages) with the devastatingly inconclusive statement, 'All the words about Hamlet, almost three centuries of words, and as many of stagings, and the adventure into the depths of the play has hardly begun'.

Even the play's most cultivated commentators have decided that it is unsatisfactory. Writing just after the Restoration, John Evelyn's disdain for *Hamlet* is symptomatic of a wish to leave behind Elizabethan boorishness and signifies the aspirations of his own neoclassical era: 'I saw *Hamlet* Pr[rince]: of Denmark played: but now the old playe began to disgust the refined age' (Evelyn 1955, III: 304).[2] Voltaire's mischievous description of the plot almost succeeds in forcing one to concede his initial premise:

> it is a vulgar and barbarous drama, which would not be tolerated by the vilest populace of France, or Italy. Hamlet becomes crazy in the second act, and his mistress becomes crazy in the third; the prince slays the father of his mistress under the pretence of killing a rat, and the heroine throws herself into the river; a grave is dug on the stage, and the grave-diggers talk quod[l]ibets worthy of themselves, while holding skulls in their hands; Hamlet responds to their nasty vulgarities in silliness no less disgusting. In the meanwhile another of the actors conquers Poland. Hamlet, his mother, and his father-in-law, carouse on the stage; songs are sung at table; there is quarrelling, fighting, killing – one would imagine this piece to be the work of a drunken savage.
>
> (Williamson 1950: 18–19)

Yet, in the next breath, Voltaire is insisting on the play's unaccountable achievements:

> there are to be found in *Hamlet* . . . some sublime passages, worthy of the greatest genius. It seems as though nature had mingled in the brain of Shakespeare the greatest conceivable strength and grandeur with whatsoever witless vulgarity can devise that is lowest and most detestable.
>
> (Williamson 1950: 19)

Hamlet causes consternation to Voltaire's Enlightenment sensibility; its mixture of the rarefied and the crude contravenes his ideals.

Hamlet retained its difficulties for the Romantics, confounding Schlegel's mathematical rigour: 'This enigmatical work resembles those irrational equations in which a fraction of unknown magnitude always remains, that will in no way admit of solution' (Williamson 1950: 38). Byron seems to intuit, in this mystery, a sublimity which both puzzles and elates him:

> I feel perplexed, confused, and inextricably self-involved; a nightmare sensation of impotence and vain endeavour weighs upon me. . . . What *is* Hamlet? What means he? Are we, too, like him, the creatures of some incomprehensible sport, and the real universe just such another story, where all the deepest feelings, and dearest sympathies are insulted, and the understanding mocked? . . . And who can read this wonderful play without the profoundest emotion? And yet what is it but a colossal enigma?
>
> (Bate 1992: 336–7)

Critics, old and new, literary and non-literary, English and non-English have struggled with *Hamlet* for nearly half a millennium. There is probably more criticism on it than on any other text, and this has spawned a secondary industry; books such as Waldock (1931), Conklin (1947) and Weitz (1965) take as their object of study not Shakespeare's play, but the plenitude of critical responses that have sought to address its problems.

Recently, however, it has been proposed that this century has seen 'the balance of academic judgement . . . tipped somewhat in favour of *King Lear*' (Hibbard 1987: 1). R.A. Foakes, in his sustained examination of the critical fortunes of both plays, entitled competitively *Hamlet versus Lear*, explains this tendency in terms of the way that *King Lear* 'speaks more largely than the other tragedies to the anxieties and problems of the modern world' (Foakes 1993: 224). Yet the *Hamlet* industry shows no signs whatever of decline; this volume is itself a further contribution to it. *Hamlet* is still the most frequently produced play in the theatre, the most commented upon, and continues to offer the most prestigious acting role to aspiring Oliviers.[3] Franco Zeffirelli's 1989 film version, starring Mel Gibson, at once capitalized upon and reinforced the play's popular appeal. The ponderous malcontent clutching a skull or meditating upon 'To be or not to be' has afforded numerous opportunities for comic sketches and advertising campaigns. Tom Stoppard's *Rosencrantz and Guildenstern Are Dead* (first performed in 1966 and filmed in 1990, directed by the playwright) projects the absurd situation of *Waiting for Godot* on to Shakespeare's most helpless characters. At the end of Bruce Robinson's comic film, *Withnail and I*

(1985), the disenchantment with the ailing Sixties is powerfully depicted as the eponymous hero, an out-of-work actor (played by Richard E. Grant), bitterly declaims 'What a piece of work is a man'. More recently, when the hero of Salman Rushdie's poignant allegory, *Haroun and the Sea of Stories*, misconnects the brain of the Hoopoe bird 'it burst into a weird little song: You must sing, a-down a-down/And you call him a-down-a' (Rushdie 1990: 169). 'Gertrude Talks Back' by Margaret Atwood, comically deflates the notions of female modesty found in Shakespeare's play and subverts the standing of the patriarchal Bard:

> And let me tell you, everyone sweats at a time like that, as you'd find out very soon if you ever gave it a try. A real girlfriend would do you a heap of good. Not like that pasty-faced what's-her-name, all trussed up like a prize turkey in those touch-me-not corsets of hers. If you ask me, there's something off about that girl. . . . Get yourself someone more down-to-earth. Have a nice roll in the hay. Then you can talk to me about nasty sties.
>
> (Atwood 1993: 17)

Alan Isler's novel, *The Prince of West End Avenue* (1995), is similarly iconoclastic, taking place in a Manhattan retirement home in which the residents are preparing an amateur production of *Hamlet*: 'Sinsheimer had instituted certain judicious cuts in *Hamlet* because of its abnormal length and because of weak bladders on both sides of the proscenium' (Isler 1995: 165). As Holderness (1987: 2) has insisted, 'Shakespeare's *Hamlet* is . . . part of the common currency of our culture, and possesses meanings and values which cannot be contained by its existence as a literary text for study, or a theatrical script'. Despite the recent formulation of a postmodern Shakespeare comprising the rejection of canonical greatness, the abandonment of ideas of organic wholeness and the rigorous questioning of established hierarchies of academic discourse, *Hamlet* retains its cultural centrality (Grady 1991: 190–246).

Hamlet's paradoxical status ought by now to be clear. On the one hand, it is the text most resistant to critical explication, a play which is construed in terms of its evasive and perversely riddling condition – Jones (1949: 22) described it, in suitably Oedipal terms, as 'the Sphinx of modern Literature'. On the other hand, it is the most popular and public of English artefacts, the most canonical text by the most canonical author of world literature, a text which defines even as it is defined by both the theatrical and educational institutions in which it figures so prominently.

II

there has been much throwing about of brains.

(II.ii.354–5)

How, then, might we situate a volume like this in relation to *Hamlet*? How can critical theory inform the study of such a play? This is not the place to rehearse the battles that resulted from the impact on world higher education of literary theory in the early 1980s, but it is worth noting that although we may reasonably have expected such a conflict to be resolved long ago, in Shakespeare studies it is still pronounced.[4] Major theoretical collections like Jonathan Dollimore and Alan Sinfield's *Political Shakespeare*, John Drakakis's *Alternative Shakespeares* and Patricia Parker and Geoffrey Hartman's *Shakespeare and the Question of Theory* (which contains a whole section on *Hamlet*) have been published now for a full decade – all appeared in 1985. Yet the opposition they encountered, which was both intellectual and institutional, has not gone away. Foakes (1993: 10) accuses theoretical criticism of attacking the 'integrity' of Shakespeare and, in a fit of extreme paranoia, describes 'a wider post-structuralist onslaught on the cultural authority of Shakespeare, who has been toppled from his pedestal' by indecent acts of 'iconoclastic smashing [and] critical arrogance'. Foakes is clearly opposed to the kinds of theoretical engagement with Shakespearian texts which a volume like this one proposes. His description of theoretically interested critics who 'seem to enjoy trashing Shakespeare, like schoolboys suddenly released from subservience to a formidable headmaster, and taking their revenge on him' might be supposed to be an ungenerous and idiosyncratic over-reaction were it not for the fact that he is not alone (Foakes 1993: 11). Lately William Kerrigan has written in truculent terms about what he perceives to be the vanity of theory. *Hamlet* is identified as a key text which needs rescuing from theoretical sophistry:

> Perhaps *Hamlet* is now a play object for contemporary critics. Their new methods and concerns give them no way to solve its mysteries and unravel its cruxes, so they paw at it, make gestures at it, and mount mischievous little runs on its margins to catch at least a bit of the crumbling old classic in their nets of inter-textuality. But this, to my mind, is cowardice, and a cowardice that leaves the world less interesting.
>
> (Kerrigan 1994: 4)

For Kerrigan, 'literary theory seem[s] to be a blank check for shallow arrogance', and he goes on to condemn it as the intellectual position of a few eccentric and over-sensitive radicals: 'We get ideology rather than ideas. . . . We get the bland modern pride known as "political correctness"' (Kerrigan 1994: 3, 32). The eminent Shakespearian, John Bayley, concurs, blending his condemnation of PC with blatant Francophobia: theory, he writes, like 'all rationalist ideology . . . is an end in itself. . . . Theory must be . . . strictly controlled both by political correctness and a Gallic domination of the abstract' (Bayley 1994: 13). In Brian Vickers's 500-page anti-theory polemic the tainted whiff of 'ideology' reappears.[5] Vickers laments the subjugation of the Shakespearian text to what he characterizes as the tyranny of theoretical orthodoxy:

> each group has a specific ideology, a self-serving aim of proving the validity of their own approach by their readings of the text. Shakespeare's plays, for so long the primary focus of the critic's and scholar's attention, are now secondary, subordinated to the imperialism and self-advancement of the particular group. . . . All of them, I argue, distort the text . . . to make it fit their critical theories or ideologies.
>
> (Vickers 1993: xii, xvi)

This description begs a number of questions; for example, what kind of critic would happily disprove 'the validity of their own approach by their readings of the text'? And what is the effect of the sly use of 'scholar'? Is it simply to suggest the relative ease and monotony of theoretically orientated criticism as opposed to the rigorous study practised by traditional Shakespearian *scholars* (including presumably Vickers)? Finally, what does the undistorted text look like, *the* transcendental and immortal version of what Shakespeare intended or what Vickers tells us Shakespeare intended, predicated on his own 'readings of the text'? For critics like Foakes, Kerrigan, Bayley and Vickers, critical practice which is hospitable to theoretical ideas developed in other disciplines – sociology, history and especially politics – is demonized as an attempt to subvert the cultural authority of the Bard and, it might be added, the senior position of such professorial figures. Essentialist mystification may be seen as the last refuge of the anti-theory lobby: Foakes (1993: 7) is typical when he says that 'literature demands not merely to be understood, but to be appreciated as an experience, and as art'.

Not only has *Hamlet: Theory in Practice* to assuage the hostility resulting from attempting to theorize Shakespeare, but it has also to exemplify the elusive discipline of putting theory into practice.[6] The *application* of theory to text is itself frequently accused of implicitly disparaging the literary text which it seeks to explore and, as we have already seen, when this text is by Shakespeare, the indictment is expressed all the more strenuously. Teaching and writing theoretically about texts, especially Shakespearian texts, is often considered to be an act of gross hubris. Theoretical criticism is regarded as an insidious cover for professional self-advancement and charged with self-glorification *at the expense* of the literary text; so Foakes laments that in

> universities, criticism has displaced literature as the source of power in English studies, for the critical processing of literature can be taught more easily than literature itself, and through the creation of journals and schools of criticism provides professional enhancement and prestige.
>
> (Foakes 1993: 7)

Vickers (1993: x) is similarly suspicious, noting 'a great amount of pushing and shoving for attention, commercial promotion, indeed self-promotion. . . . Each of the groups involved in this struggle for attention is attempting to appropriate Shakespeare for its own ideology or critical theory'.

This sort of allegation is typified by the initial reception of the first volumes of *Theory in Practice*. The *Times Literary Supplement* charged the series with depreciating literature. Based on a parodic reading of the series's 'gruesome preface', D.S. commented:

> Theory, we see, needs to be 'understood', as a whole. Those poor things, 'individual texts', on the other hand, require to be 'interpreted' to come into their own. Students, in any case, are to be encouraged to turn to them not because they are valuable in themselves but in order to be 'introduced to theory in practice'. So theory comes first; texts are not only secondary but really of interest only in so far as they can illuminate theory.
>
> (*TLS*, 23 July 1993: 14)

These remarks, although they occurred in the paper's satirical NB section (the *TLS* has not yet given serious review space to the series), rehearse a familiar charge.[7] Yet the Editors' Preface of this series (pp. ix–x above) makes clear its commitment to the literary text. One might have thought that the appearance of eleven titles specifically devoted to major canonical texts, including six by Shakespeare, would have offered prima-facie evidence of the importance the series places on literary works. Be that as it may, the Editors' Preface is concerned to prevent the construction of texts 'merely by the theoretical perspective from which we choose to regard them'. In other words, for all the animated denunciation of theoretical criticism by those who seek to protect the Bard from 'our current academic culture of political correctness' (Kerrigan 1994: 81), this series is already conscious of the manner in which it is likely to be charged with eclipsing canonical texts behind theoretical obfuscation. That this defence has been ignored illustrates the entrenchment of those who, on principle, oppose anything which sounds the least bit 'theoretical'. Despite the vociferous accusations of its antagonists, *Theory in Practice* is determined to move beyond the crude dichotomy of theory versus non-theory.

III

[Y]ou would pluck out the heart of my mystery

(III.ii.348–9)

The reasons why I have dealt with this contention at such length are intimately related to *Hamlet* itself. The play anticipates not only the interpretative difficulties which we noted at the outset but also the methodological quarrels I have just described. Contemporary theory's interest in language, pun, riddle and meaning make *Hamlet* a key text for both critical practice and metacritical discussion. *Hamlet* is principally about the frustration of sense. At the conclusion of the play, Horatio is required to provide a synopsis:

> So shall you hear
> Of carnal, bloody, and unnatural acts,
> Of accidental judgements, casual slaughters,
> Of deaths put on by cunning and forced cause;
> And, in this upshot, purposes mistook
> Fallen on the inventors' heads.

(V.ii.333–8)

This disturbing précis insists on the apparently unmotivated quality of the play. Though the audience, and Horatio, have witnessed the origins of Hamlet's motivations, personified in the Ghost, and though the desire for revenge is consistently being reinforced, we, like Horatio, are hard-pressed to explain just how we have reached this point. As Coleridge noted: 'This is almost the only play of Shakespeare, in which mere accidents, independent of all will, form an essential part of the plot' (Bate 1992: 322). Despite the play's being rigidly driven by Hamlet's obsession with the injustice he and his father have suffered at the hands of Claudius, the turn of events is haphazard.

In revenge dramas both before and after *Hamlet*, such as Thomas Kyd's *Spanish Tragedy* (1587?) or *The Revenger's Tragedy* by Cyril Tourneur (1607, also ascribed to Thomas Middleton), the protagonist's desire for revenge constitutes the play's dramatic principle.[8] Neither of these plays has a sub-plot which might pull focus from the vengeance of Hieronimo or Vindice, and although, in the case of Kyd's play, the retribution of Hieronimo on Balthazar (the murderer of his son) is the vehicle through which Andrea's ghost is also revenged on Balthazar (for the killing of Andrea in battle), Hieronimo's situation is that in which the audience are most interested, since it occupies the greater part of the play, and towards which they are most sympathetic (Andrea is a casualty of war after all). In *Hamlet* though, the play is complicated by a whole series of events and relationships which, in terms of the narrative, have the effect of compounding the revenge mission with other elements (the treatment of Ophelia, the relationships with Horatio, Rosencrantz and Guildenstern, the guilt of Claudius and the interlude of the players, etc.). Most notably, the events of the revenge plot are overshadowed by and framed within the military campaign of Fortinbras, and his assumption of power at the end of the play, for all its perfunctory appearance, places the Hamlet story in a wider political setting. In terms of the larger thematic questions which the play addresses, these other elements contextualize the revenge mission and emphasize the complexities of the social fabric of which the Prince is only a part. Thus, the force of Horatio's summing-up is in our recognition of its accuracy. The oxymoronic 'accidental judgements' crystallizes our sense both of the aleatoric nature of events and the determination of human beings to rationalize and impose patterns upon it: 'There's a special providence in the fall of a sparrow' (V.ii.166–7).

Hamlet is obsessed with the tension between indeterminacy and the imposition of definition. Its opening words dramatize this uncertainty:

BARNARDO: Who's there?
FRANCISCO: Nay, answer me. Stand and unfold yourself.
BARNARDO: Long live the King!
FRANCISCO: Barnardo?
BARNARDO: He.

FRANCISCO: You come most carefully upon your hour.
BARNARDO: 'Tis now struck twelve. Get thee to bed, Francisco.

(I.i.1–7)

The play begins in challenge, question and panic, and the response is not an answer but a counter-challenge, 'Nay, answer me'. Presumably Francisco is the soldier on duty (since we hear in l. 17 that Barnardo has relieved him), but it is Barnardo who makes the first challenge. Although Barnardo asks the initial question, he is the first to yield his identity though he does this without surrendering his name. At this point we still do not know the name of the other soldier; the play's opening question has not yet been answered. In fact, Franscisco never actually supplies an answer to Barnardo's challenge. The soldiers' exchange provides an anticipatory miniature of the Ghost's intrusion – its identity and its origin uncertain. More generally though, their challenge and counter-challenge, the maintenance of their anonymity and the swapping of roles between questioner and questioned exemplify the play's concern with the dread of uncertainty. In the First Quarto (Q1, see below) this enigmatic opening is even more pronounced. Francisco's guess at Barnardo's identity and the latter's confirmation (ll. 4–5), though they provide only small comfort, are missing here and the soldiers are identified in the stage directions only as '*two Centinels*' – they are named in the Second Quarto (Q2) and the First Folio (F). Even their speech prefixes preserve their anonymity, referring to them merely as '1' and '2'. Francisco's name does not appear at all in Q1's version of this scene ('Get thee to bed, Francisco' is also missing) and Barnardo is only identified at the line '*Barnardo* hath my place, giue you good night' (Q1, l. 12).

This bewildering opening does not simply portray the soldiers' own sense of anxiety but emphasizes the degree to which the audience are themselves involved in acts of interpretation. *Hamlet* lacks the kind of informative speeches which open plays like *King Lear*, for example. In that play the conversation between Kent and Gloucester introduces us to the political situation of Lear's court, provides us with a hint of the friction between Albany and Cornwall and initiates the sub-plot by introducing us to Edmund. It even manages to provide Edmond with a motive for his scheme to displace Edgar through his public humiliation by Gloucester. *Hamlet*, by contrast, begins *in medias res* and the play, as much as its audience, is perplexed.

The next battlement scene develops this sense of perilous ambiguity. Again, the apprehension is shared by characters in the play and the audience and, again, issues of interpretation and identity are central:

Be thou a spirit of health or goblin damned,
Bring with thee airs from heaven or blasts from hell,
Be thy intents wicked or charitable,
Thou com'st in such a questionable shape
That I will speak to thee. . . .
. . .   What may this mean . . .?
Say, why is this? Wherefore? What should we do?

(I.iv.19–23, 30, 36)

Hamlet's unresolved binary oppositions – spirit or goblin, heaven or
hell, wicked or charitable – collapse into the series of questions with
which the speech ends. But the questions about the Ghost are never
answered and the fears of Horatio and Marcellus which lead ultimately
to their attempts to restrain Hamlet physically (l. 60), stand in for
the fears of the audience who have still heard no satisfactory response
to any of Hamlet's enquiries.

In the light of our own and the characters' hesitancy in ascribing a
firm identity to the Ghost, it is appropriate that the play's other father-
figures are also accorded dubious identities. In response to Polonius's
question, 'Do you know me, my lord?', Hamlet replies, 'Excellent,
excellent well. You're a fishmonger' (II.ii.173–4). Although this
remark sounds merely ludicrous, there is method in this madness:
Polonius has just suggested using Ophelia to draw out Hamlet's
mystery, but he has done so in the language of a bawd: 'I'll loose my
daughter to him' (II.ii.162). In this sense, Hamlet's identification of
Polonius as a fishmonger, that is, a pimp, is entirely appropriate
(Williams 1994: 496).[9] Claudius, too, has his identity sexually eroded.
As Hamlet takes his leave he remarks:

Farewell, dear mother.
CLAUDIUS: Thy loving father, Hamlet.
HAMLET: My mother. Father and mother is man and wife;
man and wife is one flesh; and so, my mother.

(IV.iii.51–4)

Again, what sounds like mere antic disposition is given a serious twist:
the exchange comes after the closet scene in which Hamlet has pruriently
dwelt on the incestuous implications of Gertrude's marriage to her
dead husband's brother. Hamlet's deliberate misnomer dramatizes an
interpretative confusion shared by character and audience: is this an
incestuous marriage or not?[10]

Elsewhere the hermeneutic difficulties of the play are articulated not
in relation to identity or sexuality but to aesthetics and language.
Hamlet and Polonius's cloud conversation is almost surreal:

HAMLET: Do you see yonder cloud that's almost in shape of a camel?
POLONIUS: By th' mass, and it's like a camel indeed.
HAMLET: Methinks it is like a weasel.
POLONIUS: It is backed like a weasel.
HAMLET: Or like a whale?
POLONIUS: Very like a whale.

(III.ii.358–64)

This exchange is a manifestation of the degree to which interpretative strategies have become unfixed. In an open-air playhouse the temptation to follow the actors' focus may have been irresistible and so the problem would have had a visual as well as a verbal dimension. Polonius's willingness to 'see' the Prince's visions stands for our readiness to suspend our disbelief: 'The readiness is all' (V.ii.169). In this way *Hamlet* foregrounds its dramatic illusion even as it is practised upon us. It is no surprise, then, that some of the most stubborn interpretative difficulties cluster around the inset play.

The Murder of Gonzago, which is already confused by having an alternative title, *The Mousetrap*, reveals allegorically the nefarious activities of the King. Yet the kinship relations of the characters in *The Mousetrap* are mirror images of those in the story of King Hamlet's murder. In *The Mousetrap* the king is killed not by his brother but by his nephew, Lucianus. Hamlet is nephew to Claudius and so *The Mousetrap* can be seen as dramatizing not the murder of King Hamlet by Claudius but the prospective murder of King Claudius by Hamlet. However, the marriage of Claudius to King Hamlet's wife (following the latter's murder) clearly parallels the marriage of Lucianus to Gonzago's wife (following Gonzago's murder). *The Mousetrap* thus works on two levels: Lucianus stands both for Hamlet *and* Claudius and so the didactic function of drama – 'to show virtue her own feature, scorn her own image, and the very age and body of the time his form and pressure' (III.ii.21–3) – is maintained even while the object of its lesson is uncertain.

This question of dramatic delineation is acutely figured in Polonius's critical quandary. As the players enter Elsinore their theatrical plurality threatens to overwhelm his generic definitions: 'The best actors in the world, either for tragedy, comedy, history, pastoral, pastoral-comical, historical-pastoral, tragical-historical, tragical-comical-historical-pastoral, scene individable, or poem unlimited' (II.ii.391–4). Polonius's tortured description exemplifies the desire to impose order.

If, as with our other examples, we can extend the play's enigmas to its audience, perhaps, on this occasion, we should acknowledge its satirical double-take at the expense of literary critics. Shakespeare demonstrates the futility of an inflexible taxonomy and casts us in the role of Polonius with his fruitless terminology. *Hamlet* demonstrates the hopelessness of the attempts to pluck out the heart of its mystery. 'Explaining' *Hamlet* is as useless as consigning it to a particular genre. The play is therefore a direct challenge to traditional literary criticism which 'sets out to deliver the text from its own silences by coaxing it into giving up its true, latent or hidden meaning' (Bennett 1979: 107). It is in this way that *Hamlet* not only challenges the processes by which we make sense of things (including *Hamlet*) but also engages interrogatively with the methodological norms of literary criticism itself: 'We must speak by the card, or equivocation will undo us' (V.i.130–1). The epistemological difficulties of *Hamlet* are not merely the result of its internal puzzles, over identity, sexuality or language, but are also evidence of the inappropriateness of our traditional critical approaches.

IV

[T]hey are actions that a man might play

(I.ii.84)

As well as the play's concern with uncertainty and the way in which it challenges our critical strategies, further levels of complexity demand our attention: most crucially, what do we mean by *Hamlet*? In the discussion of any play we face the difficulty of defining our text. Which is the absolute *Hamlet*, the BBC version, Olivier's or Zeffirelli's film, or any one of thousands of stage versions?

Post-structuralist theory has radically challenged ideas of linguistic stability, and the pliancy of literary texts can be traced through to the chimera of language itself, but *Hamlet* is unstable in a more particular way, that is, as a performance text. Drama texts are inherently malleable, lines are cut, moved or transformed in production depending on medium (film, play, book), playing space (the Globe, the Blackfriars, the Inns of Court), audience, acting company and so on. Writing of *The Murder of Gonzago*, Terence Hawkes insists on the conjunction of meaning and situation. In his explanation of '*miching malicho*', the Prince's comment that 'It means mischief' can readily refer to what the play *intends now*, as a result of Hamlet's intervention; to what it is *up to*, here in Elsinore; to what, on this occasion, at this time and in this place, it *means to do*. The source of 'meaning' in this light appears almost to have migrated from the play 'itself' to the material context in which it is performed. Here and now, Hamlet seems to say to Ophelia, this is where 'meaning' will be generated.

(Hawkes 1992: 2–3)

All drama is shaped by the specific circumstances of its production. Moreover, variation may even occur in different performances of the same production as actors 'try things out', different moves, different line readings and so on. For instance, when John Gielgud directed Richard Burton as Hamlet in 1964 he proposed that Burton stab the throne on 'O, vengeance!'. Burton's response highlights the degree to which he depended on improvisation: 'I wouldn't like to rely on a prop, John, in case I change my mind in performance' (Davison 1983: 64). *Hamlet* is fully aware of the vagaries of theatre; Hamlet himself is concerned to tame the excesses of the impulsive players:

Suit the action to the word, the word to the action, with this special observance, that you o'erstep not the modesty of nature. For anything so overdone is from the purpose of playing ...

(III.ii.16–19)

Yet later, in the same scene, his grief finds exaggerated expression in a way which thoroughly o'ersteps the modesty of nature and relies on the ghoulish hyperboles of revenge drama:

'Tis now the very witching time of night,
When churchyards yawn, and hell itself breathes out
Contagion to this world. Now could I drink hot blood,
And do such bitter business as the day
Would quake to look on.

(ll.371–5)

Hamlet seems trapped between contradictory impulses, wishing to appear plausible, to hold the mirror up to nature, even while it demonstrates its compliance with literary models, like revenge drama, which are sensational and theatrical.[11] That the play foregrounds such incongruities might make the quest for a final fixed form all the more abortive.

Seeking an analogy of post-structuralist criticism, Terence Hawkes alights on jazz music: 'For the jazz musician, the "text" of a melody is a means, not an end. . . . interpretation *constitutes* the art of the jazz musician' (Hawkes 1986: 117–18). For the acting company, of course, performance is an act of interpretation and we might usefully extend Hawkes's critical model to theatre itself. Ultimately, there can be no pure *Hamlet*, no performance which transcends the material conditions of its production (McGann 1988: 111–32). For Roland Barthes, the text consists only in its various manifestations and, we might add, because theatre is a transient form, they instantly evaporate. Barthes ingeniously compares the text to 'an onion, a construction of layers (or levels, or systems) whose body contains, finally, no heart, no kernel, no secret, no irreducible principle, nothing except the infinity of its own envelopes – which envelop nothing other than the unity of its own surfaces' ('Style and Its Image', in Chatman 1971: 10). The text exists only at the moment of its performance and despite the best efforts of theatre semiotics to log and fix drama, individual performances continue to elude inscription.[12] Moreover, not only does *Hamlet* (as a play) theatrically refute notions of denotative singularity but even as a printed text it is thoroughly polyphonic.

V

Sir, I Ham a very Bad Hand at Righting

(Harrison 1987: 112)

Just as we must reject the idea of a definitive performance, so we must acknowledge that we have a multitude of textual versions to choose from. Which is the final script of *Hamlet*, G.R. Hibbard's Oxford edition (1987, the one this volume has elected to use), Harold Jenkins's New Arden edition (1982), Horace Howard Furness's New Variorum (1877)? What of the editions of the eighteenth century: Edmond Malone (1790), Samuel Johnson (1765), Lewis Theobald (1734), Alexander Pope (1725–8)?[13]

By modern standards, Shakespeare seems to have been almost irresponsibly negligent towards his own text. Not until 1616 did plays seem to merit publication in anything like a permanent form. The appearance of Ben Jonson's *Works*, in the year which saw him succeed to the position of writer by royal appointment, invested drama with an importance which, up until this point, it had lacked. Jonson personally supervised the publication of his works and a 'major principle behind this selection was certainly the promotion of the image of himself as a serious poet – something very different from a mere playwright' (Dutton 1983: 12). The contrast with Shakespeare is profound: none of Shakespeare's works appeared in folio form in his lifetime. Shakespeare died in the year Jonson's *Works* appeared, and it was not until 1623 that the first collection of his plays was published by two of his contemporary actors, Heminges and Condell. The First Folio (F) included 18 plays which had been published previously in quarto form together with several others, including *Macbeth, Antony and Cleopatra* and *As You Like It*. No quarto form of these plays has survived (if they were ever published), and had they not appeared in F they would have been lost.

In a period before copyright the publication of play-texts could make scripts available to rival acting companies. For this reason, playwrights may have been wary of publication. This would explain the non-appearance of several of the plays listed in the Stationer's Register until the arrival of F. A number of the plays that had already appeared before 1623 differ substantially from quarto to quarto. They include *Richard II* (for political reasons the deposition scene could only be inserted after the death of Elizabeth I), *Romeo and Juliet* and, most significantly, *Hamlet*.

Hamlet is extant in three quite different versions. The First Quarto (Q1), of which only two copies are extant, was published in 1603. Seven copies of the Second Quarto (Q2) are known to exist. Three of these show the date 1604 and the remaining four are dated 1605. *Hamlet* also appears in the 1623 Folio (F), giving us our third distinct text. Comparisons between the three versions reveal significant differences.[14] Most obviously, Q1 is much shorter than the other two – only about 58 per cent of Q2. The title page of Q2 announces that the edition is 'Newly imprinted and enlarged to almost as much againe as it was, according to the true and perfect Coppie' and this suggests that it was published to counter the illicit printing of Q1 (see below). In addition, Q2 and F each contain passages which are missing from the other.

F omits over 200 lines that occur in Q2, including the exchange between Barnardo and Horatio on portents that precedes the first entry of the Ghost (at F, l. 125; Hibbard, I.i.107) as well as Hamlet's disgust at the behaviour of the drunken court and his remarks on human frailty – a version of the latter appeared as the prologue to Olivier's 1948 film (F, l. 621ff; Hibbard, I.iv.16ff).[15] A significant difference between these two editions is the heavy cutting of Act IV, scene iv.

In Q2 the scene involves Fortinbras, a Norwegian captain, Hamlet and Rosencrantz. Hamlet converses with the captain, who tells him of the impending battle between Fortinbras' army and that of Poland over 'a little patch of ground/That hath in it no profit but the name' (Q2, l. 2743 + 11–12). This example of stubborn fearlessness impresses and humiliates the Prince, who has still not acted to revenge the murder of his father. In F this scene is cut to a mere eight lines and comprises Fortinbras issuing commands to the captain. But in Q2 Hamlet follows this exchange with his soliloquy, 'How all occasions doe informe against me', which occupies over 30 lines (Q2, ll. 2743 + 26–60). This final, lengthy soliloquy has often been privileged by critics and directors as the Prince's swan song, offering Hamlet's desperation as the last word in his characterization or even the play itself. For example, Bradley (1974: 112–13) writes, 'while no doubt it is dramatically the least indispensable of the soliloquies, it has . . . a great value for the interpretation of Hamlet's character'. Similarly, in his 1989 production, Yuri Lyubimov insisted on the bleak absurdity of human life by ending with an empty stage, an open grave and a disembodied voice over loud-speakers: 'What is a man/. . . a beast, no more' (Q2, ll. 2743 + 27–9). However, we should remember that this nihilistic interpretation depends upon a soliloquy that appears in only one of the three extant versions.

Though F is shorter overall than Q2, it also contains several passages peculiar to itself. Editors are uncertain whether these are 'additions' to Q2 or belonged originally to the manuscript on which Q2 was based and were omitted from it either accidentally or deliberately. Censorship is a possible reason for such omission; for example, F's ll. 1285–1315 (Hibbard, ll.ii.238–67) do not appear in Q2. The passage contains Hamlet talking to Rosencrantz and Guildenstern about the corruption endemic to Denmark – 'Denmark's a prison' and 'one o' th' worst [dungeons]'. The recent accession of James VI and I, married to Anne of Denmark, might have made the omission of this passage expedient. On the other hand, Hibbard (1987: 112) argues that the passage may have been added to F to bring 'out more fully the evasiveness of Rosencrantz and Guildenstern, which the Prince, fresh from his encounter with Polonius, so quickly detects in Q2'. The second passage missing from Q2 (F, ll. 1384–1408; Hibbard, II.ii.333–58) refers to the so-called War of the Theatres which reached its high point in 1601. Rosencrantz describes how the players have been forced to become itinerant because a company of child actors, 'little Yases' (F, l. 1387 ('little eyases', Hibbard, II.ii.335)), are now in fashion. Shakespeare seems to be slighting the companies of boy actors like The Children of the Queen's Chapel, for whom Ben Jonson composed *Cynthia's Revels* (1600) to be played at the indoor theatre at Blackfriars. Performances at the indoor theatres cost much more to attend than those at the public playhouses, such as the Globe, and yet Hamlet's concern that the 'Boyes carry it away' (F, l. 1407) suggests that Shakespeare was acknowledging the seriousness of the competition to his own company. Q1 voices this anxiety in Guildenstern's condemnation of the fickleness of the audience:

noueltie carries it [the players' reputation] away,
For the principall publike audience that
Came to them, are turned to priuate playes,
And to the humour of children.

(Q1, ll. 998–1001)

By the time the passage appears and is expanded in F this contempt for the audience has been toned down and the child actors themselves, as well as those who write for them, are criticized. The final passage found in F, though missing from Q2, is a short conversation between Hamlet and Horatio immediately before the entrance of Osric. In it Hamlet determines to treat Laertes with more respect and draws attention to their shared plight, 'by the image of my Cause, I see/The Portraiture of his; Ile count his fauours' (F, ll. 3581–2; Hibbard, V.ii.78–9). Q1 has a similar passage here but Q2 has nothing. Dramatically the passage functions to foreground the similarities between the two avengers and to highlight the nobility of the Prince. Given his determination to treat Laertes honourably, he is not in a position to refuse his challenge which is, just at that point, brought in by Osric.

Two of the three passages found in F but missing from Q2, are embryonic in Q1. This demonstrates that there is no neat or linear pattern towards a final or correct text. Although recently, editors have come to accept the idea of Shakespeare as reworking and revising his plays, we ought not to accept that the latest text is the best, the most authentic, or the closest approximation to Shakespeare's final intention. It is not the case that textual revision moves us progressively towards a more refined version; in fact, as we shall see, Q1, the earliest and most frequently condemned text, is widely thought to be the closest version to a performance script.

The three texts are substantially different in terms of their inclusion of technical or theatrical information. Only F is organized into acts and scenes; the others have no divisions (hence the necessity to refer to them in terms of line numbers). The stage directions of Q2 are much less detailed than those of the other texts. For example, in the final scene, Q1 and F detail the deaths of Claudius and Laertes explicitly with the aid of stage directions. In Q2's version the deaths are left implicit. Again, at the beginning of the closet scene F has '*Enter Hamlet*' (l. 2384) and 21 lines later it has '*Killes Polonius*' (l. 2405). Q2 has neither direction. Even the death of Hamlet, which appears as '*Ham. dies*' in Q1 (l. 2196) and '*Dyes*' in F (l. 3847), is missing in Q2.[16] Although the stage directions of Q2 are often absent, they may usually be inferred from line readings. In the case of the death of Hamlet, for example, we might reasonably assume that Horatio's lament, 'Now cracks a noble hart, good night sweete Prince' (Q2, l. 3848), is immediately preceded by Hamlet's death, but elsewhere the absence of stage directions is potentially confusing. In the final duel, F has the direction, '*In scuffling they change Rapiers*' (l. 3777), and Q1 also provides a description of the exchange, '*They catch one anothers Rapiers, and both are wounded,/Leartes falles downe, the Queene falles downe and dies*' (ll. 2169–70). Q2, however, has no stage direction here and the only evidence of the switch is Laertes' subsequent 'I am iustly kild with mine owne treachery' (l. 3785). The paucity of Q2's stage directions has led editors to assume that it is a version intended as a reading text. While its sheer length would seem to reinforce this (without cuts, Q2 is far in excess of 'the two hours' traffic of our stage' which the Prologue of *Romeo and Juliet* seems to set as a norm (l. 12)), the argument that a reading version is not in need of stage directions seems perverse.[17] If anything, without the visual aid provided by stage performances, a reading text has all the more need of stage directions which explain what is happening. If, for example, the exchange of swords is left implicit, a reader is in danger of failing to apprehend the event as it occurs. In the theatre, of course, this cannot happen since we see the exchange of swords.[18]

Of the editorial and textual problems that beset *Hamlet*, the most contentious has been the critical reception of the 'bad' quarto. Harold Jenkins's Arden edition explains its unfavourable description: Q1 'is, in the sense in which the word is now used, a "bad" quarto, one, that is to say, whose text, deriving from performance, lacks a direct manuscript link with what the author wrote' (Jenkins 1982: 19). What begins as a technical term of transmission acquires, all too rapidly, artistic, aesthetic and even ethical connotations. According to Hibbard (1987: 69), for example, Q1 is 'completely illegitimate and unreliable . . . having no direct contact with any Shakespearian manuscript, or with any transcript of such a manuscript'. Edwards (1985: 2), in his New Cambridge edition, calls it 'a much-debased version of Shakespeare's play'. For Kerrigan (1994: 113), Q1 is simply wrong, 'the many, often hilarious errors of the "bad quarto" are notorious', but Davison's (1983: 13) description stresses its imperfection in criminal terms: 'The play was first published in 1603 in a pirated version in just the manner that video tapes are pirated nowadays, inferior in content and designed to undercut the legitimate market'. As Q1's recent editors note, 'a "Bad Quarto" can readily be received as not only bad in itself, but the product of bad men, the unscrupulous Elizabethan "pirates", the ubiquitous "playhouse thieves"' (Holderness and Loughrey 1992: 15). Q1's debauchery is in the eye of the prejudiced beholder, 'for there is nothing either good or bad, but thinking makes it so' (II.ii.247).

The most widely accepted explanation of this inferiority is that Q1 is a memorial reconstruction – a text resulting either from jotting down the lines as they were spoken in the theatre or remembered by an actor who had been involved in a production of *Hamlet* and who was anxious to take the play elsewhere to profit from it.[19] In 1915, H.D. Gray suggested that the actor responsible had played the roles of Marcellus and Lucianus since these two parts are closest to the later texts and would be the ones he would best remember. Secondary roles, such as these, may have been allotted to jobbing actors rather than members of the regular company, and such a temporary member of the cast 'would be exactly the sort of man to join another company, and to concoct a version of *Hamlet* for that company to put on' (Hibbard 1987: 77).

In spite of the widespread currency of the idea that Q1 is 'a garbled form' (Foakes 1993: 89), it retains a dramatic shape very like F. This dramatic fidelity, coupled with the fact that it is only half the length of Q2, suggests that it may have been a theatrical abridgement particularly suited to regional touring. Such touring, as we have seen, occurs in *Hamlet* itself; the competition of the child companies is partly responsible for the presence of the players at Elsinore. The suggestion that Q1 is a playing version can be supported by reference to its ample and detailed stage directions, which are much fuller than those of Q2 and frequently more detailed than those of F. During the closet scene, for example, Q1 has '*Enter the ghost in his night gowne*' (l. 1551) where the other two texts just have '*Enter Ghost*'. Ophelia's entry after the murder of Polonius is amply delineated: '*Enter Ofelia playing on a Lute, and her haire/downe singing*' (Q1, ll. 1691–2). F has the less detailed '*Enter Ophelia distracted*', while Q2 lacks any local colour, '*Enter*

Ophelia'. The detail of these directions demonstrates an actor's prioritization of the non-verbal content of the play; it is more important to be on-stage when required than to be word-perfect – entries and costume cannot be 'ad libbed'. Thus, while Q1 is often considered to be poetically substandard, many critics are persuaded of its theatrical authenticity. Even those who are most disparaging about it are forced to concede its importance as something approaching an actual Elizabethan performance text: 'one catches glimpses of an acting version of the tragedy current in the early seventeenth century' (Hibbard 1987: 89). Stanley Wells and Gary Taylor refer to Q1 as the '[w]orst reported of all' the bad quartos, yet they acknowledge that for all their faults, the bad quartos 'are not without value in helping us to judge how Shakespeare's plays were originally performed. . . . they can help us to come closer than before to the plays as they were acted by Shakespeare's company as well as by others' (Wells and Taylor 1988: xxxii–iii). This theatrical archaeology is even more evident in Edwards's (1985: 24) enthusiasm: 'The one link we have with *Hamlet* as acted at the Globe Theatre is the first quarto of 1603'.

When William Poel staged Q1 in 1881, following its discovery in 1823, the contemporary theory was that it was an early version of what later came to be Q2. Poel was determined to demonstrate that the literary accomplishments of the later texts of *Hamlet* had been at the cost of Q1's theatrical immediacy: 'Shakespeare himself must have been aware of the acting value which the play had lost by its development into literary perfection. Quarto I represents more truly his *dramatic conception* than either Quarto II or our stage version' (Marvin Rosenberg, 'The First Modern English Staging of *Hamlet* QI', in Clayton 1992: 241–2). Poel's experiment was concerned to recreate the acting conditions of the Shakespearian playhouse and was performed in Elizabethan costume without scenery though, perhaps in deference to his own Victorian reservations, Poel did not (with the exception of the Player Queen), cast male actors in female roles. Rosenberg assembles a number of contemporary reviews which testify to the unfortunate quality of the performances themselves. *The Saturday Review* (23 April 1881) is typical:

It was at least to be expected that a body of people professing to be honouring Shakespeare's memory, and promoting the study of his works, should have made some effort to fit themselves for the task. The actors of *Saturday*, however, appear to have confined themselves to learning the mere words of their parts very indifferently well, and rehearsing just enough not to run up against one another.

(Clayton 1992: 243)

Despite the savage attacks on the acting, at least one reviewer spotted in the production evidence of a theatrically superior script: the *Academy* noted that

> the First Quarto is an excellent acting play, and one better constructed, dramatically, than the later and enlarged Second Quarto of 1604, which no manager now dares to play ... on account of the drag of its greater length.... The impression that the performance left on the hearer was that Quarto 1 was distinctly the representation – through whatever clouds – of a whole, a complete play that could and did well stand alone; and that this play was not merely a distorted version of the authorized text of Quarto 2.
>
> (Clayton 1992: 247–8)

The assuredness of Q1 as a performance text seems borne out by its modern productions. In 1985, Sam Walters directed Q1 at the Orange Tree Theatre in Richmond. In an interview with Bryan Loughrey, Walters insisted on its dramatic sufficiency and the way in which it manages to retain the plot of the longer versions: 'Whoever did this text, wherever it came from, nothing's removed, it's all reduced.... There's no component of the play missing.... It's all there, only compressed' (Loughrey, 'Q1 in Recent Performance: An Interview', in Clayton 1992: 126). Peter Guinness, who played the Prince, concurred and contended that the pace of the script offered a more exciting play than the other, more ponderous versions:

> I think I described the play at the time we did it ... as '*Hamlet* with the brakes off.' It's like an express train that roars out of the station at the beginning of the play, and heads for the next two hours at accelerating speed towards a dead-end at the far end of the track. The audience knows that disaster is coming, and the excitement builds simply because of the speed with which the play moves. So there is a momentum in the First Quarto that is unavoidable.
>
> (Clayton 1992: 128)

Clearly we are not entitled to posit Q1 as a performance script of the seventeenth century on the strength of its modern performability.

Nevertheless, Q1 requires that we re-evaluate it. While critics seem unanimous in denouncing it as poetically inferior to the other versions, it appears to be eminently actable and so challenges, yet again, our confidence in the fixity of Shakespeare's play, as well as our conventional notions of literary value.

VI

Words, words, words.

(II.ii.192)

The problems of *Hamlet* will not be solved by this volume. *Hamlet* is an expression of agnostic despair ('what is this quintessence of dust?' (II.ii.305–6)), a confirmation of the intellectual impotence of the age of humanism ('There are more things in heaven and earth, Horatio,/Than are dreamt of in our philosophy' (I.v.174–5)), a lament on the hollowness of human relationships ('I did love you once' (III.i.115–16)), and a trenchant critique of political opportunism ('I have some rights of memory in this kingdom,/Which now to claim my vantage doth invite me' (V.ii.342–3)). *Hamlet* offers multiple points of entry and a kaleidoscopic range of possible readings. If theory has anything to teach us about *Hamlet*, it is that singularity and totality will deform rather than illuminate the play. If *Hamlet* has anything to teach us about theory, it is that problems rather than solutions, questions rather than answers, are what we should be seeking. In the light of this mutual enrichment, we should celebrate rather than dread critical moments which recognize the scale of the issues at stake: 'the more I read of the tragedy of Hamlet the less I really understand it as a whole, and now despair of meeting with any theories that will reconcile its perplexing inconsistencies' (Halliwell-Phillipps 1879: 6–7).

CHAPTER 1

'For they are actions that a man might play': Hamlet as Trickster

MARK THORNTON BURNETT

[Mark Thornton Burnett's identification of the trickster figure in several apparently separate areas of the play is a salutary reminder of how modern our own assumptions about literary kinds might be. Even episodes that seem to carry little or no symbolic freight impart a contemporary set of meanings that are retained only imperfectly in the academic footnote. It is the simultaneity of a complex of meanings that Burnett strives to explore in this essay; not merely to add the *Hamlet* trickster to some non-temporal store of recurrent mythic tropes, but rather to use the initial isolation of a mythic figure to illuminate how a particular culture received apparently traditional and persistent signals from the fool/trickster traits – not that Polonius, or the 'mad' Hamlet or Claudius are ever consistently to be identified with these archetypes, but rather that their actions or words at particular dramatic junctures increase in significance due to the extra allusive power that a knowledge of such archetypes would help produce.

Even though a tragedy (a classically ordained kind), *Hamlet* hardly testifies to an unproblematic survival of the classical separation of styles, where the decorum of purely tragic emotions is upheld. As Burnett points out, it is in the spirit of trickery that generic purity (or fundamentalism of all kinds) is eroded and questioned. It also indicates a specific form of cultural anxiety, where the word is no longer a transparent vehicle for the known and true. Signs refuse to point straight. Burnett mentions the work of Waswo (1987) in this regard, but this could be supplemented by Martin Elsky's *Authorizing Words* (Elsky 1989), which concentrates on the interplay of an early print culture with the prejudice in favour of speech, and Ian Maclean's *Interpretation and Meaning in the Renaissance*

(Maclean 1992), which identifies specific debates over legal language and judgement.

Just as there was no common acknowledgement of decorous dramatic form in the Elizabethan theatre, the very positioning of the stage (spatially, in the twilight 'zone' of the 'liberties' and symbolically, as either a low or high, popular or courtly, entertainment) promoted an unusual freedom of response and a fecundity of wordplay and allusion. Was an actor a vaga-bond or a masterless anti-hero – or both? How transient was the auditorium in which one heard Shakespeare's language? Steven Mullaney describes this state of affairs in his *The Place of the Stage*:

> When they gazed out over their Liberties and suburbs in the sixteenth century, what the city fathers and religious authorities of London saw was a discomforting and anamorphic scene. Traditional forms of marginal spectacle were being overlaid with new forms of anomaly; traditional license was being translated into new forms of licen-tiousness . . .
>
> Companies of players organized themselves along the lines of cor-porate guilds, but to the city such imitation hardly represented social respectability. It registered instead as a bold mockery of civic hierarchies.
>
> (Mullaney 1988: 45, 47;
> see also Bristol 1985: 59–71)

This mockery has been more specifically identified as a form of 'carnivaliza-tion', to borrow a term from Mikhail Bakhtin, where the popular and com-munal forms of celebration associated with 'carnival' (fools becoming wise or beggars kings) invade the more acceptable, and so safer, genres.

This promotes literary forms that challenge the univocal and authoritative staus of the 'author', manifest in 'monologic' work. In contrast, a 'dialogue' with the audience may employ several parodic or allusive borrowings from other kinds of writing and authors, and 'carnivalization' supplies a 'poly-phonic' or multiple-voiced account with little attempt at 'closure' that would derive from the placing of such varied accents in some hierarchy. This textual openness involves the reader in an active way. As Bakhtin (1981: 280) put it: 'The word in living conversation is directly, blatantly oriented towards a future answer word. It provokes an answer, anticipates it and structures itself in the answer's direction. 'Context' cannot be confined to verbal limits.

The forms of writing favoured by Bakhtin are dynamic (as opposed to monumental) and responsive or tactical (as opposed to polemical). They may not be idiomatic in form, but they still reach out to a local readership with a focused set of meanings, and, in so doing, often have to dismantle the canonical tastes that at any one time constitute 'literature'.

Thus far, I have perhaps construed Bakhtin's work merely as an aesthetics, which would be misleading. As Mark Thornton Burnett makes clear, the stylistic variety of *Hamlet* challenges criticism to discover in it a coherence or even secure 'intention'. What is often left out of the equation is the necessary part played in the work of interpretation by a third term between the writer and the intended readership: audience-as-writer or writer-as-own-reader (for there is very little to differentiate these concepts). If the 'author' is always a *relative* concept, and never an absolute, then texts never issue from the 'individual subject'. Meaning is always in process; indeed, it is often so multiple that it forms a 'heteroglossia' of social voices so numerous in origin that it would be fruitless to try to isolate them for analysis: 'all utterances are heteroglot in that they are functions of a matrix of forces practically impossible to recoup' (Bakhtin 1981: 428). 'Carnivalized' writing is thus merely an especially marked example of Bakhtin's perception of how literature is a *social* product.

In Carnival apparently familiar relations appear strange. It is therefore a means of displaying Otherness, i.e. an alien challenge to our accepted modes of perceiving the Real by suggesting all the alternatives not accounted for by and in our ideological grasp of the world.]

NIGEL WOOD

I

In the popular pamphlet, *The Black Book's Messenger*, (1592; in Kinney 1990) Robert Greene details the escapades of the rogue, Ned Browne, realizing his career as a confessional exposé. Greene's moralizing commentary introduces the narrative, but Browne's fictionalized voice quickly takes over to control the sequence of events and to direct the readers' responses. *The Black Book's Messenger*, which constitutes one of the earliest criminal biographies, is marked by a startling finale. His filching discovered by a company of French soldiers, Browne is condemned, 'hanged . . . out at a window, . . . the rope about [a] Bar' (Kinney 1990: 205). The conclusion is further characterized by the reintroduction of Greene's authorial point of view, as the close of a life of dissimulation is subjected to one last judgement:

But note a wonderful judgment of God shewed upon him after his death. His body, being taken down and buried without the town, it is verified that in the nighttime there came a company of Wolves, and tore him out of his grave, and ate him up, whereas there lay many soldiers buried, and many dead carcasses, that they might have preyed on to have filled their hungry paunches. But the judgments of God as they are just, so they are inscrutable. Yet thus much we may conjecture, that as he was one that delighted in rapine and stealth in his life, so at his death the ravenous Wolves devoured him, and plucked him out of his grave, as a man not worthy to be admitted to the honor of any burial. Thus have I set down the life and death of *Ned Browne*, a famous Cutpurse and Cony-catcher, by whose example, if any be profited, I have the desired end of my labor.

(Kinney 1990: 205)

Throughout the pamphlet, the subliminal appeal of Ned Browne resides in his capacity to reveal marvels. The trajectory traced in Greene's vision of the criminal underworld demonstrates how the sordid and the dirty can be transformed into something rich and strange. The commonplace becomes the extraordinary; the humdrum is turned into the exotic. Dull English words are translated into vibrant vocables in Ned Browne's cant; an intrigue involving wife-swapping means that he can enjoy a *ménage à quatre*. He is a shape-shifter and a social climber at one and the same time; similarly, he performs an alchemical role, transmuting base materials into golden fantasies, a talent which is made explicit in the admission, 'The most expert and skillful Alchemist never took more pains in experience of his metals . . . that I have done in plotting' (Kinney 1990: 198), or in the description of his roistering companions who 'will tell you wonders of the Philosopher's stone, and make you believe they can make gold of Goose-grease' (Kinney 1990: 200). It is entirely apposite that the protean Ned Browne should receive his come-uppance by being consumed as a *plat du jour* by a French carnivore. The doubleness of perspective that distinguishes Ned Browne and the entire pamphlet returns in this grotesque exhumation: moralism masquerades as farce; the upstart is humiliated; even wonders are ironized. A base fate is visited upon a fantastic alchemist.

The ending of *The Black Book's Messenger*, with its nicely balanced adjudication between competing ideological tendencies, encapsulates the ways in which Ned Browne is figured in the pamphlet as a whole. At once he reflects on his crimes from his place of death and seeks salvation: he 'repented him from the bottom of his heart' (Kinney 1990: 193), Greene observes. The problem with this reading is that statements of moral intention are frequently undercut by the obvious delight that the narrative takes in the execution of anarchic impulses. *The Black Book's Messenger* is no easy repentance tract: instead, it represents an urban fantasy in which social and sexual escapism is indulged; a carnival of instant gratification, the pamphlet celebrates the various identities which Ned Browne fashions for himself and success-fully impersonates. Gulling a thick-skinned *senex*, a rich gentlewoman and a 'fat Priest' (Kinney 1990: 198), he exults in a mocking, scurrilous conduct which threatens the establishment even as he admonishes himself and entertains a will to turn convert. A chronicle of spiritual awakening, *The Black Book's Messenger* is also a catalogue of vices committed by an unregenerate, and displays a bifurcated attitude which is neatly summed up in the description of Ned Browne's two-sided coat: 'as for my Cloak, it was *Tarmosind*, as they do term it, made with two outsides, that I could turn it how I list' (Kinney 1990: 197). Like Janus, the two-faced god, Ned Browne suits himself to whatever circumstances demand, adapting himself to a proliferation of changing states of affairs. Moralist and immoralist, he plays both parts with equal insouciance.

II

Ned Browne is, in fact, an archetypal trickster, a liminal, marginalized type who undermines authority structures and uses varieties of subter-fuge to secure what are sometimes dubious or illicit ends. It is the purpose of this chapter to deploy a number of critical approaches to the trickster in a reading of *Hamlet*; to elaborate the ground-rules for such a procedure, however, some important etymological and theoretical questions first need to be addressed.

The noun, 'trick', derives from the French and Picardian form of *triche*, carrying the meanings of cheating, treachery and deceit. Allied definitions complicate the picture: a 'trick' may connote 'A crafty or fraudulent device', 'An illusory or deceptive appearance', 'A clever or adroit expedient', 'A feat of dexterity or skill . . . a piece of jugglery or legerdemain', 'A trifling ornament or . . . trinklet' or 'A habit or fashion of dress' (*OED*). Many of these meanings are linked to or played out in the action of *Hamlet*, as are subsidiary definitions of the verb (derived from the Norman and Picardian *trikier* and *triquer*), such as 'To sophisticate or adulterate (wine, etc.)' (*OED*). While the term 'trickster', meaning 'One who practises trickery; a rogue, cheat, knave' (*OED*), only dates from the early eighteenth century, the figure had a securely established lineage and was a focus of popular interest in a range of cultures and traditions.

From classical mythology and native folk-tale come a plethora of trickster characters, which would include Hermes, Prometheus, Ture,

Anansi, Wakdjukaga, raven, rabbit, spider and coyote (Babcock-Abrahams 1975: 158). The type is common to the native American as well as to the Chinese, Japanese and Semitic worlds (Radin 1956: ix). At several removes of displacement, *Hamlet* itself is partly indebted to accounts in Icelandic literature of a young man who, despite his foolishness, is still able to outwit his enemies (Ellis Davidson, 'Loki and Saxo's Hamlet', in Paul Williams 1979: 15). During the sixteenth and seventeenth centuries in general, trickster figures served as manifestations of radical energies or as narrative devices, as the works of Erasmus, the *pícaro* of the Spanish novella, and the *Luftmensch* of German literature suggest (William J. Hynes, 'Mapping the Characteristics of Mythic Tricksters: A Heuristic Guide', in Hynes and Doty 1993: 38). As far as the English Renaissance was concerned, dramatists were able to build upon the intriguing servant of Roman comedy and the vice figure of the late medieval moralities in their reinvention of a personality who challenges the forces of constituted authority in such a way as to complicate the final restitution of the social fabric.

As an example of theory in practice, however, this is not a chapter which attempts to interpret etymological niceties or to map those areas of overlap between Renaissance typologies and earlier narrative conventions. Still less does it endeavour to argue that a set of 'universal' trickster principles can be decided: the figure has attracted different meanings at different times in different cultural contexts. Employing a model of theoretical enquiry entails a confrontation with diverse textual and epistemological difficulties. In this application I am as interested in the differences between a text and a theoretical perspective as in the similarities. Where appropriate in the discussion of *Hamlet*, I will invoke a trickster anecdote, but I am also concerned to determine the broader discursive connections which throw light on the charged status of the play in its historical moment. To this end, the chapter will privilege not so much mimesis as the importance of a larger system of (what may sometimes be) quite diffuse cultural meanings and associations. The hoped-for result is to draw attention to a set of relations between the trickster theme in the play and the social, economic and political forces which lend *Hamlet* its note of specifically Elizabethan urgency.

In any discussion of the uses of theory, an acquaintance with the model adopted is desirable, and now might be the point to investigate the trickster's chief characteristics and his wider ideological functions. Unfortunately, there is no one study which performs this task comprehensively. Radin (1956) is the standard analysis, but it should be supplemented by the more recent article by Babcock-Abrahams (1975). For readers interested in the trickster as a force of resistance, Scott (1990) is informative, and some of its suggestions are (rather less evenly) developed in the anthology edited by Hynes and Doty (1993). According to these accounts, the trickster is most often perceived as one who confuses categories. As Barbara Babcock-Abrahams observes, he falls between the animal and the human, and between the natural and the cultural, and 'at the centre of his antinomian existence is the power derived from his ability to live interstitially' (Babcock-Abrahams 1975: 148). As forcefully (and related to his skill in donning disguises and changing his shape or bodily appearance), the trickster can be a foolish and intellectually resourceful figure (alternately aggressive and vindictive, comic and destructive), in whom singleness, doubleness and multiplicity, and ambiguity, paradox and inversion are abundantly evident (Babcock-Abrahams 1975: 159; Doty, Historical Overview of Theoretical Issues: The Problem of the Trickster', in Hynes and Doty 1993: 25; and 'Mapping the Characteristics of Mythic Tricksters', in Hynes and Doty 1993: 36).

The trickster's marginal status extends to his sexual and social tendencies as well as to the physical location he inhabits. Temporal and spatial distinctions are frequently disrupted by the trickster, so that conflicts with parental figures erupt and a culture's deepest taboos and restrictions are interrogated (Babcock-Abrahams 1975: 147, 154; Pelton 1980: 168). As a social subversive, the trickster uses the techniques of the *bricoleur* – who either relies upon personal qualities (such as linguistic inventiveness) to win a desired goal or who transforms materials at hand for a creative purpose (Hynes, 'Mapping the Characteristics of Mythic Tricksters', in Hynes and Doty 1993: 42) – the effect of which is to problematize a society's kinship structures and hierarchical principles (Babcock-Abrahams 1975: 178). Two instances will suffice as an illustration of this strategic ability. In African-American folk-tales, Brer Rabbit defeats Brer Wolf by drawing upon his agility and guile, while Ture, the trickster of the Azande people who live on the Nile–Congo divide in Africa, tries to convert a termite mound into a dwelling-place in order to avoid building a hut, and seduces his mother-in-law to enjoy sexual intercourse without the obligation to enter marriage (Gilbert Osofsky, 'A Note on the Usefulness of Folklore', in Osofsky 1969: 46; Brian V. Street, 'The Trickster Theme: Winnebago and Azande', in Singer and Street 1972: 92; Scott 1990: 163). In both of these cases, the trickster's actions run counter to normative familial relations, upsetting the systems of communal exchange on which a culture's continued survival depends.

At what levels of a cultural consciousness does the trickster function, and what force does the myth carry in its literary manifestations? In addressing this question, two rival interpretations come into play. On the one hand, it is argued that the trickster is an archetype with his roots in the transcendental human psyche, that he can be understood in therapeutic terms of sublimation, projection and differentiation, and that he acts most dramatically as a psychological steam-valve (Babcock-Abrahams 1975: 183).[1] On the other hand, there are social dimensions to the trickster's activities, and opinion still hesitates over pinning down the eventual ramifications of his transgressive practices. While an educative aspect is emphasized (through the narrative, the lower orders may learn to control feelings of resentment), it is also clear that the trickster opens up numerous connected (but apparently irresolvable) social meanings (Scott 1990: 164). His behaviour reinforces the rules that govern society by showing that they can be temporarily flouted; at the same time, it suggests that genuine change can be instituted, and that a new order, which subscribes to deviousness and invention as its guiding ideals, is not beyond the bounds of possibility (Street, 'The Trickster Theme', in Singer and Street 1972: 85–6, 103–4).

There is a point at which the binarisms that these arguments tend to produce, however, cannot be accommodated within the various effects of a dramatic performance. This is not to suggest that Shakespeare belongs to a more privileged aesthetic category than that of other playwrights; rather, I would contend that the Elizabethan theatre was the site for a process of negotiation with contemporary preoccupations, and that it is eventually quite limiting to interpret this aspect of the drama in terms of a logic of subversion and/or containment. A play such as *Hamlet* would seem to fit the model of negotiation with startling exactitude. The rhythms, actions and language of *Hamlet* are shadowed in the trickster's protean abilities, while the puns and disguises of Hamlet himself test but do not necessarily replace the court's political operations. *Hamlet* also resists an easy relationship with a unitary theoretical model. While Hamlet is the play's most clearly identifiable trickster figure, he is challenged by several competing tricksters (such as Claudius, Polonius and possibly the Ghost), who are in turn reflected in their split selves – Reynaldo, Rosencrantz, Guildenstern and a host of comparable intelligencers. The play delineates with an unsettling economy those abused by such covert machinations, and Ophelia is an obvious instance, but without allowing events to slip into a neat victim/victimizer pattern: if Hamlet, Claudius and Polonius are tricksters, then they are equally fools, who fall prey to their own and others' schemes. As a whole the play, which

is informed by the vocabulary and features of the popular rogue
pamphlet, stresses the rivalrous interplay of a community of tricksters,
even as it situates Hamlet as a force of resistance and enters into a
dialectic with the shaping ideological forces that lay beyond the walls
of the playhouse.

III

When Hamlet encounters the First Player, he recalls a speech from
a play, based upon *The Aeneid*, in which Pyrrhus' part in the Trojan
War is elaborated:

> 'The rugged Pyrrhus, he whose sable arms,
> Black as his purpose, did the night resemble
> When he lay couchèd in the ominous horse,
> Hath now his dread and black complexion smeared
> With heraldry more dismal. Head to foot
> Now is he total gules, horridly tricked
> With blood of fathers, mothers, daughters, sons,
> Baked and impasted with the parching streets,
> That lend a tyrannous and damnèd light
> To their vile murders. . . .'

(II.ii.443–52)

The reverberations set up by the speech will continue to be felt as the
drama progresses. What draws Hamlet to the myth is the status of
Pyrrhus as a classical trickster, who invented the ruse of the wooden
'horse' to penetrate the Trojan walls. The trickster is hinted at, too,
in the ambivalences associated with the figure: he is both murderer
(killing Priam, the father of 50 sons) and avenging hero; however, he
acts where Hamlet falters in an inertia of hesitations. Allusions to
heraldry, moreover – such as 'gules' (a red colour) and 'tricked'
(delineated with colours) – suggest that Hamlet reads the mythic hero
as an emblematic *impresa*, or as an example in an inset that can be interpreted to bolster his own intentions.[2] Although in this context
'tricked' does not connote subterfuge, the term still signals at a subsidiary level the web of treachery and deceit that the rest of the play
anatomizes.

Throughout Hamlet measures himself against tricksy classical or
Italianate forebears, only to increase an awareness of the gulf that
separates him from securing his revenge. In finding an alliance with

Lucianus – 'Thoughts black, hands apt, drugs fit, and time agreeing,/
Confederate season, else no creature seeing' (III.ii.239–40) – Hamlet
is again attracted to a dual role: the character in the play-within-the
play is both nephew and uncle, avenger and adulterer. The striking
irony, of course, is that the identifications come to nothing; despite
the macabre relish of the speech in which he promises to 'drink hot
blood,/And do such bitter business as the day/Would quake to look
on' (III.ii.373–5), Hamlet fails to act with Pyhrric or Lucianic
conviction.

Hamlet's role in these scenes sets the tone for much of the drama as
a whole. The duality and bipolarity of the trickster – among the Siouan-
speaking Winnebago of central Wisconsin and eastern Nebraska, the
trickster splits into twins (Radin 1956: 120–1; Spinks 1991: 81) – are
glimpsed in the ways in which *Hamlet* is characterized by a series of
mirror images, paired personalities, contradictory meanings and alternative possibilities for meeting the Ghost's injunctions. These variously
complementing and competing structures are apprehended in terms of
language – it is as if Horatio is searching for the lost part that would
make him complete when he announces that only a 'piece of him'
(I.i.19) is present – and in terms of situational echoes: neither Hamlet
senior nor Claudius is allowed fully to confess, and when Hamlet rails
at Gertrude in her closet, an audience may remember Laertes' parallel
attempts to control Ophelia's sexuality in Act I. Taking account of
the 'symmetrical patterns [in Shakespeare], with pairs of doubles, [and]
relationships of edged and ironically reciprocal equipoise', Joel Fineman
observes: 'In *Hamlet*, though all violence is doubled, reflexive, fratrici-
dal, Shakespeare immediately reunderstands that violence in terms of,
and makes it seem the consequence of, erotic duplicity' (Fineman,
'Fratricide and Cuckoldry: Shakespeare's Doubles', in Schwartz and
Kahn 1980: 70, 89). It is an athletic leap to the tales of the Ashanti
people of West Africa, but tricksters in different cultural locations
share conceits of equivalence that may only appear striking or strange,
and parallel each other in their mythic properties. In one tale, for
instance, 'Ogo and Nommo are [trickster] twins, the one forever
degraded for his rebellion and incest, the other castrated and sacrificed
in atonement – both punished by an almighty father' (Pelton 1980:
191). In its balances and antitheses, its conflicts and its contrasts,
Hamlet rehearses complications which resurrect the ghost of Oedipus,
who out-tricks the Sphinx but is himself tricked on learning that his
marriage is treacherously incestuous.

If the spirit of the trickster is at work behind the doubled and doubling thematic manœuvres of *Hamlet*, it is no less keenly felt in the play's action and stage business. The play's characteristic pattern of imagery centres upon acts of disguising and unfolding, as Francisco's opening words indicate: 'Stand and unfold yourself' (I.i.2). Hamlet resembles the trickster both in his predilection for black colours and in his use of a 'trick' ('A habit or fashion of dress'), which distinguishes and obscures him from the rest of the court (*OED*). Occasionally the fascination with disguise takes on an Edenic aspect, as in the rejection of the rumour that Hamlet senior was 'stung' by a 'serpent' (I.v.36) while sleeping in the orchard. The unfolding events of *Hamlet* conjure a spectrum of archetypal trickster intrigues, one of them being the satanic impersonation of the snake to corrupt innocence, introduce knowledge and engineer the fall.

But the focus of *Hamlet* is less with the tricksters of myth and legend than with Hamlet's own tricksy practices. Both in his soliloquies and in his interactions with the other characters, Hamlet replicates some of the trickster's prevailing modes of behaviour. Like the Winnebago trickster, who can change his sex and form at will (Radin 1956: 3, 4, 23), Hamlet is a potential shape-shifter, wishing that his 'flesh would melt,/Thaw and resolve itself into a dew' (I.ii.129–30), and causing political concern when the consequences of his 'transformation' (II.ii.5) become apparent. The most striking example of this skill in confusing categories can be found in Hamlet's 'antic disposition' (I.v.179), which he 'puts on' (III.i.2) to confound his opponents. It is, as Guildenstern seems to recognize, a 'crafty madness' (III.i.8), and as Hamlet later admits, he is only 'mad in craft' (III.iv.177). In this respect, Hamlet's method mimes the contours of the trickster's double identity, and what is baffling about the trickster is exactly such a mixture of foolery and intellect, of crisp witticism coupled with the seeming nonsense of mental derangement.

Discussing Hamlet's tactics, Holstein (1976: 334) notes: 'Puns, equivocations, and *double entendres* comprise his repertoire, his means of countering duplicity with doubleness, and he vanquishes Polonius, Ophelia, Rosencrantz and Guildenstern, and Osric in witplay'. In societies which lack effective means of representation, coded linguistic mockery is the only available weapon with which the powerless can communicate their grievances, and Hamlet takes full advantage of the opportunities that such humour affords. With 'wild and whirling words' (I.v.138), he confronts the labyrinthine intricacies of Elsinore's political configurations, establishing his sense of familial separateness in the phrase 'A little more than kin, and less than kind' (I.ii.65); secretly criticizing Polonius by calling him 'a fishmonger' (II.ii.174);

enigmatically referring to the weather while implying that he can see through trickery in the remark that he knows 'a hawk from a handsaw' (II.ii.374); and chiding his mother with the observation, 'Mother, you have my father much offended' (III.iv.11). It is through these language games that Hamlet is able to attack the deceptions on which Elsinore rests, and his use of tangential argument, proverbial observation and barbed paranomasia has clearly recognizable antecedents: jests and riddles are the tools of the trickster's trade.

As Gertrude testifies, 'words like daggers enter in [the] ears' (III.iv.87), changing perceptions and modifying judgements. Words, Hamlet believes, have their most devastating effect in the theatre, which he indicates after having heard the First Player's performance:

> I have heard
> That guilty creatures sitting at a play
> Have by the very cunning of the scene
> Been struck so to the soul that presently
> They have proclaimed their malefactions;
> For murder, though it have no tongue, will speak
> With most miraculous organ. I'll have these players
> Play something like the murder of my father
> Before mine uncle. I'll observe his looks,
> I'll tent him to the the quick. If he but blench,
> I know my course.
>
> (II.ii.577–87)

Failing to recognize that, in his own behaviour, he is also conforming to the type of emotional extremity which the First Player has imitated so consummately, Hamlet wonders about the ease with which an audience can be tricked into confession through the illusion of grief impersonated. As Ned Browne is able to reveal marvels, so here does the Player impress as one whose talent lies in engineering 'miraculous' transformations. His design hatched, Hamlet accordingly organizes the dumb show to bring out its qualities of 'miching malicho' (III.ii.128), recasting an older dramatic convention for new, vengeful purposes.[3] In drawing attention to the trickery beyond the 'malicho' (wrongdoing), Hamlet is here close to the trickster as *bricoleur*. The Winnebago cycle describes the attempts of the trickster, Hare, to catch the engineer of a road with a trap of nettle-weeds (Radin 1956: 75), which brings to mind the parallel efforts of Ture, the Azande trickster, who looks for formulae with which to trick people or animals into giving him what he wants: Ture's failing, as Brian V. Street comments, is that 'having got the formula to work, he overdoes it and uses up the material provided' (Singer and Street 1972: 83, 85). As the outcome of the play-within-the-play suggests, Hamlet may now be clearer about the course which he needs to follow, but he leaves behind him a court lost in mystification and sympathetic to Claudius' angry response.

Part of the impact of *Hamlet* in the theatre derives from its representation of a competition between rival tricksters, among whom can be counted Claudius and the Ghost. Hamlet, who is not alone as the play's arch-exponent of the trickster's abilities, is constantly threatened by the possibility of being outwitted by those who profess to be his closest relatives or supporters: he is forced to measure himself against the living as well as the dead. Barbara Babcock-Abrahams (1975: 155) has written that the trickster

> effaces spatial boundaries in several ways . . . he is a vagabond who lives beyond all bounded communities and is not confined or linked to any designated space . . . he lives in cells, caves, ghettos, and other 'underground' areas . . . not as normal mortals *on* the earth.

While the Ghost seems somewhat distant from these definitions as it is 'confined' (I.v.11) to 'sulph'rous and tormenting flames' (I.v.3), it is nevertheless associated with 'a more removèd ground' (I.iv.40) than that traversed by the guards, speaks from the 'cellarage', (I.v.159) and claims that it occupies a liminal, purgatorial location. Potentially misleading and refusing to divulge its full story, the Ghost suggests the trickster in a variety of ways: it only 'Looks . . . like the King' (I.i.43); has a 'figure like [Hamlet's] father' (I.ii.199); may 'assume some other horrible form' (I.iv.51); and could well be a 'damnèd ghost' (III.ii.77), itself in disguise. For much of the play an audience is left speculating about the extent to which Hamlet, the trickster, is being out-tricked by a spectral parent or an anonymous spirit. The Ghost may constitute a 'trick' in the sense of an 'illusory or deceptive appearance; a semblance, [a] sham' (*OED*), and it is a question that the play seems hesitant finally to resolve.

Injunctions may not be trusted if they come from beyond the grave; far more immediate, however, is the threat posed by those still alive, in particular by Claudius who combines the slipperiness of the politician with the *bonhomie* of an apparently trustworthy relative. Arresting juxtapositions and precise paradoxical formulations announce Claudius as one who engages in rhetorical double-play to promote his own purposes:

Therefore our sometimes sister, now our queen,
Th'imperial jointress of this warlike state,
Have we, as 'twere with a defeated joy,
With one auspicious and one dropping eye,
With mirth in funeral and with dirge in marriage,
In equal scale weighing delight and dole,
Taken to wife.

(I.ii.8–14)

In his public declarations, Claudius is rarely the beleaguered figure that
he reveals in private, pointing to a Janus-like conjuction of opposites
that is reminiscent of Ned Browne's reversible coat and the trickster's
two-sided versatility. Given the questions about the Ghost's status, it is
ironic that further evidence of Claudius' double nature should come
from its chilling address on the castle's battlements – 'lewdness [may]
court [marriage] in a shape of heaven' (I.v.54), it states – which suggests
that the past and present kings share more than a familial connection.
It is from the Ghost that we first learn of what will become Claudius'
most tricksy strategem. To 'trick' can connote 'To sophisticate or
adulterate (wine, etc.)' (*OED*), which Claudius himself practises at the
duel, thus lending a further ironic twist to the Ghost's labelling the
king as an 'adulterate beast' (I.v.42). While Claudius, like Hamlet,
is hoisted with his own petard in pursuing his scheme, he does manage
to effect the death of the prince: to the end, father and son, nephew
and uncle, are allied with and pitted against each other in what will
be a denouement of cataclysmic proportions.

Up to this point I have been arguing that the doubling structures
of *Hamlet* function to evoke mythic paradigms, and that the linguistic
games and practical business engaged in by Hamlet are an integral part
of the ways in which he constructs himself in relation to his tricksy
predecessors. To root out what is rotten in the state of Denmark,
Hamlet follows in the path of the trickster in choosing words and
theatre as the weapons with which he will secure his role as revenger.
I have also been arguing that his sense of purpose is often blunted,
from within (by Claudius) and from without (by the Ghost), making
his enterprise increasingly hazardous: the trickster invariably comes
into conflict with multiple enemies, linked through local or familial
networks, who seek to match him in duplicitous ability. The possession of a split or multiple self is, indeed, a central trickster trait, and
it is from scenes in which a trickster elects deputies to perform his
demands that much of the play's sense of secret transactions springs.

Among Claudius' split selves are Rosencrantz and Guildenstern, although their tricksy purposes are quickly exposed by Hamlet; as he remarks: 'there is a kind of confession in your looks, which your modesties have not craft enough to colour' (II.ii.277–8). While Polonius might also stand as a trickster whose inaptitude proves his undoing, he does manage to exercise a more vigorous influence than Claudius' transparent intelligencers. With typical structural sleight of hand, the play juxtaposes the willingness of Rosencrantz and Guildenstern to spy upon Hamlet with Reynaldo's initial hesitations in agreeing to follow Laertes and to act as Polonius' agent. Trickery is the watchword of these exchanges: Polonius holds that it is a 'fetch of warrant' (a justified trick) to lay 'slight sullies' (II.i.38–9) on Laertes, and that 'By indirections' can 'directions' be found out (II.i.65). Beyond Reynaldo, as his name implies, lies a long tradition of the fox as a trickster: the Winnebago cycle describes how the fox, one of Trickster's companions, steals the summer (Radin 1956: 97); Brer Fox is usually Brer Rabbit's opponent in African-American trickster folklore (Scott 1990: 163); and the narratives of the Ashanti of West Africa celebrate the transformation of Ogo, the trickster, into the 'pale Fox', who comes to be associated with 'thievery' and 'furtiveness' (Pelton 1980: 179). Unlike Rosencrantz and Guildenstern, Reynaldo disappears from the play after his first appearance, but his absence does nothing to prevent continual variations on the lineage he represents being played out in different guises and new combinations.

Although *Hamlet* is silent about Reynaldo, it is more forthcoming on the end visited upon Rosencrantz and Guildenstern, and is in general concerned to underscore the dilemma of the trickster's victims as well as the plight of the trickster himself. One aspect of Ned Browne's seductive attraction comes from his ability to charm (or gull) unsuspecting women, his philandering behaviour reinforcing an archetype of male-female relations. Much of Hamlet's venom is directed at women, although it is their supposed duplicity as well as their innocence that provokes his outbursts. We hear first, for instance, how the 'strumpet Fortune' (II.ii.484) will trick men with the illusion of a position on the 'highest mount' (III.iii.18), only afterwards to dash them to 'boisterous ruin' (III.iii.22). As the rest of *Hamlet* suggests, however, women are far more likely to be tricked than to trick themselves, which Ophelia's experience potently demonstrates. The 'trifle' is a term tied to Ophelia from the early scenes. She is warned to distrust Hamlet's 'trifling of . . . favour' (I.iii.5) and to guard against being tricked into giving up her virginity (I.iii.31–2): Polonius sums up the attitude when he states that the prince does 'but trifle/And [means] to wreck thee' (II.i.113–14). One meaning of a 'trick' is a 'trifling ornament or toy; a trinklet, bauble, knick-knack' (*OED*), and it is precisely these items that Ophelia returns to Hamlet when, under duress, she rejects his suit.[4] The major irony lost upon Polonius is that he trifles with his daughter in using her as a pawn to trick Hamlet into the revelation of the cause of his distemper, and while it is possible to read her subsequent lapse into madness positively – Phyllis Gorfain describes her as a 'Female Grotesque, a double-bodied figure of exuberant excess and mortality which dominates carnivalesque texts' (Gorfain 1991: 34) – the overriding impression is of Ophelia as a victim of circumstance and political exigency. According to Horatio, Ophelia 'speaks much of her father, says she hears/There's tricks i'th' world' (IV.v.4–5), and as her snatched refrains illustrate, the theme preoccupying her is of maidens tricked by misleading promises into yielding to men's desires: 'How should I your true love know/From another one?' (IV.v.23–4), she sings, and 'It is the false steward that stole his master's daughter' (IV.v.173–4).[5] Laertes is speaking of the tears he cannot suppress when he formulates his reaction to the news of Ophelia's death, but his mode of expression stands in ironic relation to the fate of a woman dictated to by her brother, abused by her father and engulfed by her own insanity: 'It is our trick; nature her custom holds,/Let shame say what it will' (IV.vii.162–3).

But *Hamlet* is sufficiently unpredictable in its effects to make it increasingly difficult to conceive of the play according to a binarism between the trickster and the tricked, the victim and the victimizer. At one level, it explores the situation of those who suffer by being arbitrarily manipulated; at another level, it implies that even the trickster has a vulnerable and foolish underside. If Hamlet and the split selves associated with him are tricksters, then they are equally fools who either overreach or pin too great a faith on their own abilities. Scott (1990: 162) has written: 'Occasionally the fool and trickster figures are combined, and the guile of the underdog may consist in playing dumb or in being so clever in the use of words that his enemy is misled'. This point which is taken further by Pelton (1980: 15), who observes: 'All tricksters are foolers and fools, but their foolishness varies; sometimes it is destructive, sometimes creative, sometimes scatalogical, sometimes satiric, sometimes playful'. In his Renaissance manifestation, the fool lent himself well to analyses in dramatic texts of the constraints of obligation, of the shifting balance of power relations, and of opportunities to protest against political injustices. Particularly at times of carnival, fools or boy bishops were elected; protected by a licensed impunity, they played a key role in the festival's overturning of social hierarchies, mockery of establishment figures and scurrilous elevation of sexual practices. The impermissible behaviours which they were permitted to practise were bound up with the liminal or interstitial location of the fool in early modern culture. As either natural or professional *exempla* of mental 'abnormality', fools were expected to confound normative categories and to question from the margins the institutions that lay at the centre of political life. A 1590 pamphlet describes Richard Tarlton, the fool and jester to Elizabeth I, in terms which speak eloquently of his refusal to answer to existing taxonomies: 'Well, howsoever either naturall, or artificiall, or both, he was a mad merry companion, desired and loved of all' (*Tarltons Newes Out of Purgatorie*, in Creigh and Belfield 1987: 145).[6] Pursuing the idea of the Renaissance fool's vexed relationship to contemporary classification procedures, Nardo (1991: 180) writes: 'He indulged every appetite, yet inspired awe as one touched by God; enjoyed access to the great, but remained a social nullity; inverted the social structure, and received rewards for causing havoc'. In view of the subversive potential represented in the fool, it is easy to recognize how, in *Hamlet*, the figure could be used to test the boundaries between subtle assurance and fallible misjudgement, between the trickster's craft and the crafty tricks which he must overcome if his authority is to remain intact.

An essential aspect of Hamlet's defence mechanism as a trickster is his ascription of folly to his enemies, and it is a strategy that permits him verbally to reduce the king and his most valued counsellors. In his early conversations with Ophelia, Polonius contemplates the possibility that he might be shown up as a 'fool' (I.iii.109) by Ophelia's acceptance of favours, preparing the way for Hamlet's construction of his conduct. 'These tedious old fools!' (II.ii.218), exclaims Hamlet, adding (when he suspects that he and Ophelia are not alone), 'Let . . . him . . . play the fool nowhere but in's own house' (III.i.133–4). What concerns Hamlet is not so much that Polonius, Rosencrantz and Guildenstern 'fool [him] to the top of [his] bent' (III.ii.366) but that they should pursue their tactics to a dangerous extreme, threatening to invade that interior 'mystery' (III.ii.349) which he so prizes and finally to take his life itself. For all his bumbling slow-wittedness, Polonius remains a politician and a shape-shifter (II.ii.166–7) who cannot be discounted, and in bidding farewell to him as an 'intruding fool' (III.iv.32), Hamlet suggests that he has gone beyond his customary liminal location: on this occasion, for Polonius to have concealed himself behind the arras is too close for comfort.[7]

Of course, Hamlet hopes that the 'fool' he has dispatched is none other than Claudius (only to learn that he is mistaken), and the expectation indicates that the epithet is one he reserves for particular enemies as well as for the activities of Elsinore in general. In his vilification of Claudius to Gertrude, Hamlet indicts his uncle as:

> a vice of kings,
> A cutpurse of the empire and the rule,
> That from a shelf the precious diadem stole
> And put it in his pocket – . . .
> A king of shreds and patches – . . .
>
> (III.iv.90–3, 95)

From college inventories and contemporary frontispieces, we learn that the fool wore a 'motley' (particoloured) dress (Billington 1984: 47; Laroque 1991: 131); in referring to Claudius' appearance typologically, therefore, Hamlet is recalling Iniquity, the vice of the moralities, and emphasizing the slippery duplicity to which the King is connected. Perceiving Claudius as a common criminal is a typical trickster manœuvre whereby Hamlet can reify the court, affirm his own distinctiveness and establish his father's comparably Herculean stature.

At one and the same time Hamlet draws upon the imagery and language of foolery for reductive purposes and to determine how far he might extend his criticisms of corrupt political institutions. While he generally employs the fool in a pejorative sense, he also identifies with and ventriloquizes him, excited by the possibility of an extemporized wit that transcends social and cultural restrictions. Hamlet is as much the fool as those he condemns for their foolish practices. In this respect his advice to the First Player is relevant:

> O reform it altogether. And let those that play your clowns speak no more than is set down for them; for there be of them that will themselves laugh to set on some quantity of barren spectators to laugh too, though in the mean time some necessary question of the play be then to be considered. That's villainous, and shows a most pitiful ambition in the fool that uses it.
>
> (III.ii.36–42)

Although Hamlet instructs against allowing the fool to speak out of turn, he himself interrupts during the play-within-the-play and hinders its smooth unfolding, suggesting that once again he fails to recognize the applicability of his statements to his own predilections. In this sense, Hamlet himself becomes a kind of displaced fool, and his attraction to the part is highlighted when he asks Guildenstern to play upon the 'pipe' (III.ii.334) which he has stolen from the players: the 'drum' and 'pipe' were both the fool's insignia and the instruments of his craft (Billington 1984: 43; Gurr 1987: 123).[8]

The fool with whom Hamlet identifies most closely, and for whom he attempts to speak, is Yorick, whose skull is exhumed in what could be a grotesque recasting of Ned Browne's return from the grave. Before Yorick's skull is revealed, the two clowns engage in a verbal wrestling match in which they do their utmost to out-trick each other in riddles and double meanings, looking forward to a parallel competition as Hamlet, alternating between prose and verse, contemplates his equal in 'infinite jest' and 'most excellent fancy' (V.i.176–7). Once he has mastered 'the trick to see't' (V.i.86) and has allowed his imagination to construct a history for the bones that the First Clown uncovers, Hamlet is entranced. 'Why, might not that be the skull of a lawyer? Where be his quiddits now, his quillets, his cases, his tenures, and his tricks?' (V.i.93–5) Hamlet asks, significantly reading trickery into the execution of justice, only to find that the reminder of Yorick brings home a sharpened awareness of the vanity of his own tricksy enterprise. It is the fact of Yorick's disappearance from popular consciousness and obvious inability to answer back that provokes Hamlet's despair at the futility of ambition and, in particular, his attachment to the transformatory capacities of language: as he laments, 'Alexander died, Alexander was buried, Alexander returneth into dust' (V.i.199–200). Taken as a whole, the scene introduces a sobering note: the First Clown fools Hamlet in the area where he prides himself most highly – wit-play – while Yorick, the final trickster against whom Hamlet must measure himself, serves to recall that words, too, are subject to time and that the inevitability of mortality will always outweigh the power of the jest.[9]

When the First Clown describes Yorick as a 'mad rogue' (V.i.170), a rhetorical pattern related to but different from that of foolery is reasserted. Ultimately it is not so much the language of trickery or folly that informs *Hamlet* but terms borrowed from the rogue pamphlet, so expressively reflected in Ned Browne's exploits. The phrase 'mad rogue' suggests the 'counterfeit madman' type of such pamphlets, and it harks back to Hamlet's parallel identification of Claudius as a thieving 'cutpurse' (III.iv.91). Wherever one looks in *Hamlet*, the discourse of roguery is a privileged resource. As an instance one can cite Hamlet who asks Gertrude, 'What devil was't/That thus hath cozened you at hoodman-blind?' (III.iv.72–3); and who later indicts Claudius for having 'Thrown out his angle for my proper life,/And with such cozenage' (V.ii.67–8). Here the allusion seems to be to the rogue known as the 'Hooker' or the 'Angler'; according to Thomas Harman, in *A Caveat for Common Cursitors Vulgarly Called Vagabonds* (1566), 'These hookers or Anglers be perilous and most wicked knaves', hooking 'our clothes and linen . . . out at our windows as well by day as by night' (Kinney 1990: 110, 119). For Hamlet it is a small but dangerous step to graduate from hooking clothes to angling for a life.

A trick can connote 'A feat of dexterity or skill, intended to surprise or amuse; a piece of jugglery or legerdemain' (*OED*); thus, when Laertes, pressing Claudius to reveal the truth about his father's death, exclaims, 'I'll not be juggled with' (IV.v.130), a host of tricksy associations is brought into play. The trickster himself is characterized by his fondness for juggling, although his delight in the art can land him in trouble: the Winnebago trickster, Sitconski, learns an eye-juggling trick from some birds. As Paul Radin (1956: 100) states, however, 'When he throws both his eyes on a tree . . . they remain there, and he is obliged to make new eyes of pitch'. But juggling was more often the province of the vagabond or rogue. Wandering medieval entertainers, such as the *crosán* in Ireland, combined dancing, singing, juggling and acrobatics in their performances (Harrison 1989: 46), while some rogue pamphlets concentrated exclusively on an elaboration of the practice: states Samuel Rid in *The Art of Juggling* (1612), the 'true Art, therefore, of Juggling consisteth in Legerdemain', adding 'Certain Egyptians banished their country . . . arrived here in England, who being excellent in quaint tricks and devices, not known here at that time among us, were esteemed and had in great admiration' (Kinney 1990: 267, 265). While juggling is only hinted at in *Hamlet*, the meanings it sparks off are central to the play, and extend in unexpected directions the connections between folly and trickery, trickery and roguery, adding a further elusive dimension to Elsinore and granting an urgent contemporary force to Hamlet's pronouncements.

To recapitulate: in its realization of split or multiple selves, *Hamlet* enlists the traditions of the fox, the fool and the rogue, complicating the expectation that the play can be understood in terms of a diagrammatic relationship between those who trick and those who are tricked, and stressing the trickster's failings as fully as his successes. These features of the play's dramatic method are most in evidence as the action reaches its climax: in particular, the closing stages unite the trickster motifs that have marked *Hamlet* as a whole and parallel the efforts of the characters in ways which illuminate their shared stratagems and common political procedures. Initially, however, the denouement is delayed: time plays a trick on Hamlet when he enters too late to hear

Claudius' attempts to confess at prayer. Ironically, Claudius, too, recognizes trickery's limitations, his soliloquy acknowledging that juggling with divinity is an impossibility:

> May one be pardoned and retain th'offence?
> In the corrupted currents of this world
> Offence's gilded hand may shove by justice;
> And oft 'tis seen the wicked prize itself
> Buys out the law. But 'tis not so above.
> There is no shuffling, there the action lies
> In his true nature, and we ourselves compelled
> Even to the teeth and forehead of our faults
> To give in evidence.

(III.iii.56–64)

As Claudius is realizing that legal justice can be manipulated but that there is no 'shuffling' (trickery) where God's judgement is concerned, Hamlet is determining to trick the King out of salvation by surprising him when he is drinking or 'in his rage' (III.iii.89), a resolution that proves truer in retrospect than he can anticipate. A similar parallel emerges when Hamlet turns the tables on Claudius' 'knavery' (V.ii.20) in electing Rosencrantz and Guildenstern as the bearers of the commission to have him executed. While Claudius has been attempting to cheat final judgement, Hamlet is cheating death, recalling myths of 'asocial' tricksters 'banished from the community' (Laura Makarius, 'The Myth of the Trickster: The Necessary Breaker of Taboos', in Hynes and Doty 1993: 83) and the practices of Hermes, the classical trickster and messenger, who selects or adapts those messages which he chooses to present (William G. Doty, 'A Lifetime of Trouble-Making: Hermes as Trickster', in Hynes and Doty 1993: 62)[10]. Claudius and Hamlet, Hamlet and Claudius, again come together as rivals in craft, opposed to each other and twinned in their tricksy inventiveness.

'Shuffling' is a description that returns when Claudius, discussing arrangements for the duel, imagines how the foils might be mixed to help Laertes' chances (IV.vii.113). The prompt for the tricksy plan comes from Claudius' recollection of the fantastic Norman gentleman, Lamord, whose name indicates the death-dealing properties with which he is associated:

>   but this gallant
> Had witchcraft in't. He grew into his seat,
> And to such wondrous doing brought his horse
> As had been incorpsed and demi-natured

With the brave beast. So far he passed my thought
That I, in forgery of shapes and tricks,
Come short of what he did.

(IV.vii.72–8)

The centaur-like representation of the Norman, and the fusion of the
rider and the horse, harks back to and vies with a typical Hamletian
device: Claudius is creating an emblematic *impresa*, rather in the manner of the emphasis placed upon Pyrrhus earlier in the play. Lamord
is envisaged as a figure to be read and interpreted, and as a prodigy who
can, like the trickster, work miraculous transformations. His feats of
horsemanship constitute the 'shapes and tricks' that Claudius describes;
with both terms, however, there remains a heightened secondary sense
of the dissembling that the King devises and the form that Laertes'
revenge will take.

At the duel itself, the play's key discursive patterns are deployed for
the last time. The main 'trick' is, of course, the 'crafty or fraudulent
device of a mean or base kind' (*OED*) that Claudius engineers, but
trickery saturates the scene as a whole. Despite his conviction that the
duel is 'foolery' (V.ii.162), Hamlet is fooled by the duel, dying before
he has had the chance to say more (V.ii.290), tricking the audience
into thinking that there will be some revelation. Like the trickster,
Laertes, too, is hoisted with his own petard – 'I am justly killed with
mine own treachery' (V.ii.261) – and even Horatio manages to
recognize the irony of 'purposes mistook/Fallen on the inventors'
heads' (V.ii.337–8), although his pat summary of the play's events suggests that the narrative he promises to unfold will unwittingly trick
Fortinbras rather than illuminate the subtleties and intricacies of action
that the audience has experienced. The closing stage tableau reveals
a community of tricksters, all caught in traps of their own creation,
rather like the classical trickster, Palamedes, who is executed when
gold buried beneath his tent to incriminate him is discovered (Wilson
1990: 6–7), or like Ananse, the West African trickster, who challenges
a life-size figure of sticky gum designed to scare crop-stealers, only
to be entrapped by it in the familiar 'tar-baby' sequence (Christopher
Vecsey, 'The Exception Who Proves the Rules: Ananse the Akan
Trickster', in Hynes and Doty 1993: 119). As Wilson (1990: 7) states:
'inventiveness can be outinvented; every player can be outplayed. The
typical arrogance of gamewrights and players should be viewed
ironically: anyone can be beaten, for, in the world of games, invincibility
is impossible'. As far as Hamlet is concerned, he is able, like Ned
Browne, to make a joke out of death, punning on his 'rest' (V.ii.311);

unlike the rogue, however, he is denied the opportunity properly to confess or to tell his own story.

IV

At the start of this chapter I suggested that *Hamlet* engages with ideological forces that circulated outside the Elizabethan theatre. I also suggested that the trickster figure could be used to meet a variety of psychological and social functions. In bringing the chapter to a conclusion, I would like to explore these observations in greater detail. It needs to be pointed out, first, that the theatre itself was a location for the production of meaning, and that ideology belongs as much to a play as to the society that produces it. The relationship between a text and its context is never a one-way process: both shape and determine each other in a reciprocal dialectic. The psychological and the social, moreover, are rarely separable. Both elements, with different emphases, may figure in the trickster's operations, and the categories to which they belong are not mutually exclusive.

At one and the same time *Hamlet* displays a responsiveness to political, sexual and social forces, and stands as a text which actively intervenes in historical debate. This is the sense in which the play negotiates with pertinent questions: neither unambiguously recuperative nor completely subversive, it confronts, tests and reflects upon contemporary concerns and anxieties. Without asserting that trickery in *Hamlet* is reproduced in Elizabethan institutions, it can still be argued that the play's rhythms take energy from the deceptions and adjudications, the uncertainties and polarities, that were prominent features of the period, particularly in their political manifestations. In her religious policies, Elizabeth I had to steer a fine line between Protestants who felt that the 1559 Acts of Supremacy and Uniformity did not go far enough towards a national settlement, and Catholics who protested against the extent to which the new service underplayed the role of communion and neglected Marian episcopal traditions. Both parties had grounds for claiming that they had been tricked, and, as Warren (1993: 18–19) states, Elizabeth needed 'to perform a tricky but sensible balancing-act to keep her likely (Protestant) supporters *and* her potential (Catholic) opponents reasonably happy until political circumstances made her less unwilling to tread on sensitive consciences at home and abroad'. Despite the insistence on adherence to Elizabeth as Supreme Governor of the Church of England, religious pluralism gained ground as the period progressed. The final years of the reign were plagued by the

Separatists and the Puritans, whose radical demands, sometimes for the complete abolition of authority, reached their fullest flowering during the civil war. *Hamlet* bears only a tangential relation to these controversies; nevertheless, its questions about damnation and salvation, its confusions over the intentions of supernatural presences, and its worried invocation of ministers of grace have their place in a wider context of theological turmoil and dissent. The occasionally unorthodox stance of the play – Hamlet chafes at the divine injunction that prevents him from committing suicide (I.ii.131–2), and sees 'man' not as God's 'noble' (II.ii.301) creature but as a 'quintessence of dust' (II.ii.306) – is in keeping with a larger cynicism and despair. The playwright, Christopher Marlowe, who died in 1593, supposedly declared that 'Moyses was but a Jugler and that one Heriots being Sir W. Raleigh's man Can do more then he' (Boas 1953: 251), and his sentiments find an ally in Hamlet's spurts of iconoclastic distemper, one possible consequence of a tendency towards contesting organized religion and the forms it assumed.

Trickery may have been a fear underpinning religious debate rather than its material circumstance, but discussion about the succession was certainly coloured by subterfuge at every level. In *Hamlet*, who precisely is the rightful heir to the Danish throne is never clearly determined. While isolated remarks suggest that Hamlet will accede, the rest of the play prevents such a straightforward interpretation. By referring to Gertrude as his 'jointress' (I.ii.9), Claudius suggests that she, too, has a claim, although even this argument is challenged by the later hint that the King usurped the throne (III.iv.88–93). Act V abruptly rounds off the confusions by establishing that Denmark is an elective rather than a hereditary system. Particularly galling to Hamlet is that Claudius 'Popped in between th'election and my hopes' (V.ii.66), and Fortinbras confirms that these hopes were sound ones (V.ii.350–1). The tricksy prevarications that animate *Hamlet* on the succession issue have their counterpart in speculation about Queen Elizabeth's replacement, which gained in intensity as her reign drew to a close. As I have argued elsewhere:

the 1590s show [James VI of Scotland] renewing scheming contrivances, commending himself indiscriminately to various Catholics, and corresponding with Florence and Tyrone, in anticipation of being elected to the English monarchy. Most intriguing were the letters that passed between James and Cecil in which preparations were made for the Scottish king's assumption of duties and London arrival. Complex numerological codes prevented the identities of the writers from being known; they constituted a private language designed to foil Elizabeth's intercepting agents.

(Burnett, 'The "Heart of My Mystery": *Hamlet* and Secrets' in Burnett and Manning, 1994: 37)

Like Claudius, 'bound', to 'double business' (III.iii.41), James was playing a dangerous game, courting his chances with the Queen and simultaneously promoting his candidacy with her servants. It is not that *Hamlet* casts Claudius in a recognizable political guise; rather, the play points towards the tricksy and doubling machinations that surrounded contemporary succession questions and, in representing a system still aspiring towards a coherent policy, anticipates the silences and hesitations that marked Elizabeth's refusal to acknowledge the imminent end of her line.

A woman occupying a traditionally male preserve was an ideological contradiction, a monstrous anomaly that challenged patriarchal dictates and reinforced myths about female wiles and deceit. For much of her reign, Elizabeth was forced (or chose) to compromise between asserting her political power and apologizing for the supposed vulnerability of her sex, a process which involved her in playing a variety of (inevitably contradictory) roles – princess and prince, chaste goddess and mortal mistress, mysterious virgin and wife to her people. No doubt related to the anxieties provoked by Elizabeth are the vilifying and untrusting declarations of *Hamlet*, which arraign women for their tricksy duplicity. In addition, as Elizabeth's presence on the throne offered a prompt for some women to take advantage of new social, economic and educational opportunites to improve their lives, so did the popular pamphlets of the period begin to revive interest in the dangers of women's transgressions. For Joseph Swetnam in *The Arraignment of Lewd, idle, froward, and unconstant women* (1615), a work which associates a wife's delight in wearing cosmetics with her poor economic management, women are 'crafty . . . thievish, and knavish'; they have 'ten thousand ways to deceive thee and all such fools as are suitors unto them'; and they resemble 'in shape Angels but in qualities Devils' (Henderson and McManus 1985: 193, 201, 205). There are some telling connections here with the doubling structures of *Hamlet*, with the stress placed in the play on face-painting and lasciviousness, and with the prospect of men fooled by women's manipulative excesses. Women's tricks and tricked women in *Hamlet* refract and mediate the more pressing phenomenon of shifting sexual roles in a changing early modern landscape.[11]

Early modern England was subject to rapid changes at a variety of levels. While these changes were not uniform across all parts, they still made an impact on the country as a whole. Tighter links were being set up between outlying areas and urban centres, and local communities were establishing greater connections with national administrative systems. Divisions and stratifications were increasingly apparent: the living standards of the rich and the poor were now more severely polarized, income having been redistributed towards the upper social ranks. At the village level, traditional obligations of neighbourliness were being threatened, and a three-tiered arrangement (of farmers, servants in husbandry and the poor) was giving way to a two-tiered structure, which deepened the gulf between the poor and the more privileged farming and artisan classes. In the cities, upward and downward social mobility, and unemployment and underemployment (the results of population growth, inflation and the rise of commercial enterprise), contributed to a sharper awareness of the importance of regulative offences (Archer 1991: 242–3; Wrightson 1982: 13–14, 60–1, 121–2, 140). As Agnew (1986: 7) states, 'expansion and differentiation . . . prosperity and depression . . . and . . . the seemingly inexorable commodification of land and labour' were the period's major hallmarks.

Explaining dramatic genres in 1590, John Lyly observed, 'If wee present a mingle-mangle, our fault is to be excused, because the whole worlde is become an Hodge-podge' (*Midas* (performed 1590; published 1592) in, Lyly 1902, III: 115), and his comment furnishes a means of entry both into perceptions of society and into the ideological functions served by the trickster.[12] The doubling mechanisms of the trickster might be understood as one ideological response to the spectacle of a society in flux, and as a mediator between different categories and a negotiating strategy the figure proved a convenient vehicle for elaborating a contemporary critique. An older tradition was resurrected to explore fresh structural anomalies and, in his metamorphic and provisional prowess, the trickster worked ably as a barometer of fluctuation and change, as an index of a polarized and polarizing social framework. To understand the trickster as symbolic property or a trope, or as the location where political, sexual and social meanings meet, is also to recognize the key importance of the rogue pamphlet. In these productions, questions are asked about what distinguishes a hero from a vagabond, an innocent from a practised dissembler, and even one author from another, and they are concerns which shaped a material praxis as well as a literary genre. Hamlet is indignant that 'one may smile, and smile, and be a villain' (I.v.109) in Denmark, and his worry might equally well have been applied to an England attempting to make sense of unprecedented social forms and new ideological configurations.

The trickster can therefore be seen to perform a purgative function or one that facilitates, like carnival, a release of tensions, and we have already described the centrality to *Hamlet* of carnivalesque inversions. Phyllis Gorfain (1991: 26) puts the case more forcefuly when she describes the play as 'a carnivalesque amalgam of genres and voices in its riddling tests, tricky deceptions, grotesque revenges, and cyclical saga of deaths, near-deaths, and returns'. In Elizabethan England, carnival constituted a space within which unpopular authority figures could be ridiculed, resentments discharged and social ideals scrutinized, and on occasions such as May Day and Shrove Tuesday traditional enemies, such as foreigners, prostitutes and even players, were attacked without the fear of consequent punishment from the courts. The celebratory energies that carnival embodied were essentially ritualistic in origin, and those who participated in the festival were fully aware that they played parts whose limitations and possibilities were subject to the most formal of preventive instruments. As the experiences of early modern Europe testify, however, carnival also reflected anxieties about the lower orders getting out of place, and its mechanisms could be used to precipitate revolt. For the disenfranchised classes, an opportunity to express resistance was carnival's most enticing feature. Although Hamlet is clearly of royal pedigree, the impulses he represents accord with the characteristics of popular carnival resistance. 'I have that within which passeth show' (I.ii.85), he bristles, later adding, 'I must hold my tongue' (I.ii.159) and 'who would bear . . ./The oppressor's wrong, the proud man's contumely,/. . . the law's delay,/[and] The insolence of office . . .'? (III.i.71–4). Claudius worries about the 'great love the general gender bear' the Prince (IV.vii.18), and admits that Hamlet is 'loved of the distracted multitude' (IV.iii.4). Beyond the carnival play of *Hamlet* lies the tradition of the trickster as an agent of social protest, as exemplified in the tale of Ture, the Azande trickster, who ousts Bangirimo, a local tyrant, by clinging to him under the water (Evans-Pritchard 1967: 143), or in the story of the Winnebago trickster, Red Horn, who, with his nine elder brothers, defeats the giants in a game called 'Who can shoot farthest' (Radin 1956: 119). Where *Hamlet*, so aristocratic a play in terms of the social world it dramatizes, reveals its most radical stance is precisely in its allegiance to the political potential of styles of popular entertainment.

Eventually, however, the ideological impact of *Hamlet* can be traced not to its intervention in religion and politics, and still less to its reflections on gender and social instabilities, but to its confrontation with what might be seen as wider metaphysical and epistemological pre-occupations. Waswo (1987: 50, 53) has characterized the Renaissance as a period afflicted by a semantic crisis, during which the efficacy of language as a means of access to an objective reality is called into question, and the equivalence between word and fact can no longer be assumed. With a slightly different emphasis, the concerns he addresses are also those of Agnew (1986: 9), who reads the early modern English state as one obsessed with the fact that the 'signposts of social and individual identity had become mobile and manipulable . . . the . . . principles of liquidity and exchangeability . . . were dissolving, dividing, and destroying form . . . [and] questions [were asked] about the nature of social identity'. For Agnew, these concerns centred around a problematics of representation, and stimulated speculation about the repertoire of images available with which to figure the individual divorced from religious, familial and class conventions in an increasingly market-oriented social framework.

Given the protean and unstable features of such reflections, it is easy to recognize the appeal of the trickster: his malleable form presented itself as an answer to, and an expression of, the early modern epistemological dilemma. From this perspective, it is also possible to begin to understand the appeal of the trickster in the theatre. The protean habits, dissimulating talents and self-conscious artistry of the trickster collectively signalled uncertainties familiar to the performers themselves, as they adapted to a new nexus of commercial and patronage relations. Like the trickster, who slipped in and out of categories, actors inhabited an interstitial position in the culture of the period, being courted as a lord's servants and sometimes condemned, like Ned Browne, as wandering rogues. With its own liminal location in the 'Liberties', moreover, the area outside the walls which formed part of the metropolis but lay beyond the jurisdiction of the city fathers, the public theatre, noted for its deception and trickery, its transformations and its marvels, was the most obvious forum within which such urgent questions could be ventilated. The wit and invention of the trickster, however, are finally dependent on the playwright rather than on the performer. In the balancing-act that he performed between being an actor and a dramatist, a gentleman and an upstart, a manager and a share-holder, and a resident in London and a visitor to Stratford-upon-Avon, Shakespeare embodied many of the polarities which were altering the appearance of the English landscape. In some ways, the true trickster is not Hamlet but Shakespeare, who looked to the figure, almost certainly unconsciously, as an apt emblem for the vagaries of the theatrical profession and the contradictions of his own material experience.

SUPPLEMENT

NIGEL WOOD: Is Fortinbras tainted by the trickster image at all? If he is not, then the play's efforts at closure seem positive. Here is the new hope of effective leadership.

MARK THORNTON BURNETT: I'm not sure if Fortinbras can be said to escape the tricksy deceptions that mark the play as a whole. In the opening scenes, at least, Fortinbras appears to use his attack on the King of Poland as a ruse in order to launch military operations against Denmark (II.ii.60–80), so that we can place only a partial trust in the apology to his uncle. When he next appears, Fortinbras is traversing the country *en route* for Norway, but not until Hamlet (in the Q2 version of the play) has reflected upon what he perceives to be his rival's ruthless decisiveness:

> while to my shame I see
> The imminent death of twenty thousand men
> That, for a fantasy and trick of fame,
> Go to their graves like beds, fight for a plot
> Whereon the numbers cannot try the cause,
> Which is not tomb enough and continent
> To hide the slain?
>
> (Hibbard 1987: 364–5, IV.iv.51–7)

The word 'trick' is here being used in the sense of a toy or a trifle, although there is also a subsidiary sense of pretence and deceit, begging the question that Fortinbras may have been intending to claim Denmark for himself from the start, and may only have been waiting for the most opportune moment to execute such a scheme. Of course, it is dangerous to speculate in the area of biographical fallacy, and Fortinbras remains as sketchy as his brief appearances indicate. In the restless trajectories he traces, however, there is more than a hint of another political machinator: Fortinbras is far from being a cool, clear wind that blows away Elsinore's mysteries and subterfuges.

NW: Nearly all of the equivocation you trace is exhibited in the behaviour of the male characters. They may be the main protagonists in any case, but they still stand in stark contrast to Ophelia, say. Does your analysis *need* to hook up with gender politics?

MTB: I am well aware that parts of my argument might stand accused of reifying precisely those binarisms that I seem to be at pains to reject. However, one can only respond to the specifics of the text rather than rewriting in the light of an already induced ideological orientation. New areas of enquiry would open up if it could be established that women turn the tables on their male counterparts, or if it became clear that *Hamlet* genders its representation of conflicts between rival trickster figures.

For the most part the play would appear to privilege the practices of its male tricksters over and above the women who are generally realized as their most likely victims. Without radically altering the complexion of the play, however, several details refuse to sit neatly in relation to such a one-sided reading. After the newly mad Ophelia has left the stage for the first time, Claudius instructs Horatio: 'Follow her close. Give her good watch, I pray you' (IV.v.71). When she next appears shortly afterwards, Horatio is not in attendance, pointing to a possible neglect of duty: it is certainly the case that an abnegation of responsibility is implied in Ophelia's suicide. Just possibly, Ophelia in her madness practises the tricksy craft that enables her to avoid Horatio's watchful ministrations.

While Q1 is often passed over as a memorially corrupt text, it contains a number of details and scenes that merit careful consideration. In this version of the play, Gertrude emerges as a more knowing personality than later editions would allow. She is, for instance, privately informed by Horatio of Claudius' plan to have Hamlet killed, and it is unclear if she leaves the stage when Claudius and Horatio begin their plans for the arranged duel, suggesting that she may overhear their preparations. In Gertrude's presence, Claudius later admits that 'This very day shall *Hamlet* drinke his last' (I2^r). Too much cannot be made of these scenes, but they do lead to the suspicion that Gertrude drinks the poisoned wine fully aware of the implications of her actions: she out-tricks the tricksters by choosing to take her own life.

NW: I sense a strong resemblance in your approach to the play to what has come (loosely) to be termed a new historicist reading, that is, where History is rendered as composed of textual and mythic material, and where the anecdotal is as privileged an access to the past as any more public witness. Is this your general conviction, or is it only apposite when dealing with a play as complex as *Hamlet*?

MTB: I have to say that I have several problems with new historicism as a methodological procedure. The intricate interlacing of diverse cultural products which is elaborated in new historicist criticism can come across as misleading, as rhetorical sleight of hand, as failing to take account of detailed matters of evidence, place and date. The use of the anecdote raises a number of questions, such as why particular examples are selected, and how representative can they be taken to be. All too often, it might be argued, the anecdote's paradoxical effect is to efface the marginal, to enforce a regiocentric reading of the theatre and to privilege canonically based male writers. A related cause for concern is that the use of Michel Foucault's work, and of the theories of power that he develops, tends to produce overly deterministic readings, which underestimate the attempts at resistance made by a culture's subjects. Many of these objections might be crystallized in the more urgent reservation that new historicism fails to clarify its own theoretical assumptions and methodological principles. The vocabulary favoured by new historicists – of circulation, mediation, wonder or exchange – might be dismissed for its vagueness, while a more forceful but contradictory accusation can see in new historicist work a nostalgic harking back to liberal values of freedom and autonomy, and an essentialist belief that the self can overcome the restrictions of the social process.

From the foregoing discussion it might appear as if my work is placed in a purposeful antithesis to the new historicist perspective. Despite some reservations, I have found new historicism a positive and enabling influence, although I would want to qualify my indebtedness in several respects. There will always be problems in applying a theoretical model to textual analysis, and I hope I have demonstrated the limitations as well as the possibilities involved in such an enterprise. Rather than finding in the anecdote a larger discursive field, I deploy it as a way of apprehending some of the contradictions characteristic of the culture's deepest anxieties. Similarly, the Ned Browne anecdote offers an opportunity to plot the interplay between popular and aristocratic cultural forms, an imperative which is not always acted upon in new historicist practice. My interest is in recovering marginal voices, not in an effort to pinpoint forces of resistance (although this might be part of the process) but to determine the ways in which a text negotiates with the dominant impulses of its material circumstances. In this sense, I choose to privilege neither a subversion/containment model nor one which attends to endlessly trans-gressive possibilities; instead, my focus lies with the interrogative and almost ritualistic aspects of a text's effects, and with the points of contact between negotiation in its literary manifestation and popular festive tradi-tions. The end result, I hope, is to illuminate a broader historical matrix than that suggested in the anecdote; accordingly, in the last section of the chapter, I begin to map the diverse and contradictory contexts that shape *Hamlet*, and the charged place occupied by trickery in a wide range of Elizabethan cultural transactions.

NW: Are you pragmatic in your use of theoretical material, matching its deployment to the text or texts in question, or do you have a more fixed critical bias?

MTB: As I am concerned to practise a number of critical modes and to resist being identified with a particular ideological orientation, I do tend to be pragmatic in my use of theoretical perspectives. However, I work best with approaches that allow me to ground a text in its material contexts, and to this end my recent studies have deployed mainly anthropological explorations in assessments of the role of secrecy, story-telling and gift-exchange in Elizabethan and Jacobean drama. As my essay makes clear, I am also concerned to highlight the importance of social contest in the period: this interest grows out of my ongoing research on representations of domestic master and servant relations, for which James C. Scott's work on the negotiating skills practised by both parties involved in the power equation has proved particularly beneficial.

CHAPTER 2

Hamlet: Text in Performance

PETER HOLLAND

[Performance study of Shakespeare's work takes as its main subject a rich history of interpretations. The text exists in the form of bare notation, and even then there are often conflicting and equally acceptable versions of the plays. Textual stability is often a legacy of the relatively recent growth of a scientific spirit in editing. The common assumption behind works whose existence is textual alone is to prefer the last printed edition in its author's lifetime, yet there are serious flaws in following this rule as far as Renaissance drama is concerned. As a preliminary, we might point to the fact that the copyrighted ownership of an author's words would have been impossible for Shakespeare and his contemporaries. As Andrew Gurr and others have noted (Gurr 1992: 18–22; Bentley 1971: 30), all playwrights at that time barely had contracts with the company for which they wrote. Shakespeare was probably the Chamberlain's Men's resident poet from 1594 onwards, but such writing as he was engaged in could hardly have been undertaken with its existence in print guaranteed:

> their works were written for the stage, for the playing companies, and ... the durability of print was a secondary consideration, the sort of bonus that would normally only come in the wake of a successful presentation in the company repertoire.
>
> (Gurr 1992, 22)

As Peter Holland demonstrates in relation to *Hamlet*, the existence of a play-text cannot be represented faithfully in a linguistic form. It frequently followed performance and, as any theatrical production is collaborative, the author's centralizing and unitary influence (an eighteenth-century creation in any case) need never have survived into performance – much like early drafts on the cutting-room floor. The company are likely to have commissioned the play, and the performing text was theirs. Even if a writer enjoyed an existence in print, it was rare indeed for the publisher to relinquish rights to the manuscript, as the writer had no stake in its future exploitation once the text had been handed over. As Orgel (1981) realizes, the impulse to get back to Shakespeare's original text needs to be restrained by the knowledge that that is an impossibility: the text is conditioned by many personalities, including the company of actors in the early stages of his career and certainly the prospective audience.

Does this mean that performance study is just glorified anecdotage? If there is nothing carried forward of a basic linguistic nature from play to text, then surely any individual peformance is even more evanescent and uninformative for future commentators or practitioners than even the bad quarto of *Hamlet* or each of the two (at least) versions of *King Lear*? It could be that dramatic experience is actually generically distinct from other media of expression in that it is a particularly marked instance of what McGann (1991: 69–87) has termed a 'socialized' text, where the process of understanding original or even subsequent meanings is inextricably bound up with an intended audience or multiple agents in the production of meaning.

To give an account of a dramatic experience is actually to be peculiarly alive to how text can serve and lead to performance, and how that journey might be an ironic or parodic one, where close involvement can be gauged by the degree to which these signals are deflected if not deliberately 'misrepresented'. As O'Toole (1992: 43) puts it, dramatic meaning '*emerges* – it is not laid down ... It is to a degree always negotiable, and continually renegotiable – and more than this, it is not always controllable'.

In the work of Raymond Williams, until his death in 1988 Britain's foremost Marxist cultural critic, Holland discerns an undramatic preconception that eventually qualifies most of his conclusions about drama in its full social dimension: that an investigation of contemporary staging conditions is only ever secondary to a printed play-text, and the 'structures of feeling' that are thus captured for analysis. Drama, therefore, is (without further riders or caveats) 'literature', that is to say, not different in kind from novelistic or poetic art. Holland makes the point that this is a regrettable loss of distinction, an unfortunate surrender to 'print' conventions.

The problem, therefore, is, how can *drama* (as opposed to theatre) be described and so analysed? Perhaps that is not a major concern, as performance study records but is not unduly alarmed at its own treatment of necessarily transient work. Certainly, there are those who believe performances can be described in a standard manner, but work on the problems of staging is more likely to open up fresh opportunities than it is to monumentalize.]

NIGEL WOOD

In 1954 Raymond Williams published *Drama in Performance*, a book which has some claims to be the least regarded of his work.[1] In Alan O'Connor's fine study of Williams, for instance, the book rates barely a passing mention, locating it in the context of Williams' work as a staff tutor for the Workers' Educational Association attached to the Oxford University Department of Extra-Mural Studies and underlining the connection with a form of education in which 'the emphasis was often on drama in performance' (O'Connor 1989: 9).[2] In the four hundred pages of interviews with Williams that make up *Politics and Letters*, *Drama in Performance* is referred to only twice, and on both occasions the title is wrongly given as *Drama and Performance* (Raymond Williams 1979b: 88, 192); whether the mistake is Williams', the interviewers', the transcriber's or the copy-editor's, its survival into print suggests scant interest in the book itself. Mick Wallis, who writes eloquently of the difficulty of placing drama within the institutional forms of drama in higher education, caught, as he himself was, between professional drama training and a university drama course, identifies Williams' book as providing the structure for a course he would wish to have followed 'to make sense of my experimentation, to understand the groundings and possibilities of my creative gestures, the *historicised* relationships between . . . performers and performed-to' ('Present Consciousness of a *Practical* Kind: Structure of Feeling and Higher Education Drama', in Morgan and Preston 1993: 145). But he always refers to the book as *Drama in Use*.

In part the lack of attention to *Drama in Performance* is a consequence of our apparent absorption and superficially complete acceptance of the case the book makes. The study or, as Williams terms it, 'critical essay' (Williams 1991: 15) aims to make its 'theme', the concern of its title, apparent

> in three ways: first, in the development of a method of dramatic analysis; second, in an account of the performance of certain selected plays; and, third, in the argument of certain general ideas in the relations between text and performance in drama, and of the consequences of these ideas in dramatic theory.
>
> (Williams 1991: 15)

The first two, at least, have become normative in the analysis of plays. The critical examination of drama accepts, even if it may choose not to represent, that the material conditions of performance, the theatrical context within which a play-text first appears, are valid, significant and worthwhile areas of study and that the consequence of such study may be a transformation or at least an adjustment in the process of signification which the analysis of the play seeks to demonstrate.

Williams previous book on drama, *Drama from Ibsen to Eliot*, first published in 1952 (see also Williams 1968, which is an extended version of this text), had unequivocally represented drama as the product of a group of authors, writers of literary texts rather than playwrights, whose work could be analysed solely through the published forms of those texts without reference to the performing practices and theatrical conditions within which those works may have been conceived and against which some of the work was posed by the writers. Ibsen and Chekhov, for instance, were not considered in any significant way in connection with the materiality of any form of cultural production, whether the culture of print or of theatre. Ibsen's pattern of writing, for instance, in which, through the later period of his life, the plays were written for publication in time for the Christmas market on a two-year cycle rather than published in the context of theatrical performance, does not figure at all. Chekhov's struggles with Stanislavsky and Nemirovich-Danchenko were seen, even in the revised version of the book, *Drama from Ibsen to Brecht*, published in 1968 (the same year as Williams's substantial extension of *Drama in Performance*), as the posing of dramatic problems which necessitated the intervention of 'another kind of talent – a producer's talent' in the transition from drama to theatre, rather than as a political redefinition of Chekhov's texts, a transformation over which Chekhov was effectively powerless through its interrelationship with the hierarchical structures of power within the theatre company and the disempowerment of the playwright in the circumstances of that production (Williams 1968: 120).[3]

By the end of the 1960s, *Drama in Performance* seemed to form, in Williams's work, one part of a trilogy of studies of nineteenth- and twentieth-century drama, taken with *Drama from Ibsen to Brecht* (1968) and *Modern Tragedy* (Williams 1979a). But just as *Modern Tragedy* in its reprinted form of 1977 lost its representation of the practice of drama, the example of theatre as political statement in Williams' own creative work as playwright embodied in his play *Koba*, *Drama in Performance* as a critical representation of the analysis of the practice of drama receded from attention, soon falling out of print, while *Drama from Ibsen to Brecht* and *Modern Tragedy* continued to be widely sold, widely prescribed for undergraduate courses and, it would seem, widely read.

My concern here with the publication and revision of Williams's writing and the context of its production and reception will, I hope, have resonances with the investigation of the texts of *Hamlet* in print culture and theatrical culture later in this essay. Like *Hamlet*, *Drama in Performance* exists in three texts, two published in the writer's lifetime and one edited after his death; the question of authorial revision, augmentation and the recontextualization through the work of the editor can reasonably be seen as having some parallels. *Modern Tragedy* (Williams 1979a) changes substantially when *Koba* is excised, even if one can comfortably respect Williams' critical judgement in the decision to remove a disappointing play whose shortcomings seemed only to mark the gulf between Williams' acuity as critic and his abilities as playwright; and the book is transformed again when it is both placed historically and framed by the adding of a new 'Afterword' for the 1979 edition, defining the gaps and redefinitions necessitated by the contemplation of tragedy across the intervening years, a fine act of critical self-consciousness.

But the textual changes and the changes in the context within which the books are presented also represent something of the difficulty of placement of the study of drama in performance within Williams' work and within academic work more generally (see Wallis, in Morgan and Preston 1993: 129–62). O'Connor (1989: 89–91) and Holderness ('Introduction', in Williams 1991: 12) both emphasize the WEA's significance in the generation of *Drama in Performance* but it is not clear to me *why* teaching for the WEA should have placed 'an emphasis . . . on drama in performance'. Certainly many of Williams' later essays returned to the consideration of drama in terms of its cultural and materialist practice: it is there in 'Theatre as a Political Forum', for instance, Williams' contribution to a collection of essays on 'avant-garde culture and radical politics' (in Timms and Collier 1988: 307–20). It is also centrally present in the essay Williams contributed to the *Festschrift* for M.C. Bradbrook, a volume he co-edited ('Social Environment and Theatrical Environment: The Case of English Naturalism', in Axton and Williams 1978: 203–23).

That study of the social and theatrical determinants on a specific form of naturalism, a form of drama on which he had repeatedly written, was an especially appropriate contribution to such a *Festschrift* for, if Williams is often placed in a context defined as 'Cambridge English' and understood to mean early contact with Leavis's journal, *Scrutiny*, and the examination of drama as literature occasionally observed in a historical context, then 'Cambridge English' also includes the work of M.C. Bradbrook, the honorand of the volume. O'Connor and Holderness both suggest that Williams' determination to research drama was, in the 1940s, 'a very independent, if not eccentric path' (Williams 1991: 9), and the latter suggests that the decision to 'approach drama as a medium of performance and as a cultural form was a similarly risky and unsupported venture' (Williams 1991: 9). But Bradbrook's work on English Renaissance drama as a cultural form of theatre practice, from *Elizabethan Stage Conditions* (Bradbrook 1932) onwards, was always centrally and unequivocally concerned with 'drama as a medium of performance'. By the time of the *Festschrift*, she was a professor in Cambridge's English Faculty, Mistress of Girton College, Cambridge, and a figure of immense authority in British Shakespeare studies. But her reputation was already considerable at the time Williams began his explorations of drama in the 1940s. Her career is as representative of 'Cambridge English' as the more literary approach against which *Drama in Performance* is placed and within which *Drama from Ibsen to Eliot* had been written.

Scholarship like Bradbrook's lies firmly behind the generalizations about the conditions of performance which open Williams' discussion of *Antony and Cleopatra* in Chapter 4 of *Drama in Performance*. Yet the exact and exacting recreation of those conditions which typifies her work modulates rapidly in Williams' detailed examination of the play into an imaginative and imaginary process of reading as watching. When Williams comments concerning that what 'we notice about [Philo's opening] speech is that we are being moved at once into the heart of the action' (Williams 1991: 68), the 'we' of his analysis has less to do with a posited identity with members of the audience at the Globe than with the response of an intelligent and responsive group of readers. While later parts of the chapter may investigate the use of the elements of the Globe playing-space, for instance the distribution of the characters across the stage in Act IV, scene iii, the performance of the boy actors or the use of the space for Cleopatra's monument (Williams 1991: 72–83), the audience for Williams is not constituted as a group of early seventeenth-century playgoers but as a 1950s reader trying to see what is missing in the act of reading the play, trying to create imaginatively and responsively the implications of Elizabethan staging as an indication of the restrictiveness of literary analysis. The analysis of performance is designed to supplement and verify the kind of analysis of a play's 'structure of feeling' which Williams had proved himself perfectly well able to articulate and investigate without reference to performing conditions elsewhere in his writing.

For if in one light *Drama in Performance* is unquestionably a key inaugurating text in the development of a discipline of stage-oriented, performance-conscious criticism, Williams' brilliant essay does so from within the discipline of 'English studies'. Williams' approach may support that poor relation in the academy, theatre sudies, but it does so by a form of appropriation for a more traditionally acceptable field of study. Williams' pioneering work on television, in, for example, *Television: Technology and Cultural Form* (Williams 1974), and on film, in, for example, his early book with Michael Orrom, *Preface to Film* (Williams and Orrom 1954), establishes the fundamental difference of these forms so that his analysis is within the context of what would now be seen as cultural studies and media studies. But the work on theatre has as a looming anxiety – the question of how to locate drama as a sub-form of literature, a problem Williams never fully resolved.

In one of his most important statements about drama, 'Drama in a Dramatised Society',[4] Williams identified as a modern development the extension of drama beyond the confines of the theatre: 'Drama is no longer . . . coextensive with theatre; many dramatic performances are now in film and television studios' (Williams 1984 11). But drama here, and elsewhere in Williams, is a form of writing, effectively held as distinct from theatre, although the distinction is rarely pursued. It would be possible to argue that the essay itself explores as some sub-species of dramatization certain areas within which that act of writing is subordinated to a point of virtual invisibility – in advertising, for instance, which is seen as a field within which actors 'deploy the same or similar skills' to those they use in a play 'which we can all specify as dramatic art' (Williams 1984: 16). It would also be possible to argue that Williams is often trying to write here about theatricality rather than drama, as if a more accurate title for the essay would be 'Theatre in a Theatricalized Society'. Further, his exploration of dramatization does not seem to prove its distinctive modernity (which here means late twentieth century), for much of the recent work on, say, English Renaissance society has demonstrated the theatricality and dramatic form of, for example, preaching or pamphleteering, so that, in Stephen Greenblatt's analysis of Harsnett, the theatricality of exorcisms, which can be seen as 'stage plays fashioned by cunning clerical dramatists and performed by actors skilled in improvisations', leads quite reasonably into Shakespeare's use of the same concept in *King Lear* (Greenblatt, 'Shakespeare and the Exorcists', in Parker and Hartman 1985: 169).

Drama, for Williams, is a written text generated by an author whose position is not only analogous to but also fully to be identified with the practice of a novelist or poet in the generation of that species of writing called literature. At the opening of his investigation of 'the social history of dramatic forms', for instance, Williams writes revealingly that:

> The dramatist, like the poet or novelist, works in language to create a particular organization of experience, but the nature of the organization, in his case, is in terms of performance; the words

he has arranged will be spoken and acted by other artists, the actors, in the normal process of communication. Already, by virtue of this, and in spite of the fact that the relation between text and performance, the literary work and the acted drama, varies greatly in different periods and societies, the extension from an individual creative activity to a social creative activity is clear.

(Williams 1965: 271)

Though the form of communication is performance, the processes of theatre here become no more than the vehicle enabling the mediation and transmission of the product of the individual writer to the audience. Drama is here explicitly a 'literary work', performance an intervention in that text, the dramatist different from poet or novelist only in so far as performance is specific to the cultural production and reception of the dramatist's literature.

For Williams, then, the play is an object generated in advance of production and unaltered by production. The printed text seems for him simply to represent the essential and essentialized document for critical analysis, a literary work in its ideal form: 'When a dramatist writes a play, he is not writing a story which others can adapt for performance: he is writing a literary work in such a manner that it can be directly performed' (Williams 1991: 159).

That performance transforms the drama in ways more substantial and more troubling than by bringing this platonic text on to the stage does not seem to occur to him. The collaborative process of making theatre, the 'social creative activity' Williams identified, may, of course, transform as well as generate that which is written. If, in most theatre, rehearsal begins with something approaching a complete text, we can easily recognize not only that in some forms of theatre the 'literary work' is only developed through the practice of making theatre, writing becoming a consequence of the improvisation or communal investigation of the materials out of which the piece of theatre is made, but also that in such theatre there may be no writer, no individualized creator, let alone one whose work precedes the processes of performance. While Williams is glancingly aware of this problem, he is frustrated by it since if the performance is 'not accompanied by publication . . . we can know the work only in performance' (Williams 1991: 159). But, even in cases where the written text precedes the generation of the production, the text may be substantially rewritten, either by the playwright or by the performers, and that rewritten text may form the basis for a new version of the text in the form which Williams uses as the basis for his kind of analysis, a published edition of a piece of writing.

It is no accident, then, that in *Drama in Performance* Williams should choose Ingmar Bergman's *Wild Strawberries* as the work to exemplify the apparently different relationship between text and performance in film. Williams writes of film as a case where the object is both 'a single recorded performance' and 'in itself the dramatic production' (Williams 1991: 148). Though in film we often 'have no access to the script which is the written form of this work . . . Bergman has published what he calls his screenplays, and discussed their relations to his finished work' (Williams 1991: 148). But 'script' occludes the substantial differences between varying forms of the 'written form' in their placement in the process of production. A script may be that which the writer first offers for film production; or the text as rewritten by the writer or other writers to accord with the demands of the director or others in the process of pre-production work; or the camera script marked up for shooting; or a record, according with conventions of published screenplays, of that which has been shot. Far from being anterior to performance, script may in film effectively be subsequent to that which already exists. Bergman is unusual, both because he is the writer of the script for his films and because the published form of that script may differ substantially from the film as made.[5] These differences may in part be caused by the problem of notation (a topic to which I shall return), so that, as Williams quotes Bergman writing, the 'only thing that can be satisfactorily transferred from that original complex of rhythms and moods is the dialogue' since 'the script is a very imperfect *technical* basis for a film' (Williams 1991: 148, 150). But Bergman dissociates himself from the category of 'author', distinguishing between writing and film-making,[6] so that the function of this 'text' is only as preparation and clarification for the process of filming, thus denying its accessibility for analysis in Williams' terms.

As Williams accepts, the written play is a very imperfect technical basis for a theatre production. But *Drama in Performance* is 'concerned with . . . *the written work in performance*: that is to say, the dramatic structure of a work, which we may realize when we read it as literature, as this actually appears when the play is performed' (Williams 1991: 18). Williams' model for performance, the transfer from something written to something performed, is also the revelation – or at least the making available for perception – of the dramatic structure. It is a simple and idealist concept of the relationship between text and performance. If, as I have suggested, two of Williams' three aims in the book are accepted, the third is the most vexing and difficult: 'the argument of certain general ideas in the relations between text and performance in drama, and of the consequences of these ideas in dramatic theory' (Williams 1991: 15). While Williams is concerned throughout with the question 'what, historically, is the relation between a dramatic text and a dramatic performance' (Williams 1991: 15–16), he is not concerned, in writing of plays with theatrical performance, with the precise question of what that 'relation' might mean as it affects the definition of the printed text. For a play-text as published both defines itself and may itself be defined in terms of that relationship. The self-definition and the external definition may be substantially at variance.

As an example of this problem let me take David Garrick's performance of *Macbeth*. In January 1744, Garrick played Macbeth for the first time. *Macbeth* was not a play particularly admired in the 1740s; the usual performance text was still Sir William Davenant's version written and performed in 1663, with its spectacular scenes for the witches and careful balancing of the Macduffs against the Macbeths. The Davenant text, while theatrically and commercially effective, satisfied neither Garrick's interest in the role nor his adulation of Shakespeare. In preparing to play Macbeth, Garrick, for the first time in his career, transformed the traditional text, preparing *Macbeth* as well as his role.

When the production opened, billed as being 'as Shakespeare wrote it', Quin, who had played Macbeth successfully for years, was justifiably confused: 'What does he mean? Don't I play *Macbeth* as written by Shakespeare?' (quoted in Murphy 1801, 1: 71). As Orgel (1988: 15) comments,

> Twenty years earlier a producer could have expected to attract audiences by advertising a wholly new *Macbeth*, bigger and better; Garrick's assertion, the invocation of the author to confer authority on the production, marks a significant moment in both theatrical and textual history.

In a way that marked an unprecedented collaboration between the theatre and the new traditions of Shakespeare textual scholarship, Garrick had paid minute attention to the opportunities offered by the latest scholarly research. His primary text was that prepared by the scholar Lewis Theobald in 1740, the most recent edition available to him. But Garrick also consulted Warburton, whose edition was finished, though not published until 1747, and, of course, his friend Samuel Johnson, using some, though by no means all, of the suggestions for emendation and restoration, even for repunctuation, that Johnson had made in his pamphlet *Miscellaneous Observations on the Tragedy of Macbeth*, written but also not yet published by the time of Garrick's performance.

The resulting play-text is not Shakespeare purified. Some lines are still as rewritten by Davenant. Davenant's recognition of the potential for theatrical display offered by the witches was one Garrick could hardly have resisted and, while there was less flying than in Davenant, there was still plenty of song and dance in these scenes. Some parts of the original were still effectively unplayable: there could be no Porter, only a brief appearance by a polite servant; Macduff's son becomes a silent presence, so that the scene concentrates on the pathos of Lady Macduff, and the on-stage child-murder is cut, too; nor can Malcolm be allowed most of his self-accusations in the scene in England.

Garrick's text is over 250 lines shorter than Shakespeare's but he found space to write in a few necessary linking speeches, to cover cut material, and, inevitably, to include a proper dying speech for Macbeth to replace Davenant's single line for the dying Macbeth ('Farewell, vain world, and what's most vain in it, Ambition.').

> 'Tis done! The scene of life will quickly close.
> Ambition's vain, delusive dreams are fled,
> And now I wake to darkness, guilt and horror.
> I cannot bear it! Let me shake it off. –
> 'Twa'not be; my soul is clogged with blood.
> I cannot rise! I dare not ask for mercy.
> It is too late, hell drags me down. I sink,
> I sink – Oh! – my soul is lost forever!
> Oh! (*Dies.*)

Davenant's version, first published in 1674, is announced on its title page as 'Macbeth, A Tragedy. With all the alterations, amendments, additions, and new songs. As it's now Acted at the Dukes Theatre'. There is no mention here either of Shakespeare or of Davenant. The text is that version of the play being performed at the time. When Garrick's version was finally published, in Bell's edition of Shakespeare in 1773, it is offered as 'Macbeth, A Tragedy, by Shakespeare, as performed at the Theatre-Royal, Drury-Lane. Regulated from the prompt-book, with permission of the Managers, by Mr. Hopkins, Prompter'.[7] Again, the published text makes explicit its theatrical transformation. But the version as performed in 1744 was publicized as authentically Shakespeare's, something it clearly is not. Garrick's additional lines are not a matter of scholarly emendation, the attempt accurately to represent that hypothesized, but yearned for, originating authorial text, the literary text, which the accidents of transmission of manuscript and the processes of printing have blurred. They are an actor's attempt to provide himself with the right closing speech, a form of dramatic interpolation premised on the actor's need to die heroically and morally, according to canons of performance practice and dramatic theory appropriate to the moment of production.

Garrick's performing text is more authoritatively Shakespeare's than any version performed that century; it is less authoritatively Shakespeare's than the versions represented in the tradition of eighteenth-century scholarly editions. In its published form it exemplifies the growing bifurcation of Shakespeare editions into separate literary and theatrical forms. It is not difficult to separate out Garrick's additions to the Shakespeare text as evidenced by the First Folio (F, 1623). Nevertheless 'the relation between a dramatic text and a dramatic performance' (Williams 1991: 15–16) needs clarification 'historically' at this moment in the subsequent history of *Macbeth*.

But the relationship may be occluded much earlier in the history of the transmission of a play-text and in the history of the play's performance. In an article written while he was at work on the New Arden edition of *Hamlet*, Jenkins (1960) set out to define what he called, in the title of the article, 'Playhouse Interpolations in the Folio Text of *Hamlet*'. Identifying a number of short passages, 'ranging from single words to passages no more than a line in length' which are present in F but missing from the Second Quarto (Q2, 1604–5), Jenkins wondered whether the words or phrases were 'omitted by the Q compositors or ... perhaps ... never stood in Shakespeare's manuscript at all' (Jenkins 1960: 31). Jenkins pursues John Russell Brown's suggestion, in a study of the compositors of Q2, that the passages might 'have no stronger authority than that of a scribe or the players' promptbook' (quoted in Jenkins 1960: 31–2). Among the passages Jenkins is concerned with are Hamlet's last words or, more accurately, sounds as they appear in F: 'O, o, o, o'. As Jenkins (1960: 41) notes, 'hardly anyone since Rowe has been willing to add the 'O, o, o, o' with which F represents his dying groans'. But if the editorial tradition since Rowe in 1709 has silenced that which F offers to follow 'The rest is silence', it has also tended to remain silent about it: Furness's massive New Variorum edition of 1877 has a brief comment from White (1854) judging F's four sounds 'the addition, doubtless, of some actor' (note *ad loc.*). Jenkins himself, following his editorial theory, cuts the 'O's without comment, recording them in the collation. Wells and Taylor (1986) include 'O, O, O, O!' since they are following F, but do not comment on it.

In his superb Oxford edition, Hibbard (1987: 352) transforms the sounds into a stage direction and amalgamates it with the stage direction that appears in F ('*Dyes*'): '*He gives a long sigh and dies*'. Hibbard's justification (in a footnote) for 'thus "translating" F's "O, o, o, o.", which has been the object of unjustified derision' is a suggestion of E.A.J. Honigmann (1976: 123) who argued that such sounds in Elizabethan plays should be seen as 'crypto-directions', directing 'the actor to make whatever noise was locally appropriate. It could tell him to sigh, groan, gasp, roar, weep'. But the examples Honigmann gives for transforming the early text's 'o' sounds into an editor's stage direction (decoding the cryptography) are far clearer: when the Doctor comments of Lady Macbeth's 'O, O, O!' (V.i.49–50) 'What a sigh is there!' (V.i.51) it does not seem unreasonable to choose to represent the 'O's as '[*A long sigh.*]', as Honigmann suggests.

But it is not so clear what Hamlet's 'O, o, o, o' represents. In a long and extravagant commentary on them, Rosenberg (1992: 923–4) defines them as 'inarticulates', indicating,

> apart from the pain of dying, something of the final mystery of Hamlet's last perception. An *O* of a murmur? a wonder? a laugh? a shock? a groan? *Os* can be most eloquent. (Try them.) ... His last utterances – *O, o, o, o!* – far from bringing his polyphony to rest, can leave it still open-ended, dissonant.

A recent flurry of articles has been generated by the 'O's in F. Brown (1992a: 28–9) described them as representing '[What] Burbage the actor added':

> What can this mean? Did Burbage believe he needed extra time to express pain or disbelief, or to struggle or panic? We have no idea what the four *O*'s were intended to mean and still less notion of what Shakespeare thought about them ... but this addition ... serves to remind us that, however serious Hamlet's last words were intended to be, they had to be spoken while he faced the physical reality of death itself.

By 'Hamlet's last words', Brown meant 'The rest is silence', so that the 'O's are excluded from such 'serious' consideration. In a response to Brown, Mehl (1992: 183) suggested that the sounds 'are the earliest commentary on Hamlet's silence we have and they may well be part of Shakespeare's own revision of the play' and that 'whatever their precise meaning, they confirm the impression that at this point in the play it is not so much "multiplicity of meanings" that is the issue, as the ultimate failure of language'.

Mehl bases his defence of the F passage both on its critical potential (as a moment on which the ingenuity of the critic's investigation of the play's meaning in general or at this specific point can reasonably be expended) and on the possibility of its source being Shakespeare (specifically, Shakespeare as the reviser of the text available in Q2). Maurice Charney's defence is based on the frequency of occurrence of such sounds elsewhere – 'O-groans occur in *Othello*, *King Lear*, *Macbeth*, and in many Elizabethan and Jacobean plays. They were a fairly conventional emotional gesture . . . especially associated with death' (Charney 1992: 188) – and on their possibly authorial source. Significantly, though Charney does not indicate it, the 'O's in *King Lear* are present in the Quarto text but not in the Folio; they are present in that text which has tended to be critically undervalued as subject to playhouse 'corruption' rather than in the text traditionally assumed to be more substantially Shakespearian.

Brown returned to the problem, defending his position with the aid of Jenkins' argument for playhouse interpolation and attacking some of the growing case made by Wells and Taylor and by Hibbard for the Shakespearian origin of the variations in F, part of the argument for seeing variations between certain quarto and folio texts as the product of Shakespeare's rethinking of the plays during their existence in the repertory of the Chamberlain's Men (later renamed the King's Men). Brown (1992b: 280–1) finds F's 'O's unacceptable not only for bibliographical reasons but also because 'the repeated cry contradicts several of the most obvious meanings of the preceding words', because 'the cry is too vague in effect' and because it contradicts Horatio's definition of Hamlet's death as a breaking heart which Brown sees as 'a nearly silent death' in Elizabethan drama. Brown (1992b: 281–2) goes on to offer an explanation of how the 'O's might have been inserted in the playhouse copy and why they might have been preserved.

While Brown's argument is a well-managed piece of bibliographical reasoning, it is driven by his intense dislike of sounds whose addition he finds 'inflate the drama', which 'might be sensational and puzzling', which 'devalue the effect of Hamlet's words, . . . risk sentimentality . . . [and] obliterate the silence that would otherwise follow "silence"' (Brown 1992b: 283). Ultimately, to accept the addition is 'to believe that Shakespeare wished to finish Hamlet off with something that was vacuous in comparison with his many words' (Brown 1992b: 283). And, of course, Shakespeare cannot possibly be vacuous. The bibliographical argument is constructed to justify a notion of Shakespeare's greatness, an assumption that apparently cannot be maintained if the sounds are authorial.

At the root of the debate lies a belief in the recovered authorial text, a text quarried out from behind the accretions of overlay deriving from the practice of printing house and playhouse. The literary text, the text written by Shakespeare, is assumed explicitly or implicitly to be the sole object of critical enquiry, and any argument that suggests that the source of F's copy is Shakespearian must be supported by those who find potency in F's 'O's and rejected by those who find them unacceptable. The critical sophistication of the meanings extracted from or imposed on the 'O's is irrelevant. Mehl's (1992: 183) belief, for instance, that 'the Folio's blunt statement that the wonderfully rich rhetoric of the Prince has faded into inarticulate sound before it is finally reduced to silence' has to be justified and buttressed by the possibility of the sounds' being 'part of Shakespeare's own revision'. Brown's belief that the sounds are not Shakespeare's means that their contradiction of 'The rest is silence' cannot be accepted and worked into an argument for such a subversive sound, a denial of the silence that the over-verbal Hamlet offers. That which is not Shakespearian must be discarded. Anything else would threaten the integrity of the object of analysis, an object that must be perceived as being generated by a single consciousness, that imaginative and imagined subjectivity that constitutes Shakespeare.

At one significant stage of his defence, Brown notes that the page of F (sig. 2Q1ʳ) on which the 'O's appear contains a large number of stage directions not present in Q2: '*They play.*', '*Play.*', '*In scuffling they change Rapiers*', '*Hurts the King.*', '*King Dyes.*', '*Dyes.*', '*and shout within*' (added to Q2's '*A march a farre off.*') and '*with Drumme, Colours, and Attendants.*' (added to Q2's entry for Fortinbras and the Ambassadors[8]) as well as the stage direction '*Dyes*' for Hamlet after 'O, o, o, o'. Brown (1992b: 282–3) comments:

> It is hard to see why Shakespeare should bother to add this information. With the exception of the exchange of weapons and the off-stage shot all is clear enough to an experienced reader of the text; and these two directions can also be inferred with only a very little thought – there is no other way of playing the scene so that its words make sense.

The reader of Q2 is a book-buyer, a person choosing to purchase a quarto edition of a popular play, perhaps influenced by the strong statement on the title-page that the text is 'Newly imprinted and enlarged to almost as much againe as it was, according to the true and perfect Coppie'. But the readers of the text that Q2 later printed were not book-buyers but members of the theatre company, people who were undoubtedly 'experienced readers' but whose aim in reading was less the critical analysis of a literary text than the preparation for performance of a theatrical text.⁹ For them the addition of stage action was a necessary part of performance; that this material reappeared as stage directions, added either by the prompter or by someone who had seen a performance, is unsurprising. That makes explicit what Brown accepts is implicit in Q2 does not make it less accurate, even if it might appear to Brown less sophisticated since it does not rely on the reader's competence and sustained attention to draw out those directions which can be 'inferred'.

But the way in which stage directions can be 'inferred', the extent to which they are present, is not static. In the last chapter of *Drama in Performance*, Williams sets out the 'Argument: Text and Performance'. After exploring the two senses of the word 'drama' – 'to describe a literary work, the text of a play' and 'to describe the performance of this work, its production' (Williams 1991: 159), itself a contentious definition – he outlines four kinds of dramatic action and then the varying relationship of what he sees as the four elements of performance (speech, movement, design, sound) to the 'literary text' according to these four kinds of dramatic action: acted speech, visual enactment, activity, behaviour (Williams 1991: 159–63). The four kinds of action are differentiated here, in a sequence that is implicitly chronological across the history of drama, according to their presumed adequacy, that is, according to the extent to which the text in performance can be adequately deduced from the evidence of the printed text. In 'acted speech',

> when a text of this kind – e.g. the *Antigone* – is set in the known conditions of performance for which the dramatist was writing, the full detail of the performance is seen to be prescribed . . . In such a case, the dramatist is not only writing a literary work; he is also, by the use of exact conventions, *writing the performance*.
> (Williams 1991: 162)

In 'visual enactment', 'the text exactly prescribes the performance, by stage direction, or by necessary inference from the verbal design' in those cases where the enactment is 'fully conventional'. In 'activity', words are subordinate to physical action, so that 'there will usually be scope for considerable variation in performance' (Williams 1991: 162), thereby freeing the text for such variations or representing its inadequate ability to prescribe, depending on whether performance is seen as supplemental or altering, though Williams is here markedly neutral as to whether performance is an interference in the integrity of the literary text. The fourth and final category, 'behaviour', is one where 'there can be no exact relation between the arrangement of words and the method of speaking them' and hence 'the performance' will inevitably be an 'interpretation of the text, and hence subject to wide variation' (Williams 1991: 162–3). In this category the performance 'is based less on the text than on a *response to the text*' (Williams 1991: 163).

Williams' schema, as the culmination of *Drama in Performance*, is implicitly a suggestion of historical changes both in the relationship between text and performance and in the conditions of performance themselves. If 'behaviour' is the mark of a particular definitional aspect of the modern play, it is also the mark of a definitional aspect of the modern performance. Every performance of *Hamlet* now is inevitably an 'interpretation of the text, and hence subject to wide variation', but it is clear that, moments like the duel apart, most of the text of *Hamlet* is perceived by Williams as embedded in the category of 'visual enactment'. The ascription of a play to a category would seem then, at the very least, to be an aspect of the moment of performance.

But it is not clear to me how one can know or test the adequacy of the literary text as a prescribing of convention-bound performance, since we lack any significant detail about the performance even of *Hamlet*, one of the most successful of all English Renaissance plays. The assumption underlying Williams' placing of the text is close to that of Coleridge, who saw contemporary performances as interventionist interpretations (Williams' 'behaviour'): as the reporter of his fifth Bristol lecture (1813–14) had it, 'He had seen Mrs. Siddons as Lady, and Kemble as Macbeth – these might be the Macbeths of the Kembles, but they were not the Macbeths of Shakespeare' (Coleridge 1962, 2: 230). Coleridge believed that Renaissance performance undercut the presence of the performer so that 'the idea of the *poet* was always present, not of the actors, nor of the thing represented. It was at the time more of a delight for the intellect, than amusement for the senses' (Coleridge 1962, 2: 68). As Jonas Barish (1988: 33–4) comments, 'odder still is the notion that such a state of affairs – had it existed – could have been a desirable one, that a Shakespeare play in the theatre would have been all the better for having the colour and density bleached out of it'.

Coleridge's version of performance both bleaches and cleanses, removing the intervention of performer and allowing an unmediated form of access to an originating genius, the writer of the literary text. He shares with Williams the notion of play-text as written and preceding that which makes possible performance. But that need not be the case. Edward Bond's play, *Restoration*, was first published in 1981 at the time of the play's first performance at the Royal Court Theatre. The pressures of time, the need for the play-script to be available in the theatre by the time of the première, meant that, as a note in the edition, presumably by Bond, states, 'The script here represents the play as it was towards the end of rehearsals for the first production' (Bond 1981: 2). This careful definition of the moment of evolution of the text represented by a particular edition is not uncommon in modern plays: Howard Brenton's *Weapons of Happiness*, for instance, was first published with a note that 'This text . . . is that of the first day of rehearsal of the National Theatre production' (Brenton 1976: 8). Bond's note went on to anticipate a further version, to be 'published by Methuen Modern Plays in due course'. But this future text is given an extraordinary valency: the 1981 text, the script as it existed late in rehearsal, 'must not be taken as the basis for future productions'. The future edition is to be 'a definitive, post-production version of the play'. Bond's play is then to be rewritten, the value of the process of rehearsal and performance assessed, the worth of altera- tions made by the author or suggested by director or performers established by their inclusion or exclusion from the 'definitive' text. The decision, the validation, is lodged with Bond, the writer re-establishing control over the text through the copyright in the published editions and the processes of production of text for those editions. The script late in rehearsal, a script already, I assume, bearing traces of the inter- relationship of text and performance, is explicitly prevented from being a script for subsequent performance, for re-production, those future productions that will take place without Bond's controlling presence authorizing textual change.

In 1988, *Restoration* was produced by the Royal Shakespeare Com- pany in the Swan Theatre at Stratford-upon-Avon and accompanied by 'a programme/text' containing the full text of the play. But this version is not that text published in 1982 and anticipated as 'definitive' (Bond 1982); it is, instead, a 'newly revised edition'. While the 1981 text indicated how one might enquire about performing rights (by contacting Bond's agent, Margaret Ramsey) on the same page as it refused the use of this version of the text as a basis for performance, the 1988 text establishes Bond's copyright in the revision without any mention of its potential use for performance.

The case of *Restoration* demonstrates a contemporary author's attempts to sustain control over the text in its most literary form, its materiality as a book, and over its future theatre production. There have been repeated attempts to theorize the nature of performance- orientated criticism, to define the textuality of performance, to wonder whether performance is indeed a text.[10] All are attempts to chart the route from *mise-en-page* to *mise-en-scène*, to wonder about the definition of the written text in relation to that which will or might occur in performance. In different ways each renegotiates the relationship of text and performance that Williams set out to explore in *Drama in Performance*. They do so within an awareness and an informing control offered by not only the possibility of performance but also the facts of performance, that material that theatre history can make available.

From a different perspective, Harry Berger has tried to respond to what he has called '*textual dramaturgy* – that is, to indications of staging given by the Shakespeare text' (Berger 1987: 135).[11] He has formulated three modes of reading: the first, a '*theatrical* model of stage-centered reading', respects both 'the psychological constraints that playgoing imposes on interpretation, and the theatrical circumstances (the "structure of theatrical relationships") that reading must attend to'; the second, a '*literary* model of stage-centered reading', respects the circumstances but not the constraints; and the third 'ignores both' (Berger 1989: xiii–xiv). Berger's work is an intelligent attempt to model, for a mode of criticism that is not directly concerned with that which has been done in the theatre, a recognition of the text's potentialities for theatrically aware but not theatrically constricted criticism.

But Berger's method – and the concerns of those interested in the textuality of performance – fail to consider the nature of the text under examination. If, recently, there have been attempts to find new methods of notating performance,[12] there is also a long and immensely scholarly tradition of attempts to disentangle the nature of notation in English Renaissance texts, the tradition out of which Jenkins' assumption of the need to eradicate traces of playhouse interpolation derives. I shall need here to return to the nature of the three early printed texts of *Hamlet* and to review recent accounts of their origins, not in order to decide on the relative merits of competing arguments but in order to uncover the presuppositions that implicitly underpin their uncovering of the sources of the printed texts.[13]

We can assume that the process of transmission in the Elizabethan playhouse began with a written text provided by – or, occasionally, stolen from – a playwright.[14] This manuscript, usually called 'foul papers', represents the play often with numerous loose ends, deletions, interlineations and other evidence of the process of composition. Throughout this essay I have been referring to the playwright as a singular entity, but Elizabethan playwriting was often collaborative: in the case of Shakespeare it is generally accepted that, for instance, *Two Noble Kinsmen* and *Henry VIII* were written by Shakespeare and John Fletcher and that there is no single originating author; many – perhaps most – of the plays for which Philip Henslowe made payments were the work of more than one author (see Foakes and Rickert 1961). In the theatre, the foul papers needed to be copied and, either before or, more commonly, after the copying, the play was marked up by the 'plotter' for the preparation of the prompt-book.[15] The prompt-book was, again usually, the document authorized by the Master of the Revels, licensing the play for performance. There may have been, on occasions, an intermediate stage in which the foul papers were copied by a scribe before they reached the theatre workers.

The printer's copy, that version of the play available to the compositor setting the play, may derive from any one or a combination of these manuscripts (foul papers, intermediate transcript or prompt-book). One version may have been read against and corrected from another. In the case of a printed edition subsequent to the first, the earlier edition may be used as copy, marked up with alterations derived from any of the manuscript versions. There may also have been manuscript versions prepared for use outside the playhouse, for instance the transcripts prepared by the professional scrivener, Ralph Crane, usually for a patron's private library. Any of these stages, indeed any act of copying, printing or preparation for performance, may, of course, 'corrupt' the text; accidental errors or misreadings alter the text in ways which may be intended neither by the playwright nor by the transcriber. Interlineated passages or marginal additions may be put in the wrong place; first and second versions of the same passage both included where one should have been omitted; any number of possible transformations accomplished. One might, quite reasonably, see the majority of these as blurrings of a recoverable original, a literary object which Williams and others investigate. The work of editors and of textual bibliographers might, with varying degrees of success, disentangle the text from these blurrings.

But, as Gary Taylor notes, 'the prompt-book is a socialized text, one which has been communally prepared for communication to a wider public', and a text's 'progress from a private to a socialized mode' may involve modification (Wells and Taylor 1987: 15). Of the numerous varieties of modification, the principal forms might reasonably be summarized as follows: censorship (words or passages refused by the Master of the Revels); actors' interpolations and excisions, whether or not accepted by the dramatist; additions by another hand in the subsequent run of performances (like the additions to Kyd's *Spanish Tragedy* for which Ben Jonson was paid); additions, alterations or excisions made by the original dramatist (the category of authorial revision); and abridgements or other alterations made for different theatrical purposes (such as for touring, where the available cast may have been smaller). There was also the modification caused by memorial reconstruction, the transcription of a performance through the work of a shorthand reporter and/or through the reconstruction of the complete play from the memories of one or more of the actors who had played it.

Any or all of these modifications could be introduced at any one of the numerous stages in the process of production of a particular printed book, itself the sole surviving witness in the case of by far the majority of English Renaissance plays. When John Heminges and Henry Condell, fellow-members with Shakespeare of the King's Men, prepared the First Folio, they recognized that the volume had not been in any way overseen by Shakespeare himself. Their hope was that their edition both included plays never before published and, in the case of some of the plays that had been printed previously,

> where [before] you were abus'd with diverse stolne, and surreptitious copies, maimed, and deformed by the frauds and stealthes of injurious impostors, that expos'd them: even those, are now offer'd to your view cur'd, and perfect of their limbes; and all the rest, absolute in their numbers, as he conceived them.
>
> (F, sig. ĐA3ʳ)

As Margreta de Grazia has shown, Pollard's argument in 1909 that this passage referred not to all quarto editions (many of which the Folio editors *had* used in the preparation of their edition) but only to those quartos that the Folio editors had not used (for example, *Hamlet* Q1 of 1603), had the effect of justifying and purifying the patrilineal line of descent of editions from Shakespeare through F to the long litany of the editorial tradition. The study of the printing house undertaken by the New Bibliography was

> not primarily to learn more about the mechanics of printing the book; it is to differentiate the non-Shakespearian from the Shakespearian . . . Once the habits and quirks of the compositors can be identified, the alien matter can be eliminated from what Shakespeare is imagined to have put on paper.
>
> (de Grazia 1988: 70–1)[16]

But the plays of F are not unmediated by the interventions of accident and modification. The F text of *Hamlet* is, as far as Taylor is concerned (Wells and Taylor 1987: 396–402), derived from foul papers, transcribed into a prompt-book, in turn prepared by Shakespeare into a version incorporating a number of revisions (by Shakespeare and the actors) made in the course of the experience of the play in repertory performance, and checked against or contaminated by the use of previous printed editions (for example Q3, 1611).

It is generally accepted that the copy for Q2 was 'foul papers'. The logic of the tradition of editing, that tradition which searches for the Shakespearian behind the non-Shakespearian, was therefore to edit from Q2, to purify the text, from those accidents of the printing house which affected the printing of Q2, by careful reference to a text (F) which was held not only to betray traces of further printing-house incompetence but also to show the additional problems of playhouse incompetence. This line of argument was most strongly established this century in the two volumes of John Dover Wilson's long study, *The Manuscript of Shakespeare's 'Hamlet'* (Wilson 1934), a work that in its title established its search for a document that does not survive. Its latest strong formulation was by Philip Edwards who, ending his discussion of the textual problem of the play in his edition for the New Cambridge Shakespeare, summed up:

> I believe there was a point when Shakespeare had made many alterations to his play, mostly reflected in cutting rather than adding material, some of which he may have made after pre-liminary discussions with his colleagues among the Chamberlain's men. The play then became the property of these colleagues who began to prepare it for the stage. At this point what one can only call degeneration began, and it is at this point that we should arrest and freeze the play, for it is sadly true that the nearer we get to the stage, the further we are getting from Shakespeare.
>
> (Edwards 1985: 31–2)

One does not have to call the process 'degeneration' at all. The frozen text Edwards aimed to create is based on a notion of the transfer of property that excludes writing from performance and denies the possibility that actors could ever contribute effectively to the making of a literary text for theatre. As de Grazia (1988: 81) comments,

> what bibliographical treatments of Shakespeare resist is non-authorial writing; that is, a play text recording a wide array of collective and extended contributions and transformations. And what critical treatments evade is non-authorial meaning; that is, discourse representing the interplay of the cultural and economic activities in which performance and publication are involved.[17]

Even the labour of those bibliographers whose work has investigated the extent to which variations between editions demonstrate the presence of Shakespeare as a reviser of his own plays, the search has been for Shakespeare separated out from non-Shakespeare, for that object in which a modern culture 'characteristically invests a good deal of intellectual capital' (Hawkes 1986: 76). For, if we accept that Shakespeare's plays were written 'not for publication but for performance' and that they were, 'in their inception at least, not books but scripts, designed to be realized on the stage' (Orgel 1988: 6), then critical approaches have to consider the sheer length of *Hamlet*, a text too long for Renaissance performance without cutting. Orgel (1988: 7) suggests that 'Shakespeare habitually began with more than he needed, that his scripts offered the company a range of possibilities, and that the process of production was a collaborative one of selection as well as of realization and interpretation'.[18] Certainly many English Renaissance plays were published marking their differences from the version performed, but only two, Marlowe's *Tamburlaine* and Jonson's *Sejanus*, record those differences as cutting for publication. Elsewhere the printed text incorporates material that, for example, in the case of Webster's *The Duchess of Malfi*, 'the length of the play would not beare in the presentment' (title-page, 1623).[19]

Q2 may witness a potential for performance but it is not, in itself, a witness of performance, neither in the external definition through bibliographical study of its printer's copy nor in its self-definition. Where the title-page of Q1 emphatically defines itself as *Hamlet* 'As it hath beene diverse times acted by his Highnesse servants in the Cittie of London: as also in the two Universities of Cambridge and Oxford, and else-where', Q2 emphasizes only its extent as a printed book ('Newly imprinted and enlarged . . . '). Q1 uses the standard form of presentation for printed Renaissance plays, identifying the published text as a record of past performances ('as it hath beene . . . acted').[20]

But Q1 is the most vexing of the three early texts. Usually vilified, Q1 has recently begun to be examined afresh as part of a more general re-evaluation of the so-called 'bad quartos'.[21] A pirated text, printed without the permission either of the theatre company or of the printer who had claimed it in the Stationers' Register, the copy for Q1 may have been derived from a memorial reconstruction or an abridgement for a touring company or even a version played at the Globe or some mixture of all three; it may be based – at, depending on the way the evidence is viewed, very different degrees of distance – on a Shakespeare version prior to either Q2 or F or between the two or after the text that lay behind F.[22]

There is no doubt both that some version of the text lying behind Q1 was performed and that Q1 itself can still be performed.[23] But its evidence is perplexing. When it indicates that the mad Ophelia enters, at IV.v.20, 'playing on a Lute, and her haire downe singing' (sig. G4ᵛ), Q1 most probably records that *an* Ophelia did that, not that Shakespeare prescribed either hairstyle or prop, or even that either was the case in performances at the Globe by the Chamberlain's Men.[24] That the first is a 'conventional theatrical representation of madness' (Wells and Taylor 1987: 408) does not prove that it was actually a conventional practice at the Globe. Madness is often theatrically represented through a convention of dress: in Japanese Noh theatre, for instance, female madness is indicated by folding the actor's robe back from the right shoulder (see for example, Keene 1970: 107, 135). Williams' argument might suggest that the Q1 stage direction is a moment where 'the text exactly prescribes the performance'. But, since Q1 might represent a theatrical provenance quite other than the work of the Chamberlain's Men and hence quite other than the source of Q2 and F, we cannot assume that Q1 is sufficient to define the mode of representation, the transition from text to performance, for Globe performances. The exact prescription, as Williams observes, can only operate where the action 'is fully conventional'. Q2 and F, at this point, fall into the category of Williams' rider: 'In other cases, the text does no more than prescribe an *effect*, of which the *means* must be worked out in performance' (Williams 1991: 162).

A similar problem occurs in the closet scene when Q1's direction for the entry of the ghost of Hamlet's father specifies 'Enter the ghost in his night gowne'. Both Wells and Taylor and Hibbard adopt the direction (at III.iv.95). In a footnote, Hibbard (1987: 282) carefully and accurately identifies this as 'the only indication we have of how the Ghost appeared in this scene in Shakespeare's day', since it seems more likely that this direction has entered Q1 as a report of performance rather than as a suggestion for future performance, that the stage direction is descriptive of practice rather than prescriptive. But, though Hibbard sets out other advantages the costume offers, the stage direction does not indicate that this was how the Ghost appeared in performances that used the F text which Hibbard is editing.

The precision of such stage directions in Q1 is a temptation, encouraging assumptions about the relationship of text to performance. Williams' argument about the nature of text depends on an assumption that text can – or, at least, at moments of the history of drama, did – represent adequately the performance. Textual minutiae though these two moments in Q1 *Hamlet* may be, such precise information as the stage directions suggest emblematizes the difficulty of extrapolating from a printed text whose status is so frustratingly imprecise. While we cannot identify with certainty the circumstances of those performances with which the text of Q1 might be connected, we cannot possibly know the degree of connection with Shakespeare that such stage directions might represent. If we reject the critical approach that seeks only to pay homage to the imagined author, the theatre offers an awkwardly messy alternative: not one from which the author has been removed but one 'in which complex interaction between author and stage often occurs and in which the author may be precisely *not* a rarefied presence behind the playtext but a collaborator in the process of performance' (Dillon 1994: 76). But what sort of collaborator?

The three early texts of *Hamlet* offer three witnesses of different states of a text, three modes of possible connections to different moments of performance. Properly considered, they dissolve the unitary notion of the play, of a play-text, which has underpinned critical approaches to the play. They constitute three moments, the only three extant versions, out of the myriad forms Shakespeare's play might have taken in the early seventeenth century. Text, the written or printed evidence of the author's writing, is no more stable, fixed or unitary than the history of performances. But the examination of text in all its disturbing fluidity opens up the relationship of author to theatre in ways that most literary analysis disregards.

The problem this essay has tried to investigate is one embodied in the institutionalization of the disciplines within which we work: students and academics within a faculty of English find it difficult to resist the structures of thought, the academic equivalents of Williams' 'structures of feelings', that enclose and encode the essential literariness of the material investigated. The development of cultural studies in Britain, a development in which Williams played a crucial and inaugurating role, has not altered the distance from the materiality of theatre practice, the only circumstance within which and against which the detail of the printed text of a play can make sense, for students working outside departments of drama and theatre studies. While textual bibliography and the history of the book continue to grow as academic interests, such concerns rarely filter through to undergraduate work. All these academic fields have their provocative and necessary connection to the analysis of the status of speech and stage directions within each of the three texts of *Hamlet* and to the analysis of the generation of meaning in the Renaissance or modern theatre.

Part of the answer lies in the careful consideration of the least-used sections of any edited text of a Shakespeare play: the account of the text and the textual collation. It also lies in the sustained use of the numerous facsimiles of early texts, quartos and folios, now readily available. The answer is not a method or a theory so much as an awareness of the nature of the sources for the work, the limits and possibilities in the textual witnesses to the place of Shakespeare within the processes of production both of text and performance. Only then can the blur that masks the edges of the conceptualization of a text of *Hamlet* in critical analysis be clarified.

George Bernard Shaw, reviewing a production of *Hamlet* in 1897, began wryly: 'The Forbes Robertson Hamlet at the Lyceum is, very unexpectedly at that address, really not at all unlike Shakespear's [*sic*] play of the same name' (Shaw 1932, 3: 200). But what is 'Shakespear's play'? In the context of the material practice of performance, the identification of the text as a literary object created by the unitary subjectivity of the playwright disappears. In the context of the complexity of textual transmission to print in the English Renaissance, the identification of the printed text with that concept of the literary object is not tenable. Williams' schematized system of relationships between the literary text and the culture of performance simplifies and occludes. As Shaw, later in his career, would have been the first to appreciate from his own experience as playwright, the link of text to performance is anything but straightforward.

SUPPLEMENT

NIGEL WOOD: Taking up Williams's line and his treatment of play-texts as 'texts', this could be part of a recurrent debate that cuts to the heart of any critical act, or, at least, any materialist analysis. As Walter Benjamin commented in his sixteenth thesis on the 'Philosophy of History', all 'historical materialists' need 'the notion of a present which is not a transition . . . in which time stands still' (Benjamin 1970: 264). Your consideration of a theatrical state of affairs denies this 'notion' its full force. What are we studying if not textual 'snapshots'?

PETER HOLLAND: One of the problems with some approaches to theory is that they seek to sort and order the messiness of history and the messiness of the practice of writing and publication. Theatre, as anyone who has worked in it knows only too well, is the messiest form of all: it involves large numbers of people, each offering a specific creative input; it is triumphantly ephemeral and hence shifting; it still seems impossible effectively to notate and record, even with videotaping. Hence it offers a field of continual shift and slippage, an imprecision to set against that yearning in theory, the basis of its analytic work, a desire for precision and immutability.

We are, of course, studying 'snapshots' but the difficulty is to know what these murky photos show. Are the three 'snapshots' offered by the three texts of *Hamlet* images giving different witnesses of the same thing, an idealist, perfectible version of the play, or are they holiday snaps of something always in process? Is the thing that each grainy black and white, badly developed picture shows a performance or an act of printing? Is it a text or a witness of production?

It would be consoling to behave, as critics have till recently, as if none of this were germane to literary analysis and as if the history of the theatre's own treatment of a play were of significance only for theatre historians, since it post-dates the author's release of the text. But the text is not released in such a fashion, least of all in the context of Renaissance production, and especially when the playwright was also an actor-sharer in the company. If we accept some implication of the act of performance in the analysis of the text, then we are obliged to go beyond the textuality of print towards that to which play-texts gesture, the fact or possibility of performance. But the picture is still left as a troublingly or provocatively unclear witness. To overextend your image, it is rather as if when the holiday prints come back from the developers, they show you places you are no longer quite sure you ever visited.

NW: Is there such an item as 'dramatic' form that can exist across periods?

PH: If you mean by that, is there a concept of, say, 'tragedy' that is transhistorical, then the answer must be 'certainly not'. Forms are themselves participants in historical process, both as they are replicated and extended and as they are re-viewed. The *Hamlet* that Garrick perceived in the mid-eighteenth century is not the *Hamlet* that Kenneth Branagh perceived in the 1980s. Neither is the influence of the text, the form it is perceived as offering or obliging subsequent writers to consider, a fixed object. The study of dramatic form must be a cumulative history, a history both of change and development but also of the subsequent histories of earlier texts.

NW: Granted that all play-texts are 'special cases' at some level, is *Hamlet* just a marked instance of all plays?

PH: Yes, of course it is. I have come across very few cases of plays which, when you investigate their textual history, prove to have been written in a single and unaltered form. The striking exceptions at the point of the playwright's finally relinquishing control over the text are writers like Jonson, Brecht and Beckett: Jonson because he takes tight control over the printed version in creating the volume of his *Works* published in 1616 (a decision that influences Congreve in publishing his *Works* in 1710); Brecht, because, in spite of the changing nature of the text in performance, he publishes model-books, instruction kits for production; Beckett, because he, predictably, goes a stage further and, in the television versions he made late in his life, creates the notion of the definitive authored and authorized performance.

What marks *Hamlet* out, though, is the extreme nature of the gap between the early textual evidence and the dominance of an assumption that we know what *Hamlet* is in the enormous volume of writing and thinking and performance of the play. As George Hibbard points out in his edition, even the assumption that Hamlet delays (remember Olivier's voice-over at the beginning of his film version telling the audience that *Hamlet* is 'about a man who could not make up his mind') is rendered problematic by the textual evidence: in F, where the text cuts the whole of the soliloquy 'How all occasions' after Hamlet has seen Fortinbras' army, it is easy to argue that Hamlet never delays at all. Recent work on Shakespeare as a reviser of his plays has tended to focus on *King Lear* so that we now have parallel-text editions of Quarto and Folio, both solemn facsimiles and modernized student-friendly versions, and the Wells–Taylor Oxford edition prints the play twice over. We have also had productions that have sought to explore Quarto and Folio texts (for example, Hytner's Folio-based version for the Royal Shakespeare Company). But the implications of the textual problems in *Hamlet* have not yet been followed through either by critics or by actors and directors working on performances of the play. When Adrian Noble directs an 'uncut' *Hamlet* with Kenneth Branagh for the RSC (1992) or Peter Hall does the same with Stephen Dillane at the Gielgud Theatre (1994), they are assuming that the conflated text is the ideal version of the play and hence that more is better. It often is – though it can also be intolerably boring! – but it is not therefore more 'Shakespearian', a more accurate representation of the extent of the text.

NW: Is there some point in attempting to arrive at the 'expected' or 'standard' existence of Shakespeare's text, so as to explore fully departures from it?

PH: There have already been 'expected' or 'standard' forms of the text but the forms change. In the divergence between theatre editions and scholarly editions that began in the eighteenth century, each creates its own version of the standard text: for the theatre it is that version which is currently the staple form for performances in the theatre; for the critic it is that version which is held at a particular moment to represent most accurately the version that Shakespeare wrote. What we might now dislodge within the second category is the assumption that 'what Shakespeare wrote' is the aim of textual archaeology rather than 'what Shakespeare's company performed'.

Most literary analysis of Shakespeare is written as if there is a 'standard' form, the version enshrined in whichever edition the critic happens to be using. I just wish we might get into the habit of wondering what that edition seeks to represent. At least, for all its other faults, the Wells–Taylor edition is perfectly clear about the relationship between text and performance that its version of the texts tries to make manifest.

CHAPTER 3

Explaining Woman's Frailty: Feminist Readings of Gertrude

SHARON OUDITT

[Sharon Ouditt's reading of *Hamlet* is simultaneously a review of how feminist readings intervene in accepted critical estimates of the play. At the same time as they develop insights from psychoanalytical, historicist or sociological work, they have a common political goal: to render visible women's contribution to the historical process or, within literary texts, to account for the silences and repressions that the 'female' attracts. Thereby, a simple quotation of the words on the page cannot supply proof of how this *hidden* voice exists or can work.

In Elaine Showalter's 'Ophelia: The Responsibilities of Feminist Criticism' (in Parker and Hartman 1985: 77–94), the contest for meaning occurs extrinsically to the text. Ophelia is 'mad', and Gertrude lustful and a negligent mother, yet these conclusions, which may pose as innocent extrapolations from the text, actually stem from the patriarchal stereotyping of femininity. Where, therefore, might we find Ophelia? Not in any secure 'real' sense can criticism define some genuine article: 'There is no "true" Ophelia for whom feminist criticism must unambiguously speak, but perhaps only a Cubist Ophelia of multiple perspectives, more than the sum of her parts'. In exposing the 'ideology of representation', however, Showalter also points out how aware feminists need to be about their own political and historical relation not just to the text but also to the occasion of their critical work: its audience and its particular cultural tasks (Parker and Hartman 1985: 92).

This is why 'facts' about the past are not reliable material. Anthropological scientism actually has a great deal invested in its 'factual' rhetoric, as any reader of Simone de Beauvoir's *The Second Sex* (1949) or Luce Irigaray's *This Sex Which Is Not One* (1977; Irigaray 1985) will discover.

Women must define themselves aside from the snares of being just reflections of how men would require them to be. For de Beauvoir, it was essential to discover that 'no man really is God' (de Beauvoir 1972: 622), and that women are not born as stable reference points but constructed as such. For Irigaray, the problem is rather to do with the search for a language apart from that uttered within patriarchal terms. In her exploration of gender difference, 'a feminine language' (so often relegated to the margins) works to 'undo the unique meaning, the proper meaning of words, of nouns: which still regulates all discourse'. This inevitably questions the assumption that there is somewhere a primal unity, for all such ordering presupposes description, and possession. For Irigaray, there is 'no feminine meta-language':

> The masculine can partly look at itself, speculate about itself, represent itself and describe itself for what it is, whilst the feminine can try to speak to itself through a new language, but cannot describe itself from outside or in formal terms, except by identifying itself with the masculine, and thus by losing itself.
>
> (Irigaray 1985: 65)

To this extent, it is *positively* illogical, and the 'unruly' or 'mad' woman (see the language of Ophelia in Act IV, scene v, where she is allowed to initiate discourse for the first time) is elusive and consequently disruptive.

For Lawrence Stone, for example, in his massively influential *The Family, Sex and Marriage in England, 1500–1800* (Stone 1977), the available record, assembled according to 'orderly', which is to say masculinist, premisses, confirms femininity as the passive 'Other' to male prerogative and control – an instance where an unsparing empirical account actually colludes in the silences visited on women at that time. Ouditt's eclectic review of feminist positions attempts to open up their positive disruption of surface order to view, and, in so doing, joins several critics whose accounts of the otherwise mute voices of resistance obey no clear rules or formulae (see Jardine 1989: 68–102; Erickson 1991: 23–30; Berry 1989: 134–65; and Lorraine Helms, 'Acts of Resistance: The Feminist Player', in Callaghan *et al.* 1994: 102–56).]

NIGEL WOOD

Introduction

What might feminism offer to Shakespeare studies? Or, to reorder the proposition slightly, what might Shakespeare offer to feminist studies? What kind of relationships exist between the archetypal symbol of English literary heritage and the textual wing of a political movement bent on stripping bare and eradicating the structural inequalities between the sexes?

In fact, the intersections are many and fruitful, and one might detect a gradual evolution in feminist approaches. Lisa Jardine describes her 'growing tide of personal irritation' at the 'reverence' of early feminist critics for Shakespearian 'realism' (Jardine 1989: 1); Lynda E. Boose, on the other hand, is unhappy with Marxist critic Kate McLuskie's argument that the only viable position open to feminist readers of Shakespeare is radical resistance. McLuskie's line is that to imagine Shakespeare as an advocate for feminism is merely a sentimental attempt to co-opt his authority (Boose 1987: 723). Elaine Showalter takes the debate a stage further in her essay on representations of Ophelia. Here she outlines and implicitly dismisses three possible feminist approaches: first, the idealist pursuit of the 'real' Ophelia; second, a French psychoanalytical approach that would see Ophelia as 'nothing', 'the cipher of female sexuality to be deciphered by feminist interpretation'; and third, the construction of Ophelia as 'the female', the weakness and emotional instability which needs to be jettisoned from the patriarchal world of the play before Hamlet can act (Showalter, 'Representing Ophelia: Women, Madness, and the Responsibilities of Feminist Criticism', in Parker and Hartman 1985: 78–80). Showalter's modest responsible and historically researched feminism, conscious of the 'age of critical hubris' which it inhabits, takes the path of considering Ophelia in her particular historical representations, from the seventeenth century to the present day, and thus produces a character of 'multiple perspectives'; a cultural icon, which takes on the preoccupations of its age, whether on-stage, in paintings, or in lunatic asylums, rather than the '"true" Ophelia, for whom feminist criticism must unambiguously speak' (Parker and Hartman 1985: 92).

Faced with these developing approaches, it is as well to remember that feminism is a living, political practice with a range of goals. It constantly questions its own aims, blindnesses, methods and assumptions from a number of perspectives. Showalter's essay raises some recurring criticisms within feminist theory, explicitly and implicitly. These might be summarized as follows:

1 Its tendency to idealize, universalize or essentialize women, that is, to see women as fundamentally the same and similarly victimized and misrepresented by patriarchy, irrespective of race, class, sex and historical differences.
2 A tendency to celebrate madness in women as a form of deviation from the suffocating patriarchal symbolic order; to see women as culture's victims, slipping through the gaps in rational representation.

3 Its preoccupation with questions of identity, ideology and discourse at the expense of a radical political analysis; in the name of diversity it has fragmented, lost sight of its original goals.

Not all of these criticisms are valid all of the time. Some refer to particular approaches, and there is no doubt that feminism is presently characterized by its diversity, by a global as well as a local framework, by its attention to culturally specific detail, by the scope of its objectives and objects of study. For some, a populist political agenda can seem alienating – for example, Diana Fuss on Tania Modleski: 'Why . . . do I find Modleski's concluding invocation of "female empowerment" so distinctly *disempowering*?' (Fuss 1989, 28).[1] For others, feminism's basis in women's experiences (the personal as the political) can appear tiresomely unprofessional – for example, Lisa Jardine on Marilyn French: 'French's book reveals rather depressingly clearly the common misapprehension that to be a literary feminist is adequate qualifications [sic] to make one a specialist feminist critic' (Jardine 1989: 8, n. 15).

Feminist literary theory is often said to have begun, in the context of second-wave feminism in the late 1960s, with the recognition of a mismatch between the experience of women readers and the representation of female experience in texts, resulting in 'images of women in' studies. This gave way to the rediscovery of lost narratives, lost heroines, lost writers, whose recovered stories began to redress the balance, tell the other side, put the woman's point of view. This, however, did not answer the problem of 'femininity'. What is it? How is it constructed? Where and in what form does it exist? Social and psychoanalytical studies were useful here in analysing difference, questioning the universality of female identity, theorizing 'otherness'. And thus arose the question of cultural blindness, the recognition that white, Western middle-class concerns had routinely been privileged above those of other races and classes, in ignorance of the complexities of sexuality and the effects of imperialism. Subsequently came the development of sophisticated theories concerned with destabilizing hierarchies, reconstructing coalitions, recognizing diversity, announcing that there are many ways in which to be a feminist. What begins as 'This does not meet with my experience' ends with a similar kind of recognition, but from a scholarly, political and theoretical base that has taken on some of the implications of 'difference' rather than being a reaction to the experience of feeling excluded from a patriarchal interpretative game.

Feminism, then, is not 'simply one thing'. The précis above is intended to give an impression of a theory that is, and always has been, on the move. It is a theory that is not an originary fable but a social and cultural practice. It changes, develops, revises, reflects, is lashed against, regroups, is over, is poised on the brink of a revolution – in relationship with the cultural register of its day. It may come as no surprise, then, that I should request the tolerance of the reader and deviate slightly from the standard format of this series. Contributors are generally expected to take a single, influential, theoretical text, identify its main features, then apply it to a single, influential, literary text. There is, however, such diversity within feminism that I would consider it impossible to do justice to the range of responses – by both critics and students – if I were to take a single voice and consider it representative.

Instead, I should like to consider three perspectives and the interpretative possibilities that they present. This will not solve the problem of representativeness, but it will go some way towards articulating the kinds of concerns with which feminism is engaged and against which readers can test their own responses. In order to mitigate the potentially fragmented effect that this approach may have, I have chosen pieces that relate directly to the play itself, and particularly to the role of Gertrude. These are Rebecca Smith's 'A Heart Cleft in Twain' (in Lenz *et al.* 1983), Jacqueline Rose's 'Sexuality in the Reading of Shakespeare: *Hamlet* and *Measure for Measure*' (in Drakakis 1985) and Lisa Jardine's *Still Harping on Daughters* (1989). I have chosen these in order to represent three different feminist perspectives, respectively 'reading as a woman', psychoanalytic, and materialist feminist. These perspectives exemplify particular preoccupations in feminist literary theory that concern, first, the different interpretation that a woman reader might bring to a character that has traditionally been analysed (and in the case of a play, produced, both in the theatre and on screen) by men; second, arguments centring on the 'inscrutable' nature of female sexuality, and the burden of guilt borne by women for social, sexual and aesthetic failure; and third, the effect of summoning a broad cultural and historical framework of ideas and practices concerning the changing roles of women in the Renaissance period, accompanied by an alert scepticism about the omniscience and objectivity of literary criticism.

The individual essays raise specific issues concerning the nature and limits of interpretation. In the meantime, however, I should like to set up three basic questions which underpin feminist theoretical enquiry. The first is whether women read differently from men. Does the different experiential ground of women's lives inevitably produce alternative readings? The spectrum between the responses 'yes' and 'no' is vast and is complicated by many questions often stimulated by the idea of 'difference' itself: that between men and women, that which arises from sexual orientation, class, race, relationship to power, and that which is constructed internally, on the level of subjectivity, that is to say, the many different ideologies, discourses, social, sexual and aesthetic practices that intersect in any one person, or subject. The second is to ask what feminism *does* to texts. Does it expose patriarchal attitudes? Locate articulations of femininity as 'other'? Investigate the immediate context in order to cut through 'universal' ideas of femininity? The third, and related, question asks what is the *object* of feminist study. This might be the words on the page, myth, ideology or discourse – the form of speech that constructs concepts of gender and its social operations. Equally, it could be femininity itself (its social sexual, verbal, aesthetic manifestations), historical documents, theatrical conventions, inheritance laws, religious change – the complexity of the social environment in which a text was originally produced, and in which it continues to be produced in different historical periods. All of these possible approaches, in feminist criticism, are situated in the context of wanting to produce social change. That desire is their common feature.

Rebecca Smith, 'A Heart Cleft in Twain'

Rebecca Smith's essay on Gertrude ('A Heart Cleft in Twain: The Dilemma of Shakespeare's Gertrude') was first published in 1980 in *The Woman's Part: Feminist Criticism of Shakespeare* (Lenz *et al.* 1983). It is representative of the kind of approach Elaine Showalter, in a germinal essay, called 'the feminist critique'.[2] That is, in taking male-authored texts as the object of study, it seeks to reveal patriarchal attitudes particularly through the representation of female characters as stereotypes, whose role is to further male fantasy.[3] Smith sets out to unlock the prison house of misconceptions that has resulted in a historically consistent, but nevertheless inaccurate portrayal of Gertrude. The interesting thing about this essay, though, is that it does not criticize Shakespeare for his part in a patriarchal conspiracy. He is – at least partly – exonerated from blame. The guilty parties are the other male characters and 'most stage and film directors' (she names Olivier, Kozintsev and Richardson), who 'have simply taken the men's words and created a Gertrude based on their reactions' (Lenz *et al.* 1983: 194). We can gather two things from this: first, that Smith considers Shakespeare to exist somehow above and beyond the boorish chauvinism of his interpreters (and his characters) as a liberal humanist of exceptional sympathy; and second, that there is a 'real Gertrude' for whom Smith must speak. This seems to suggest a certain naïvety about literary 'realism': the dubious conviction that literary characters are accessible as 'people'. If we accept this stance, then the essential Gertrude can be properly recognized from an analysis of the words she herself speaks – rather than the things said about her by the Ghost and by Hamlet. The suggestion is that a proper interpretation can only be attained by reading against the grain of the male-originated comments and listening attentively to what she has to say for herself. Smith is thus reading as a woman; offering a 'herstory'[4] of the dowager Queen. She is Gertrude's advocate, defending her against false accusations of lasciviousness and cunning.

Smith's line of argument is that Gertrude is portrayed as a sex object by the Ghost, Hamlet and Claudius, and that this is an unjust represen-tation. She is 'the ultimate sexual object' in Olivier's Hamlet (Lenz *et al.* 1983: 195) and seen 'in quite heightened terms as a sexual *object*' by the triad of male combatants (1983: 207). Her self-representation, however, does not add up to the same thing. Instead, when we listen to her alone, we are presented with 'a quiet, biddable, careful mother and wife' who 'obviously loves both Hamlet and Claudius and feels pain and guilt at her inability to please both' (1983: 201, 204). This, we are told, is the Gertrude that Shakespeare created (and who has nothing to do with the one described by the Ghost, Hamlet, etc.). So the lascivious Gertrude is a projection by the 'jilted' husband and anx-ious son who cannot bear the idea of his mother remarrying. The real Gertrude needs to be rescued from the portrayal of sexual objectifica-tion and seen for what she is: 'a compliant, loving, unimaginative woman' who marries Claudius 'probably because of her extremely dependent personality' (1983: 207). Smith admits that Gertrude is not fully rounded and densely layered, that she appears in only ten of the twenty scenes and takes up only 3.8 per cent of the dialogue (1983: 199) and that she, Smith, is probably only outlining another stereotype ('malleable, submissive . . . solicitous of others at the expense of herself' (1983: 207)), but she maintains that this is a more positive stereotype than that of the temptress and that it 'more accurately reflects the Gertrude that Shakespeare created' (1983: 208).

One could point out here that this 'Gertrude', distinct from the whole play, merely creates a further problem: how to understand the part played by dramatic gestures (even those that are performed when Gertrude is not needed on-stage) over and above excerptable speeches assigned to her. The relative paucity of words she utters does not decree how significant such speech actually becomes within the *dramatic* text.

For instance, the single line 'But look where sadly the poor wretch comes reading' (II.ii.168) sounds so alternatively in the context of the male voices in the scene (Polonius on the cause of Hamlet's madness, Claudius' businesslike efficiency), that it gathers enhanced attention to itself. The projection of Hamlet's fears and logic during the Player Queen's speeches in Act III, scene ii, should not be confused with any *propria persona* utterance from Gertrude, yet it could still be influential when we observe Gertrude's relationship with Claudius in Act IV, scene i, and the apparent pragmatism with which she initially reflects on Ophelia's mad fit at IV.v.14–16. Does this information provide a context for the full reversal of Gertrude's perspective at her lyrical account of Ophelia's drowning (IV.vii.141–58)? Or are we simply overlaying inappropriate novelistic reading conventions that assume the construction of characters along 'normal' patriarchal lines, that is, 'knowing' another person on the strength of how they are permitted to utter? If so, the noting of female silence comes dangerously close to the assumption that Renaissance women had no characters at all.

The interpretative categories that Smith uses resemble many of those in books such as Dale Spender's *Manmade Language* (1980), that seek to emphasize women's nurturing, caring, enabling capacities (see for example, Dinnerstein 1976; Chodorow 1978; Sara Ruddick, 'Preservative Love and Military Destruction', in Treblicot 1983). Gertrude does not say very much, as indicated above. When she does speak, she usually asks questions or 'voices solicitude for the well-being and safety of other characters' (Lenz *et al.* 1983: 200); she demonstrates 'perspicuity' and intuition and her actions are similarly unlascivious. She rarely appears without her husband, and does what he tells her; she scatters flowers on Ophelia's grave and wipes Hamlet's face with a napkin during the fencing match. In short, she is not a whore, she is a good mother who made a mistake in marrying Claudius (not much perspicacity there) and who has been unfortunately branded ever since. She cannot be made responsible for the imagination of a dead husband and a tormented son.

What is puzzling about this is not this particular reinterpretation of a character whose portrayal has been coloured by masculine obsession and fantasy (which element of the analysis is, surely, perfectly credible), but the apparent need to think of characters as though they are human beings, as though there is an essential Gertrude to whom the right-minded critic with appropriate interpretative equipment can gain access. Smith admits that, as a speaking part, it is pretty sparse; Showalter comments that Shakespeare did not really leave a great deal of evidence on which to base that kind of detective work (Showalter,

'Representing Ophelia: Women, Madness, and the Responsibilities of Feminist Criticism', in Parker and Hartman 1985: 78). Jardine (1989: 4) simply considers Smith's approach 'endearing'. A lot of this is a matter of critical fashion, and it is perhaps a little cheap to criticize a critic for holding assumptions that are not presently in vogue; nevertheless, let us see how this estimation of Gertrude helps with the business of interpretation. Three questions suggest themselves. First, was Gertrude involved in the murder of her first husband? Second, did she have a sexual relationship with Claudius before the murder? And third, do we need definitive answers concerning either matter? The first two recur in analyses by critics who try to assess Gertrude's character and role in the play, and are considered by Smith. The third arises from a critical consideration of Smith's approach.

'When speaking to Hamlet, the Ghost does not state or suggest Gertrude's guilt in his murder, only in her "falling-off" from him to Claudius (I.v.47)' (Lenz et al. 1983: 201–2). It seems indeed to be the case that the Ghost accuses only the 'serpent' Claudius of 'stinging' his life – and of seducing his wife. It could be (if she were involved in the murder) that the Ghost had no knowledge of it, or that he wants to enlist Hamlet's vengeful passion purely against Claudius in order that he should immediately lose the crown, while Gertrude can be left to the heavens and to her own conscience. On the other hand, Gertrude, unlike Claudius, at no stage admits guilt of any specific crime. When faced with Hamlet's implied accusation, 'almost as bad, good mother/As kill a king and marry with his brother' (III.iv.29–30), she merely retorts 'As kill a king?' (III.iv.31). Smith suggests that she exclaims this in horror (Lenz et al. 1983: 202); it could be horror or disbelief at the extraordinary sequence of events – first Hamlet, with no provocation, kills Polonius, then, expressing no immediate regret for this, he retorts that it is not quite as bad as murdering a monarch. Hamlet could be mocking his mother, who may understand his jibe and be faking innocence. On the other hand, Gertrude, as far as we are aware, has no knowledge at this stage that Claudius was responsible for her first husband's death, so there need be no guilt either on her own account or on Claudius' – merely bewilderment at Hamlet's extraordinary and violent behaviour, accompanied by the strange flux of his imagination (all of which is of a piece with his 'antic disposition' and vile treatment of Ophelia during the play). Why on earth, she may be wondering, should he think that I killed his father? Or, even more difficult for the critic eager to attribute blame to her, what on earth is he talking about? The scene continues. Having understood Hamlet's professed intention to 'wring [her] heart' (III.iv.36), she asks two questions: 'What have

I done, that thou dar'st wag thy tongue/In noise so rude against me?' (III.iv.40–1), and 'Ay me, what act/That roars so loud and thunders in the index?' (III.iv.52–3). These questions seem to indicate innocence, or at least a lack of understanding as to why her 'o'erhasty' marriage should produce such tempestuous emotions in her son. It is only when Hamlet has been through the 'counterfeit presentment of two brothers' (III.iv.55) and demonstrated the grace and majesty of the one as against the 'mildewed ear' of the other, that she cracks a little and admits to seeing 'black and grainèd spots' in her soul (III.iv.82). This might, of course, be her greatest virtue, that she is ruthlessly self-critical of negligible faults. She then implores Hamlet to 'speak no more' several times until his passionate flow is interrupted by the appearance of the Ghost.

Hamlet's line of attack concerns his mother's irrational choice and unthinking sexual response. It is not until line 88 that he names Claudius 'A murderer and a villain', and these epithets might be taken by her to be metaphorical, or yet another symptom of Hamlet's hyperbolic frame of mind. Whether she believes him or not, she cannot bear to hear any more either against herself or her second husband. One might easily assume that she knew nothing about it.

But how far-reaching was her involvement with Claudius? Many critics argue that the Ghost's description of her 'falling-off' (I.v.47), his description of Claudius as 'adulterate', the description of lust sating itself in a celestial bed and then preying on garbage (I.v.56–7) amounts to a clear implication of Gertrude's guilt. She is clearly guilty in the Belleforest source. The term 'seeming-virtuous' (I.v.46) seems to imply duplicity in marriage, the comparison between his love, that was faithful to its marriage vows, and hers all add up to a reading that condemns her for adultery (cf., for example, Bradley 1974: 134). Smith, however, maintains that she is innocent. She points up the ambiguity in the Ghost's narrative – it cannot be clearly concluded that he is describing simultaneous events rather than a close sequence of events. It might appear equally immodest to marry hastily after the death of a husband, without leaving due mourning time, and thereby revealing an unwarranted sexual appetite. The sequence of 'falling-off' and 'declin[ing]/Upon a wretch' (I.v.50–1) might equally have taken place after the King's death as before it. The time-scale is brief. The same could be said of the celestial bed/preying on garbage sequence (I.v.42–57). Hamlet's concern, Smith insists, is with the *speed* of his mother's remarriage and with her apparent betrayal of the memory of King Hamlet – this is what 'makes marriage vows/As false as dicers' oaths' (III.iv.45–6) (Lenz *et al.* 1983: 202–3).

This reading of Gertrude as a solicitous matriarch, her heart 'cleft in twain' by her equal loyalties to her son and to her husband, releases her from the female stereotype of 'lascivious whore' even if only to place her uncomfortably close to its dumb and vulnerable counterpart, characterized by unreflective passivity. Both interpretations are drawn from the same information – the words on the page – plus a general cultural sense of what women's roles might be in a violent and vengeful setting. It is that latter, unacknowledged source that persuades critics to supply the parts of the drama omitted by the dramatist; that is, to make whole and coherent that which is inevitably sparse, ambiguous and driven by forces other than the creation of a full range of psychologically consistent characters.

The process of attempting to answer the questions concerning Gertrude's guilt and adultery lead one to consider whether or not those questions should require a definitive answer. And this in turn recalls my earlier comment on the nature and limits of interpretation in the framework of feminist criticism. The text can never be autonomous. It invites readings, and the nature of that process is not bounded by the horizon of the text, no matter how close the reading becomes. The text does not provide definitive answers to those questions concerning Gertrude's guilt or otherwise; it is the act of intervention on the part of the critic that might decide this, and that act is, in this case, performed with the explicit intention of preventing the occlusion of the female by the male; preventing the silence that is the result of heeding only the play's main (male) protagonists. So the nature of this interpretative act is interventionist, radical, aligned to the feminist cause of rescuing women from silence, obscurity and the presumption of guilt.

The limitations of Smith's interpretative strategy coincide with assumptions concerning the close reading of 'character' in a dramatic text. The shortage of verbal evidence on the part of Gertrude herself, allied to the exclusion of non-verbal, performance elements that might shape the direction of the play combine to produce a reading based on conviction rather than certainty. The ambiguity, in any case, leaves us as readers/audience in a similar position to that of Hamlet: we do not know. We are invited to interpret, and we may do so on the basis of textual evidence, in an attempt to undo the repressive interpretations that have dominated discussions of Gertrude. But, in the context of a practice of close reading, a discursive, interventionist strategy leaves us not with 'knowledge', but with an angle, a position from which to speak and interrogate, and one buttressed by the weight of a firm ideological commitment which extends to cultural practices beyond literary criticism.

Jacqueline Rose, 'Sexuality in the Reading of Shakespeare'

Jaqueline Rose is best known for her feminist and psychoanalytic criticism (see Rose 1982; 1991; 1993). Her essay on *Hamlet* appeared in *Alternative Shakespeares* edited by John Drakakis, which sets out to dismantle the 'myth' of Shakespeare (Drakakis 1985: 24); in her own book, *Sexuality in the Field of Vision* (Rose 1986); and again in the Norton edition of *Hamlet* (Hoy 1991), Rose moves away from direct concentration on the play and from any attempt at a direct 'reading' in the light of psychoanalytic theory, and looks instead at the concept of 'femininity' and the way it has been used to explain away the short-comings of Shakespeare's most problematic play. Her object of study, then, is not 'women' or 'Shakespeare', but the common ground of 'language, fantasy and sexuality' in which 'the woman occupies a crucial, but difficult place' (Drakakis 1985: 95). In this essay, language, fantasy and sexuality are seen to circulate in literary, literary-critical and psychoanalytical texts – namely *Hamlet*, T.S. Eliot's 'Hamlet' (Eliot 1975: 45–9) and extracts from Freud and from Ernest Jones.

Rose addresses the same initial problem as that addressed by Rebecca Smith: that Gertrude stands accused of lasciviousness. This is linked to the question of the play's 'problematic' status: that it has been described as an aesthetic failure because it demands too much of the act of inter-pretation (Drakakis 1985: 95). The two accused, then, the woman and the play, form the focus of an essay which looks at the relationships between sexuality and aesthetic form and finds that it has been all too easy to make the woman bear the burden of failure when the cause really lies elsewhere, in the failure to integrate the self both within language and subjectivity. In other words, critics such as Eliot are looking in the wrong place and with misguided motivations when they scapegoat Gertrude. A more fruitful focus of attention and more appro-priate motivations, Rose suggests, can only be properly discovered using the tools that have arisen from the study of psychoanalysis within a post-structuralist framework.

Eliot is first in the dock, and is called to account for adopting the attitude of a literary policeman: a 'particularly harsh type of literary super-ego', whose general tendency towards repression (which was to find other outlets in political terms) demanded the too-neat resolution of linguistic, sexual and aesthetic complexes (Drakakis 1985: 102). Rose explains her questioning of Eliot's influential assumptions with reference to his concept of the 'objective correlative', which he developed in his essay on *Hamlet*. The objective correlative is 'a set of objects, a situation, a chain of events which shall be the formula of that *particular* emotion; such that when the external facts [. . .] are given, the emotion is immediately evoked' (Eliot 1975: 48). In other words, the route towards experiencing the 'particular emotion' is external to, and not to be confused with, the emotion itself. Proper artistic control means that the emotion must be brought under control in the mind of the artist and rendered in an aesthetically contained and objective form. The problem with *Hamlet*, in Eliot's eyes, is that there is a mismatch between the character of Gertrude and the emotional excess that she has apparently generated in her son. The emotional effect that she has on the play thus causes it to veer out of aesthetic control, Hamlet's mother being an inadequate stimulant of Hamlet's reaction to her: 'his disgust envelops and exceeds her' (Eliot 1975: 48).

So, Eliot suggests, Gertrude is to blame for the play's artistic failure. Which is not to say that the play lacks interest: indeed it is, according to Eliot, 'the "Mona Lisa" of literature' (Eliot 1975: 47). Rose picks up this analogy, precisely because we see Eliot using another image of a woman to convey the play's failure: 'Like the *Mona Lisa*, *Hamlet* is a flawed masterpiece whose very failing acts as a pull on spectator and critic alike. Its very imperfection brings with it the power to seduce' (Drakakis 1985: 96). So the idea of undecipherability, of the enigmatic, of that which lures only to refuse to yield up its meanings, is transferred between play and painting with the woman as common, and deceptive, currency, implicitly denigrated by male authority.

In *Hamlet*, then, sexuality is unmanageable. Gertrude's impropriety provokes disorder and tumult. To Hamlet it is disgusting: he cannot control his response to it. It is horrific. And this excessive emotional reaction, the object of which is too insubstantial a dramatic presence to warrant it, leads to a problem of interpretation: 'how to read, or control by reading, a play whose inscrutability (like that of the *Mona Lisa*) has baffled – and seduced so many critics' (Drakakis 1985: 98). Rose's argument is that Eliot's criticism operates on the principle of strict control and proper example. He demands formal constraint in the body of works that comprise the 'Literature' that is worthy of that status. Formal constraint is exemplified by the objective correlative, which 'carries the burden of social order itself' (Drakakis 1985: 98) in that it forces emotion into the strait-jacket of object. And Gertrude's character, in its weakness and deficiency, is indicative of the crisis that occurs when the (ever-present, but none the less) unknowable, the incomprehensible in social and affective life, refuses to be contained by aesthetic form. Rose is thus setting up a comparison between the objective correlative and social order. The former is to art as the latter is to life – but they are linked by an unacknowledged concern with what is considered proper behaviour in the normal world.

Rose's real interest is not so much in Eliot's critical formulations in themselves, as in the surprising resemblance that they bear to psycho-analytical concepts. Her essay progresses along lines that are more associative than linear, and her next move is to indicate the similarity between Eliot's formulation and the psychoanalytic account of subject-ivity. Just as Eliot (1975: 49) sees the dangers of the 'inexpressibly horrible' threatening to upset aesthetic form, so psychoanalysis sees speech, or utterance, as open to disruption by the ungovernable forces of the unconscious. The more obvious manifestations of this are found in dreams, slips of the tongue and jokes, but ordinary language use might be similarly affected. Where Eliot (1975: 49) observes the 'buffoonery' of Hamlet's unchanelled emotional excess delivered in the form of puns, repetitions and other instances of word-play, in the light of psychoanalysis we could equally see traces of the unrepresentable (the unconscious). Thus aesthetic coherence (which Eliot detects in many other Shakespeare plays) is perilously close to aesthetic collapse. One false move and the Bard, instead of displaying masterly control, 'slips off the edge of representation itself' (Drakakis 1985: 99). In other words, the insistence on control always bears traces of its flip side, chaos and disorder, and the example of psychoanalysis suggests that readers and critics should be aware of their proximity. This need not necessarily result in Eliot-style condemnation of the work in question, but might, on the other hand, open up new avenues of enquiry.

In another associative move, Rose points up the similarities between the (psychoanalytic) Oedipal drama and Eliot's cultural theories in his essay 'Tradition and the Individual Talent' (Eliot 1975: 37–44). The former is central to the Freudian psychoanalytic theory which accounts for the division of human subjects into male and female and for the direc-tion of desire on to its appropriate object. The boy child, for example, perceives his father as a rival for his mother's love and fantasizes about killing him in order to possess the mother. Fears of castration, however, which the father, the source of all authority, threatens, persuade the child to relinquish desire for his mother and move towards identification with the father, on the understanding that one day he, too, will be similarly empowered. In 'Tradition' the artist must submit to something outside himself and surrender to the tradition which precedes and surrounds him. Just as the son pays his debt to the father and thus becomes a male subject, so the artist pays his debt to the dead poets and thus becomes a poet. Either son or poet may, of course, fail to submit: alternative claims may prevail over those of patrilineal tradition. Rose's point is that, as well as this being another scenario suggestive of the capitulation to order of the growing (literary and social) subject, it also recalls the numerous pleas for appropriate mourning in *Hamlet* which go unheeded, or remain unresolved (Drakakis 1985: 99–100). The play is, of course, noted for its palpable inadequacy of mourning (of King Hamlet, of Polonius, of Ophelia): 'a beast that wants discourse of reason/Would have mourned longer' than Gertrude, in Hamlet's eyes (I.ii.150–1).

Having set up a literary-psychoanalytical context in which order is repeatedly asserted and frequently fails, Rose returns to the issue that it is a woman who is seen as the cause of excess and deficiency in the play and a woman (the *Mona Lisa*) who symbolizes this in Eliot's essay. She now relates this to the drama of sexual difference, as described by Freud, where woman *is* failure in representation, *is* something deficient, *is* lacking or threatening to ordered systems, whether these be aesthetic or sexual (Drakakis 1985: 100).[5] This can result in fetishization or mystification – or inscrutability. Enter the *Mona Lisa* once more: again, it is evoked as that which cannot be controlled, managed, that which is in excess, that which is not an 'objective correlative' to the range of emotions which it seems to produce – but this time Rose is setting this in the context of psychoanalysis and reveals Freud's similar interest (at around the same time) in the enigma of the representation of 'the contrasts which dominate the erotic life of women' (Freud 1953–74, 11: 108; cited in Drakakis 1985: 101). Rose's deduction from this is that Eliot's invocation of the *Mona Lisa* suggests that what seems unmanageable to a rigidly controlled aesthetic theory is 'nothing other than femininity itself (Drakakis 1985: 101). So what needs explanation is not why Gertrude is so inadequate as an object for the emotions generated in the play, but why she should be expected to support them. Why should Gertrude be responsible for her son's feelings towards her? Why does she bear the guilt? Why does Hamlet not concentrate more on his revenge project and less on her sexuality? Woman embodies a whole range of fantasies concerning sexuality, disruption, seduction, reserve, voracity, cruelty, compassion, grace – many of which are seen lurking behind *La Gioconda*'s smile, and many of which are projected on to Gertrude, the scapegoat for the failure of the play. Rose's point is that behind Eliot's reference to Leonardo's painting lies a whole history of the fantasies that woman embodies and is required to uphold. Furthermore, the burden of guilt, like the male-orientated construction of femininity, falls unfairly, displacing attention on to a fetishized concept of woman and away from more demanding considerations concerning language and subjectivity.

Thus

> writing which proclaims its integrity, and literary theory which demands such integrity (objectivity/correlation) of writing, merely repeat that moment of repression when language and sexuality were first ordered into place, putting down the unconscious processes which threaten the resolution of the Oedipal drama and of narrative form alike.
>
> (Drakakis 1985: 102)

So Eliot's aesthetic demands are ethically oppressive. He blames the woman for the play's lack of resolution on the level of form (she is not an adequate objective correlative) and theme (she obstructs the resolution of the revenge plot). Femininity, as Rose puts it, 'is the image of that problem' – is the concept through which that problem is represented. As a locus of lack of representation, of excess, of inscrutability, femininity is a focus for the threat of disintegration, on both literary and psychic levels, that can rise through the cracks in normative representation at any time. Gertrude disrupts the surface of the representation of Hamlet – both character and play.

An account of readings by Ernest Jones and D.W. Winnicott (Drakakis 1985: 109–15) brings Rose on to the question of interpretation through the psychoanalytic concept of resistance: this is where meaning disguises itself, is overwhelming or escapes. It is not a question of simple concealment, but represents the 'truth' of a subject 'caught in the division between conscious and unconscious which will always function at one level as a split' (Drakakis 1985: 116). Interpretation can only move on when resistance is seen not as obstacle, but as process. Hamlet's problem is that he cannot act. He also cannot make sense of, cannot *interpret* his immediate situation. The fact of being unable to interpret what the intervention of the Ghost means, what Gertrude's change of sexual partner means, what Ophelia's behaviour means, 'leaves the relationship between word and action held in unbearable suspense' (Drakakis 1985: 117). The tension between words and actions, the difficulty of interpreting the incapacity of words (in this case 'revenge') to complete themselves in action (to kill Claudius) provides the productive focus of critical uncertainty. Rose suggests that Gertrude has been a kind of victim of this tension: 'Failing in a woman, whether aesthetic or moral, is always easier to point to than a failure of integration within language and subjectivity itself' (Drakakis 1985: 118).

The kind of 'failure' of which Gertrude stands accused could only be upheld within discourses based on coherence models – and coherence models which take partriarchy as the norm. Rose is suggesting that Eliot's repressive desire to see *Hamlet* conform to the aesthetic coherence of Shakespeare's 'more successful' plays is of a piece with an attitude that ignores the gaps and chasms in representation, that seeks to smooth over interpretative inconsistencies or to arraign them for breaking the law of aesthetic unity. Rose is suggesting that the critic should turn his or her attention away from apportioning blame for shortcomings in the literary meritocracy, and instead turn towards subjectivity, which is not unified, but is a space, cross-hatched with a multiplicity of conflicting drives, desires and duties. In this way femininity might cease to become a scapegoat for the incoherence of the human subject.

Lisa Jardine, 'Wealth, Inheritance and the Spectre of Strong Women'

The approaches that we have examined so far have considered Gertrude's 'character', in an attempt to come to a more accurate understanding of her role in the play than that traditionally portrayed. These approaches have analysed why Gertrude takes the 'blame' for the play's 'failures', from a psychoanalytic perspective that considers 'femininity', not only as it is represented in the play, but also in terms of the history of myths and fantasies that it supports and which are read into the play by critics, psychoanalytic and otherwise.

The third approach looks to the place of the female subject in history and fits somewhere between the categories 'new historicist' and 'materialist feminist'. Lisa Jardine, in her updated preface to *Still Harping on Daughters*, describes her ambivalence towards the discovery that she was considered as part of a general critical trend 'loosely called the "new history"' (Jardine 1989: viii), and also describes her debt of intellectual gratitude to American feminist psychoanalytic critics, in particular Coppélia Kahn and Carol Neely. Valerie Wayne, in her introduction to *The Matter of Difference: Materialist Feminist Criticism of Shakespeare*, outlines a rift between feminism and new historicism in which the latter is criticized for its apolitical and élitist tendencies (Wayne 1991: 4–5).[6] Lisa Jardine's description of her own method aligns her more with materialist feminism, and it is within this broad theoretical context that I should like to consider her.

She states that, in her case, 'the move *forwards* towards a new fusion of methodologies and material from cultural history and text studies was made in order to retrieve *agency* for the female subject in history' (Jardine 1989: viii). Her object is to build back in for woman her place in history as agent as well as receiver of masculine ideologies. She does this by 'treating the individual female subject in the drama as a "cultural artifact". . . . I look for the subject in history at the intersection of systems of behaviour, customs, beliefs, out of which, I consider, personal identity is constructed' (Jardine 1989: viii–ix).[7] By using the term 'cultural artifact' she is distinguishing her approach from those who see characters as 'people' and from those who seek to understand concepts such as 'femininity' in terms of their relation to ahistorical psychic drives – that is, from the two approaches we have already considered. Catherine Belsey describes materialist feminism's 'concern with the social and the economic, as opposed to the purely psychological, and with historical difference, as opposed to the universal and essential categories of 'woman' or 'patriarchy' ('Afterword: A Future for Materialist Feminist Criticism?', in Wayne 1991: 257). In other words, 'the past is another culture' (Jardine 1989: ix). Our access to it and to those subjects who participate in it should be formed by an understanding of the values and practices of that culture, which give shape and meaning to individual action and to representation. Jardine's practice, then, is to offer detailed historical documentation concerning, for example, the changes in education, the effects on women of religious reform and the complications involving inheritance laws as 'avenues of approach' to the representations of women in Renaissance drama (Jardine 1989: 6). She does this not with the conviction that the plays offer an accurate reflection of the social scene or articulate explicitly the changing views on 'the woman question' (for this see Dusinberre 1975) but with the belief that plays are one form, among others, in which concern about social change is registered.

Now, how does this help with the question of interpretation? What form of activity is involved in putting into practice this broadly historicist, materialist, feminist theory? Perhaps, first of all, we should say that Jardine (1989: 6) rejects the status of 'theory' for her analysis and calls it instead 'a practice of feminist interest in literature'. The heuristic work, she suggests, involves detailed contextualization of the plays, in which social formations, conventions and practices are seen as intersecting systems, which are articulated in the form of texts or subjects. For our purposes here, Jardine's chapter on 'Wealth, Inheritance and the Spectre of Strong Women', coupled with other documentary evidence (gathered by materialist critics such as Catherine Belsey and

Sara Eaton[8]), can help put Gertrude in the context of beliefs concerning women, power and sexuality in the Shakespearian period.

Belsey speaks of the 'silence' of women in the period: women were

> enjoined to silence, discouraged from any form of speech which was not an act of submission to the authority of their fathers or husbands. . . . [T]hey speak with equal conviction from incompatible subject positions, displaying a discontinuity of being, an 'inconstancy' which is seen as characteristically feminine.
>
> (Belsey 1985: 149)

Their legal position was in flux, their position in the family ambiguous, their power position in the state non-existent. Some women did resist, but they were nevertheless 'placed at the margins of the social body, while at the same time, in the new model of marriage they were uneasily, silently at the heart of the private realm which was its microcosm and its centre' (Belsey 1985: 150). The notable exception was, of course, Elizabeth I. Perhaps this can help us out with an explanation of Gertrude's relative silence in comparison with the psychological weight that she bears in terms of Hamlet's relation to her as his mother. The 'positions' from which she speaks are normally as Claudius' wife, and as Hamlet's mother – for example, at I.ii.68–73 she bids Hamlet, 'cast [his] nightly colour off'; in Act III, scene i, she obeys Claudius' request that she leave, but only after she has expressed the hope that Ophelia's 'virtues' will restore Hamlet's sanity; in Act III, scene iv, however, the closet scene, which Gertrude opens by criticizing her son's behaviour, Hamlet names her conflicting roles and his own troubled relation to them: 'You are the Queen, your husband's brother's wife,/But – would you were not so – you are my mother' (ll. 16–17). Her heart is 'cleft in twain' when the demands of her present husband and son, the present occupants of her familial microcosm, pull in opposite directions. Her 'inconstancy' is notorious. But instead of looking for a psychological motivation that could explain her 'frailty', we might consider instead her awkward *duty* to speak from the position of Claudius' wife. When Hamlet reminds her of the qualities of her former husband, all she can do is request his silence ('speak no more' (III.iv.80)): her past life, her past position as King Hamlet's wife, is at odds with her present position. She can do little more than try not to acknowledge the discontinuity and thereby to maintain some kind of dignity in the role in which she presently has, as it were, a speaking part. Hamlet's attention to her lack of judgement – 'what judgement/ Would step from this to this?' (III.iv.71–2) – and lack of constancy –

'O shame, where is thy blush?' (III.iv.74) – elicit no explanations.
This is the consequence of remarriage in the Renaissance period. One is
a wife, and then, one is a wife. There is no opportunity to explain
the discordance in the sequence. Gertrude's single, terse comment on
female prolixity – 'The lady protests too much' (III.ii.216) – is perhaps
not so much an admission of her own sexual laxness as an indication
that verbal excess is either not an appropriate aspect of female
behaviour, or that it is positively dangerous in such a threatening
patriarchal world. However we interpret it, it seems to suggest the
difficulty of making the autonomous female voice heard, especially for
one in her 'cleft' position.

We can add to this Jardine's (1989: 69) point that the 'female hero
moves in an exclusively masculine stage world, in which it is the task
of the male characters to "read" her'. This is almost exclusively what
happens to Gertrude (and largely what happened to Elizabeth I).
Gertrude is 'read' by the Ghost and by Hamlet who find in her 'frailty',
a 'falling-off', absence of reason and an unseemly lasciviousness. The
atmosphere surrounding these assessments of her motivations is thick
with sexual accusations, which we can take as an accurate judgement
or leave as the overheated imaginative response of a husband in hell
and distraught son. As far as Gertrude is concerned, the rest is silence.
Contemporary sources warn against 'dishonest' behaviour. Ophelia is
given a good talking to by her brother and her father: 'weigh what
loss your honour may sustain/If . . . you . . ./ . . . your chaste treasure
open/To his unmastered importunity' (I.iii.29–32); 'Tender yourself
more dearly,/Or . . ./ . . . you'll tender me a fool' (I.iii.107–9). Women,
in general, were assumed to be the 'Image of sweetnesse, curtesie and
shamefastnesse' (quoted by Jardine 1989: 76, from Boccaccio 1963: 177):
any sign of sexual awareness would brand a woman as Eve or Magdalene
rather than Mary (Jardine 1989: 77): Gertrude would thus have been
seen as 'wanton' because of her rapid remarriage, irrespective of her
son's vile imaginings.

Widows, however, were often expected to remarry in the sixteenth
and seventeenth centuries, despite the Church's emphasis on the
chastity of widows and the assumption that they would remain true
to the man they married with God's blessing. As Jardine (1989: 83)
puts it, 'the widows of wealthy men were married off again with quite
undignified haste where those responsible for them considered it finan-
cially advantageous to the line to do so'. Gertrude's own status is
deeply ambiguous. It does seem that Claudius was probably elected
King by a group of elders – he 'Popped in between th'election and
[Hamlet's] hopes' (V.ii.66) – and that he married Gertrude once this

position was secure, rather than her bestowing the monarchy on him by marriage (which even now is not possible in English law). It is also not clear whether one can assume that Shakespeare had English or Danish law in mind – or, whether his original audience would have had any knowledge of Danish law. This operated on the principle of elective monarchies, although, according to Jas. Howell, in 1632, the last three kings of Denmark had ensured, before their deaths, that their eldest sons were confirmed as successors (Jenkins 1982: 434).

Jardine (1989: 192) argues that Gertrude's remarriage excites in Hamlet a 'suppressed fear of female interference in patrilinear inheritance'. This focuses his revulsion at her remarriage because it places in question his own position as successor to the throne. According to the (English) law of *tail male*, the estate passes from eldest son to eldest son, and thus would pass next to Hamlet. If Hamlet were to remain childless, however, his paternal uncle Claudius and his offspring would then be next in line. This would be the case regardless of the marriage of Claudius to Gertrude. The fact of their marriage, however, means that a child born of that union would displace Hamlet. This might explain Hamlet's insistence that Gertrude 'go not to [his] uncle's bed' (III.iv.155) in an age of unreliable contraception. The whole scenario – lust interfering with inheritance – would make Gertrude guilty of the disruption of patrilineal tradition irrespective of any conscious intention on her part.

Jardine's (1989: 93) argument is that the question of inheritance adds a dimension to Hamlet's reaction to the marriage that a modern audience would probably miss, at the same time as it renders Gertrude 'guilty' by the simple fact of her having a (potentially interventionist) sexual role in a drama that circles around patriarchal power. She comments that the inheritance theme is subsidiary in the play, but that it nevertheless sheds some light on the supposition of Gertrude's culpability (in the absence of any 'proof' of her involvement in murder or adultery) and on Hamlet's obsession with her sexual relations with Claudius.

Sara Eaton, in her essay on 'Defacing the Feminine in Renaissance Tragedy' (in Wayne 1991) makes the basic point that the female characters of the period give less of an impression of their physical and psychological fullness than do the males: 'their expressions of desire, of will, of being, their explanations for their actions, rarely add up to the complicated declarations of interiority common to male characters by the 1590s' (Wayne 1991: 186). This is clearly the case with Gertrude, who is notably silent on her own motivations. Eaton also comments on the increasingly private treatment of female sexual misdemeanours, at a time when women's lives were gradually being redefined as domestic (Wayne 1991: 191). What is interesting is that while punishment was private, the theatrical space publicized it, most notably in somewhat later plays such as Webster's *The Duchess of Malfi* or Heywood's *A Woman Killed With Kindness* (Wayne 1991: 193); male protagonists are frequently concerned with female virtue (a concern that dominated the public performances of Elizabeth I), and punishments are often enacted in private spaces – such as the 'closet' in which Hamlet upbraids Gertrude. 'Men's power to punish is made visible by their actions, and is rarely questioned, demonstrating the power of the patriarchy to construct the "realities" of women's lives' (Wayne 1991: 193). Lust is not to be permitted to interfere with inheritance.

Eaton's essay does not refer directly to *Hamlet*. Its implications suggest, however, that one might interpret Gertrude's silent suffering, her plea that she should hear 'no more', as an indication that she has no way of answering Hamlet's accusations; that her role as wife determines one set of loyalties at the same time as her role as mother sets out another. The men surrounding her continue to interpret *her* life in terms of *their* lives. Her silence and passivity make her an object on to which their demands (and deepest fears), in all their contradictions, are projected. When Ophelia speaks in her *own* voice – actively, without status – she utters 'things in doubt/That carry but half sense'. Perhaps more crucially, according to Horatio, 'Her speech is nothing' (IV.v.6–7). The single occasion when Gertrude acts in *propria persona*, in defiance of Claudius' wishes, she drinks poison, the prelude to her own extinction.

A reading of Gertrude as a subject in history, then, offers explanations for her silence and for the presumption of her guilt that rely on an understanding of the ideologies concerning marriage, inheritance and submission to authority that were current at the time.

Conclusion

What, then, are the problems in each of these three approaches, and how do they help us to interpret Gertrude?

It has already been suggested that Rebecca Smith relies on the idea of re-presenting Gertrude 'as she really is', stripped of the voyeuristic trimmings imposed upon her by the masculine eye and mind, solicitous in her maternal duties. This is a 'rereading' in the light of an alternative vision – a woman's – and one that takes account of the ways in which the accretion of stage and screen representations of Gertrude constructs a dominant cultural vision of her which should be challenged. Jacqueline Rose does not attempt to offer us a clear interpretation of who Gertrude 'is', or what her role is in the play. She suggests instead that the cultural construction of 'femininity', with all its fantasies of seduction, cunning, grace, etc., have blinded critics such as Eliot to the essence of the play's 'problem'. Eliot 'blames' Gertrude for the play's failure. In doing so he is revealing his own authoritarian insistence on order and missing the point. The point is that subjectivity and language are infinitely complex systems, criss-crossed with incompatible motivations and unknowable drives which rarely resolve themselves in any easy or 'unitary' meaning. The reason for Hamlet's inability to act is not necessarily something 'inexpressibly horrible' that concerns his relationship with his mother, but might equally be read as an articulation of the nature of subjectivity itself. The weight of interpretative activity that Gertrude seems to require is not an aspect of a fault in the play's construction, but a comment on the way language and subjectivity operate. The feminist point here is that Gertrude is absolved. Rose is indicating a cultural obsession with the 'inscrutability' of femininity and the way that it tends to serve as a decoy, an easy target, deflecting attention from areas perhaps more analytically complex, but less susceptible to the combination of seduction and blame.

The Jardine approach offers us a Gertrude who is a 'subject', that is, who is constructed by the cultural position of her femininity at a particular historical moment. The interpretative problem here is in gaining access to the specifics of that historical period and in combining this, in all its conflicting multiplicity, with a reading of a notoriously unstable text. Many feminist Shakespearians who take this path seem to do so with a sense of modesty, combining detailed scholarship with a recognition that they are producing a contribution to an ongoing project (Jardine 1989: 6–7; Wayne 1991: 23–4). And this seems an appropriate point on which to conclude. Feminism, by its very nature as a political programme as well as an aspect of literary study, is a continuing project. The contributions to it and the readings of Gertrude considered here form part of a changing cultural and critical history. They are interventions, committed to a form of social change that will undo the inequalities between men and women. As such they read against the grain of a predominantly patriarchal and conservative cultural inheritance in order to undermine the tendency to represent women in terms of common stereotypes and to shed some historical, cultural, analytical light on the particular circumstances in which femininity has been constructed.

SUPPLEMENT

NIGEL WOOD: In Janet Adelman's *Suffocating Mothers* (Adelman 1992) Gertrude's 'maternal body', the intrusion of her mark on masculine identity and its destabilizing effects, casts a long shadow (see Adelman 1992: 11–37). She regards the matter of female characterization as bearing more or less directly on masculine identity as well as signs of the female. This seems a manœuvre that is not catered for in your review of feminist positions. I wonder whether you could say more about the particular challenge the 'mother-figure' sets in Shakespeare or other texts?

SHARON OUDITT: I think that there is something of this implicit in Rose's reading of Eliot's position, and that is precisely what she – Rose – is steering clear of. The 'inexpressibly horrible' that Eliot describes bears some relation to the 'horrific maternal body' to which Adelman alludes. It seems to speak to an invocation of 'deep fantasy', of the Oedipal forces that align the female body with the power to engulf, to render into nothingness, to emasculate? Perhaps it speaks more to male fantasy about women than to female experience. This doesn't mean, of course, that it is invalid as an approach: it's very useful in elucidating a masculine fear of femininity that troubles so many texts – Shakespearian and other – and in explaining the inability of this particular kind of masculinity to 'grow up', that is, to perceive women in any function other than the maternal/sexual. The best example in a modern text that I can think of that explores both sides of this kind of figure (positive and negative) is Mrs Ramsay in Virginia Woolf's *To the Lighthouse*. She is oceanic in some respects, but also limited and limiting, preventing the younger generation from outgrowing her dictates while she still lives. She does indeed cast a long shadow – over Lily Briscoe's canvas. But that's another story.

NW: Is there a contradiction between the impulse towards public or general meanings in materialist approaches and the private histories uncovered in psychoanalytic readings?

SO: Not in so far as the personal and the political, or the general, are elements of the same continuum in the context of women's oppression. There has been some considerable friction between psychoanalytic approaches (commonly characterized as 'French') and social, or materialist approaches (often described as 'Anglo-American') and, while I don't want to suggest that there is no distinction, I think that the idea of the 'subject' has provided a lot of common ground. That is to say, psychic meanings are also social meanings. The forces which make up the unconscious are socially as well as privately induced. The subject is a kind of battleground in which drives, ideologies, discourses struggle against each other and in which the private is barely distinguishable from the public. We can see this in all three readings of Gertrude that I've outlined: the private meanings which the Ghost and Hamlet apply to her are aligned with public ideas of what it means to be female. Her silence, confusion, lack of coherence, whether it be explained in the language of personal motivation or public duty, seems to be a product of the inevitable 'inconstancy' of woman's position when she has a number of roles to play and each is viewed separately from a male-orientated perspective. I think the two approaches are complementary rather than contradictory.

NW: You state on p. 91 that several of the disagreements within feminist criticism could be attributed to 'critical fashion'. Are there approaches that are distinct from transient cultural forces?

SO: Perhaps the word 'fashion' suggests a capriciousness that I didn't really intend. I can't imagine an approach that is not inflected by the cultural and historical forces of its day even if aspects of that approach remain stable across long periods of time. In the case of feminism (in the recent term) emphases have shifted, alliances have been established, changes have been made – it has been a learning process for all – but many of the core considerations are still there because our culture has not yet been able to change them.

NW: How would you confront the common resistance to feminist critiques that emerges whenever it is pointed out that what is now held as an article of good faith just could not be true of Renaissance perceptions?

SO: First, I would say that this is not a problem borne by feminism alone. I don't think any approach, from practical criticism to present-day postmodernist preoccupations, can entirely divest itself of the prejudices – conscious and unconscious – of its time. Then, I would say that feminism, like a lot of other politically inflected theories, is by nature interventionist. That is, it is not trying, by some mysterious act of transhistorical osmosis, to get to and re-experience the object of its study, in the historicist and literal terms derived from that object's temporal location. Feminism is, on the whole, conscious that there is historical and cultural difference between Renaissance perceptions and those of the present day. Its concern is to elucidate the position, roles, cultural existence of women at that time *and* to unpick the silencing of women's issues in literary criticism that has dominated our cultural understanding of that period since. It reads against the grain, when that grain is characterized by patriarchal attitudes, in an effort to analyse the effects of those attitudes. And to examine the various ways in which women, who are not always perceived by feminists as victims of a patriarchal conspiracy, have dealt with them.

CHAPTER 4

'Vnfolde your selfe': Jacques Lacan and the Psychoanalytic Reading of *Hamlet*

NIGEL WHEALE

[Wheale's essay provides the context for a critical reading of Jacques Lacan's discussions of *Hamlet*. It begins by paraphrasing Lacan's arguments as they apply to the Prince and his father, Gertrude, Ophelia and Laertes, while also establishing descriptions of some key terms in Lacan's psychoanalytic theory. It then considers how Lacanian analysis might contribute to performance theory and our responses to productions. Finally, it evaluates critically Lacan's interpretation of the father–son relation in the tragedy, identifying errors and misreadings, and supplying contextual details which qualify his psychoanalytic approach.

A traditional view of the means by which we attain expression in language derives from the basic assumption that it involves a compromise between our unconscious desires and the public negotiation with an inherited language. Whenever we enter linguistic self-consciousness, we give ourselves up to a pre-existing system of signifiers assigned individual meanings by such a system. Lacan noted that, alternatively, we take up 'subject-positions' within a distribution of relations (for instance, male/female, I/you), and so are not totally in charge of our meaning. Indeed, it is a condition of our use of language that meaning is rendered unstable – never captive, but always in view. For Freud, our unconscious drives cannot be expressed through language. If desire is formless and unknown, language apparently supplies form and intelligibility – a clarity quite foreign to the language of the unconscious which is too instinctive to be fully semantic as traditionally understood. Lacan refuses this division between a pre-existing unconscious and its ensuing expression, as he regards the unconscious as emerging simultaneously with language, which actually *structures* our desires. (This is why Lacanian phraseology and written style is so complex, obliging the reader to 'work through' to the specialized associations of the signifier.) As Colin MacCabe describes it, this 'play' between imagined presence and the inevitable absence of non-linguistic corroboration *produces* the unconscious and its unadmitted desires (see MacCabe 1979: 6–7). Lacan's reading of Freud recovers some of the realization that these desires are not biological instincts but rather 'drives' activated by a sense of lack or prohibition. What is at stake here is a sense of 'character' or 'subject' as traditionally understood. When a child perceives itself reflected in a mirror for the first time, it is led to identify with an image that promises unity and distinctiveness. Lacan regards this as a misrecognition, based on the *desire* to possess such unity yet which is never actually experienced, and is termed by him as the 'Imaginary' state. This identification with an image, a 'dyadic' mental structure, is a pleasurable activity and yet one to be invaded by a third and intrusive term. With linguistic maturity, there is an inevitable entry into a system of differences (present/absent, here/there, as well as male/female), which Lacan calls the 'Symbolic', associated with the Father's prohibition of incestuous desire. The easy equivalence of a 'signifier' (the child) with its reflected 'signified' (the image) is thus disturbed and the direct path to reality thwarted. Instead we grow to associate with an endless relay of *linguistic* and so hollow signs. Lacanian literary criticism derives from the realization that, just as the unconscious might be structured *like* a language, it may be an effect *of* language. The metaphors of a literary text figure the unconscious rather than represent it in the signified. The usual formulation (since Saussure's linguistic work) is that the signifier is sustained by what it signifies ($\frac{s}{S}$). The bonding may be arbitrary, as a physical object such as a hairy quadruped that barks can be a 'dog', 'chien' or 'Hund', yet once locked into the specific *langue*, the bonding becomes a secure one. For Lacan the algorithm should be better expressed as $\frac{S}{s}$, where the signified 'slides' beneath a signifier which 'floats'; the bar between the two signifying a division rather than a relation, that is, the signifier obeys no 'law' of the signified. For Freud, the unconscious expresses itself through dream images which may be 'condensed' (a combination of several at once) or be 'displaced' (a constant shift of significance from one image to a contiguous one). Lacan calls these rhetorical features the 'metaphorical' and 'metonymic' respectively.

Both of these textual tendencies are symptomatic of a response to the obstruction of desire. The metaphor transforms the apparent 'signified' (for example, 'the ships ploughed the ocean'), whereas metonymy always supplies allied references rather than similar ones to the apparent 'signified' (for example 'the pen is mightier than the sword', 'the decisions made by Downing Street'). This obliquity or evasion is not a route, however indirect, to some signified deeper 'meaning', the unconscious desire. It is the very condition of language that it is never able to speak of what it desires to say. Consequently, when I use the first-person pronoun, 'I' am assigned a subject-position, in a symbolic sense, but not describing the disjointed self at all. There is always an *absence* at the centre of our determination to represent, and we cannot avoid either providing a substitute for or deferring such contact with the realm of desire in and through language. Literary expression, as with all linguistic use, provides a constant stream of signifiers, which only ever attain temporary meaning retrospectively, through the noting of their difference from one another. The desire to express the inexpressible is a mechanism which unsettles the symbolic order's impositions of meaning. In practice, however, no one can define one's matrix of desires so as to control it, that is, in Lacan's terms, to occupy the position of the Other. Despite this, we continue to use language to attempt just that: to become the origin and so guarantor of meaning.

A 'subject' can thus never be an autonomous observing non-participant. Similarly, the text will never be fixed in form and content. On the contrary, it is riddled (quite literally) with discontinuities and inconsistencies to the point where it is always 'decentred', free of governance by a fixed authorial subject. Similarly, readers may feel that they are grasping meaning in their readings, yet it is more the case that the narrative appropriates its readers through their transferred and projected desires.]

NIGEL WOOD

Freud's legacy to literary criticism has been at best dubious. Jacques Lacan began his seven seminars on *Hamlet* by making a review of the psychoanalytic literature on the play, but even he found that 'the writings of analytic authors are far from enlightening' (24: 19).[1] Freud's own writings on art and literature have often been dismissed as 'vulgar Freudianism', that is to say they are criticized for being schematic and reductive, and the most productive psychoanalytic criticism tends to have been written by literary critics who have appropriated elements of psychoanalytic theory for their own purposes. Ruth Nevo, for example, makes a psychoanalytic reading of the 'late play' *Pericles* which focuses on all of those aspects in the drama which criticism has traditionally found to be unsatisfactory. By considering the apparent absurdities and elisions in *Pericles*, Nevo finds that 'precisely because it is closer to primary process, [that is, to the workings of unconscious materials] more anomolous, 'crude', absurd, strange, [it is] a representation of elemental and universal fantasy of great power' (Nevo, 'The Perils of *Pericles*', in Sokol 1993: 151).

Freud himself characterized the appropriation of psychoanalytic ideas by untrained amateurs as 'wild psychoanalysis', and disapproved of what he took to be the misapplication of his science. What contribution can it make to literary studies? Three broad objections are often made against psychoanalysis, both as a clinical practice and a method of cultural analysis.

The most damaging refutation of Freud is made by philosophers and historians of science who deny all methodological validity to psychoanalysis. Because its results cannot be falsified, it does not have the status of a physical science; the conceptual diction of psychoanalysis has to be accepted in order to be able to draw psychoanalytic conclusions. That is to say, the model delivers only those results which it has already prejudged, and its efficacy cannot be measured against any free-standing criteria (MacIntyre 1971; Gellner 1993).

Second, it denies conscious decision and rationally-based behaviour, replacing them with the promptings of the unconscious, which cannot be directly known by any individual. This kind of objection was made to Freudianism at a very early stage, and was effectively formulated, for example, by the Russian formalist theorist, V.N. Voloshinov. As a critic from a resolutely materialist tradition, Voloshinov (1987: 83) argued that historical process and social circumstance entered into consciousness through the dimension of communication, understood in its broadest terms: 'What we call "the human psyche" and "consciousness" reflect the dialectics of history to a much greater degree than the dialectics of nature. The nature that is present in them is nature already in economic and social refraction'. Therefore, for Voloshinov, the Freudian unconscious was a mystification of essentially social processes. This argument in some ways anticipates Lacan's revision of Freud, as we shall see.

Finally, from the point of view of cultural studies, psychoanalysis often seems to be fundamentally unhistorical, suspending vital contextual information in favour of supposedly timeless, psychical structures, and reducing contingent details to one primordial, recurrent pattern of development. Vickers (1993: 287) criticizes Ruth Nevo's psychocritical reading of *Pericles* on exactly these grounds: 'Ignoring historical criticism, theatrical convention, genre, rhetoric, and Renaissance theories of literature, the Neo-Freudian critic approaches a nonrealist literary form with expectations derived from realism and finds – incoherences'.

These are genuine problems which we need to confront when thinking about Lacan's interpretation of Shakespeare. But in defence of literary criticism based in psychoanalytic thought, we can argue that for our own period Shakespeare's *Tragedy of Hamlet, Prince of Denmark* (whatever it was for previous audiences and readers) is first and foremost a tragedy about tortured minds – the traumas experienced by

Hamlet, Ophelia and Gertrude, perhaps even Claudius – so we must make a serious attempt to test the adequacy of contemporary psycho-analytic accounts of the play. Freud 'reduces' so much in the psyche and culture to a primordial conflict between parents and children through the Oedipus complex, yet that conflict is so obviously close to the centre of the *Tragedy of Hamlet*, that psychoanalysis ought to provide a special interpretative access to the material. What follows can only be a brief and closely defined discussion of Jacques Lacan's remarks about *Hamlet*, and is properly only the starting-point for anyone's more extended engagement with Lacan, which must inevit-ably also be a reading of Freud.

Lacan's writing is notoriously difficult, partly because its author intended to imitate the complex processes of repression and evasion which are central to Freud's account of psychical structures. He did this so as to make the reader more conscious of these mechanisms, though whether this strategy can be said to be effective is very debatable. But as well as being conceptually complex in this way, Lacan also had recourse to diagrams and equations of an apparently mathematical rigour, which seem to confer a kind of systematic logic to the evasions of his prose argument. Lacan's critics object to what they describe as his pseudo-logical and wilful obscurity, arguing that if an idea is worth anything, then it should be clearly articulated. Freud's own expository style, after all, is celebrated for its persuasive clarity, which was recognized in his lifetime with the award of the Goethe Prize. And in common with other compatriot intellectuals such as Michel Foucault and Roland Barthes, Lacan disdained the use of careful scholarly apparatus; he was not scrupulous about referencing and textual preci-sion. It is also probably fair to say that his influence has been much greater in academic cultural studies than in any established psycho-analytic or therapeutic practice, and this again has raised doubts about the nature of his achievement (Roudinesco 1990).

Although he made a fairly extensive review of the earlier criticism on *Hamlet* at the beginning of his seminal-discussions (24: 19–23) Lacan did not follow contemporary literary criticism at all closely, and seems to have been uninfluenced, for example, by the work of Roland Barthes: 'His own readings of *Hamlet*, Poe, *Athalie* and *Antigone* are essentially thematic and are subordinated to a search for supports for or illustrations of psychoanalytic theory' (Macey 1988: 6). Therefore this account of Lacan's discussion of *Hamlet* supplements his literary commentary with arguments from elsewhere in his psychoanalytic theory. Despite the scandals and schisms which attend Lacan's career and its legacy, one of the most helpful guides to his work can still conclude that 'Lacan is the only psychoanalyst of the twentieth century . . . whose intellectual achievement is in any way comparable to Freud's' (Bowie 1991: 203). How effectively is this achievement brought to bear on Shakespeare's play?

Jacques Lacan's Seven Seminars on *Hamlet* (March–April 1959)

Lacan's reading of *Hamlet* is a provocative, speculative discourse, edited together from seven sessions of the open seminar which he initiated in November 1953 and which continued annually until the year before his death in 1981. The complete text of the seminars is still in the process of being established from transcripts. In other words the original seminar was itself a performance, relying on the aggressions and fixations of a lively debate, and there are passages where the speaker seems to be casting around to find an effective form for his argument; at other times he seems to feel the need to persuade his audience that this excursion into literary analysis bears any relation at all to his main business, which in 1959 was the interpretation of *désir*. We will return to this apparently tendentious analogy between Lacanian psychoanalytic performance and theatrical event in the next section.

I will now give a selective paraphrase of the psychical functions which Lacan attributes to the main roles in *Hamlet*. This will inevitably foreshorten (and also coarsen) Lacan's own account, but it will provide us with a simplified Lacanian schema which can then be tested against our own responses to Shakespeare's play, in reading and in performance. References indicate where Lacan's arguments can be followed in greater psychoanalytic detail.

Hamlet: the Subject Divided in the Symbolic

Freud was drawn to the poets and dramatists, he said, because they had already articulated in metaphorical form the truths which only he could formalize in psychoanalysis: 'In their knowledge of the mind they are far in advance of us everyday people, for they draw upon sources which we have not yet opened up for science' (Freud 1953–74, 9: 8). Lacan endorses this interrelation towards the end of his first seminar on *Hamlet*: 'poetic creations don't simply reflect psychological constructions, they give birth to them' (24: 17). For Freud, *Hamlet* was a modern elaboration of Sophocles' *Oedipus Tyrannos*, and Lacan cannot ignore this reading, but he recasts it for his own purposes: 'the psychoanalytic tradition sees in Oedipus' crime the quintessential charting of the relationship of the subject to what we call here the Other, i.e., to the locus of the inscription of the law' (26–7: 34; 42).[2] Lacan employs Shakespeare's play as a means of considering 'the place of the object in desire' (26–7: 37; 47), rather than for yet another account in the classical Freudian vein of the inescapable 'family romance'. This is the contest between children and their parents which produces gendered identity and social conformity through the process of the Oedipus complex. This, inevitably, remains Lacan's theme, but the Oedipal experience is cast in new terms: 'The drama of *Hamlet* is a kind of mechanism, a structure, a bird-catcher's net, where human desire is articulated, and precisely in the coordinates which Freud established for us, to reveal the Oedipus and castration' (24: 24).

Lacan restructured Freud's topography of id, ego and superego in a way which committed each individual psyche to an external, intersubjective scheme of meanings. Lacanian cultural theorists welcome this innovation because it focuses attention inescapably on the linguistic dimension, and appears to compensate classical Freudian psychoanalysis for its apparent failure adequately to account for social interaction. Writing in 1966, Lacan himself claimed that he was revealing the true contribution which language makes in Freud's conception of the psyche (Lacan 1977: 34ff.), but it is certainly possible to argue that Lacan consistently misrepresents Freud's arguments about language and the unconscious: for Freud 'the drives need to be silent, inscrutable, unavailable to mere talk, if psychoanalysis is eventually to rejoin biology in a unified science of man' (Bowie 1991: 53).

The peculiar relationship between subjectivity and eloquence which makes the early modern period so fascinating does seem to be what drew Lacan to this play in particular: 'To understand the Elizabethans one must first turn certain words around on their hinges so as to give them a meaning somewhere between the subjective one and the objective one' (26–7: 44–5). Lacan's three terms which articulate the psyche are the Imaginary, the Symbolic and the Real, and they tie 'subjectivity' and 'objectivity' so closely together that they effectively abolish any such distinction. Unfortunately for our immediate purposes, the seven seminars on *Hamlet* do not make any extensive direct reference to these categories because the audience/reader is assumed to be already familiar with them from previous work: 'The ins and outs of the play *Hamlet* will enable us to get a better grasp of the economy – very closely connected here – of the real, the imaginary, and the symbolic' (26–7: 31; 39). Therefore these key terms will be established in this discussion using the role of the Prince as an example of the subject who labours within their triadic structure. The three classifications are capitalized in this discussion to distinguish them from their non-specialized uses.

Lacan introduces *Hamlet* as 'the drama of an individual subjectivity, and the hero is always present on stage, more than in any other play' (26–7: 8; 12); this is not in fact accurate, since Richard III has a larger share of his own text than does Hamlet, but the emphasis establishes the focus of analysis on a subject-in-language. Probably the most fruitful emphasis that Lacanian criticism can bring to this play lies here: the subjectivity created by any role (in reading or through performance) must be understood in its complex relation to the structures of desire and signification. These are simultaneously subjective, inward to the particular individual, and objective in that they are enabled by externals such as language and social convention. To put this in a very condensed form which can be elaborated in the remainder of this section: the Prince is an exemplary type of the way in which subjectivity is deprived of that which it most desires, and is therefore neurotically driven through a narrative of unsatisfactory substitutions, until it finds a kind of fulfilment which is only obtained at a total cost. 'There is a level in the subject on which it can be said that his fate is expressed in terms of a pure signifier, a level at which he is merely the reverse side of a message that is not even his own' (26–7: 8; 12).

As this statement indicates, Lacan's major revision of Freud attacked any notion of a coherent and unitary structure in the ego. The individual is redescribed as a 'subject', which is a space 'subjected to' the pulsions of the dominating orders under which it labours. Lacan's conception of this human subject is of a consciousness which is intrinsically riven, and whose motor energy in fact derives from this radical incoherence:

> Let me say simply that this is what leads me to object to any reference to totality in the individual, since it is the subject who introduces division into the individual, as well as into the collectivity that is his equivalent. Psychoanalysis is properly that which reveals both the one and the other to be no more than mirages.
>
> (Lacan 1977: 80)

The splits or ruptures which, according to Lacan, constitute human subjectivity begin with the child's earliest sensory experience, to which the infant – deriving from 'infans', the unspeaking – is subjected before it has even the illusion of control over its body or the external world. The Imaginary is therefore that dimension of consciousness which is fundamentally sensory, derived from perception. It is laid down in the child's earliest relations to the body of the mother, which becomes the focus for the most intense fantasies and hallucinations on the part of the child. Illusions of plenitude and bliss are established in this period, and they are the type of all utopian hopes and desires in adult life. Hamlet's strange remark to Rosencrantz and Guildenstern might be seen as this kind of delusory, infantile megalomania: 'O God, I could be bounded in a nutshell and count myself a king of infinite space' (II.ii.252–3). But the falsity of this kind of Imaginary bliss is evident both to Lacan and to Hamlet – '. . . were it not that I have bad dreams'. Central to the Imaginary is the alienating experience of the mirror stage (*le stade du miroir*), where the child constructs an illusory coherence for itself as it begins to gain a greater sense of bodily autonomy (this is defined more closely below, in relation to Hamlet's duel with Laertes).

Both the Imaginary and the mirror phase establish fractures within the subject; the next catastrophic split is introduced by the order of the Symbolic. This is the all-powerful dimension of language and abstracting representation, which is omnipotent because (for Lacan) it necessarily controls the expression of the Imaginary and the Real. Like the mirror phase, the Symbolic offers the subject a sense of autonomy since utterance seems to organize desires and intentions for the self. But the Symbolic is another supremely alienating structure because it defines the subject within the totality of culture, and lays down the Law: this is the function of the figure of the castrating Father who coerces male and female infants into conventional gendered behaviour. In other words, the Symbolic functions for Lacan as the Oedipal process.

The third term in Lacan's fundamental triad is the Real. This is (of course) more complex than any simple idea of 'reality'; it elaborates Freud's notion of the reality principle, the inordinate, crushing demands of the world which coerce and ultimately overcome each individual's pleasure principle. And it is also perhaps to be compared with Sartre's idea of the 'practice-inert', the brutal resistance of things which oppose existential choice, and yet which is the precondition of doing anything at all: 'Language is a kind of vast reality, what I would call a *practico-inert* entity . . . something which encompasses me and from which I am able to take things' ('The Writer and his Language' 1965 in Sartre 1973: 77). But the Real is distinctively Lacanian because it is also a textual phenomenon, akin to the narrative of history which will not exempt us, and to which we only have access via the Symbolic. The Real is utterly inimical to the Imaginary. Fortinbras – 'Strong Arm' – might be thought of as the personification of the Real, existing in a different dimension to Hamlet, an adroit worldling who successfully repairs the narrative of political succession after the Prince's interlude of catastrophic subjectivity.

Hamlet immediately places the issue of identity before us: Barnardo's question to Francisco which opens the play asks 'Who's there?', but he is answered only with a mirroring demand, 'Nay, answer me. Stand and unfold yourself.' (In the Q2 text of 1605, following the convention of the period, the pronoun is written as two words, 'vnfolde your selfe', conveying a separated sense of selfhood that accords with Lacanian division in the person.) Barnardo replies not with his own name, but by citing the name of Denmark's metaphorical father: 'Long live the King!' This supreme political signifier guarantees his own identity, which, mirror-fashion, he can now allow Francisco to grant to him in return. But this guarantor of the Symbolic is, we know, an empty signifier, representing Claudius and not old Hamlet. This is a small-scale demonstration of the ways in which Hamlet's own identity is founded on the Name-of-the-Father, which is synonymous with his own. The apparition which appears to the Prince is not precisely his father, but a neuter principle, designated by 'it' (I.iv.37ff.). In conference with this Symbolic-father in Act I, scene v, Hamlet describes what is effectively the installation of the patriarchal Law in his consciousness, as derived from this fantasm. He will purge his memory of 'All saws of books, all forms, all pressures past' (I.v.100) so as to leave a single, abiding 'commandment' within the 'book and volume' of his brain (I.v.103). This kind of doubling of terms ('book and volume') has been noticed as a feature of the play's language, and is a recognized rhetorical trope in the period, called *hendiadys* (Wright 1981). From a Lacanian perspective it might be described as an active demonstration of the insidious prolixity of signifiers which can only be defined differentially, that is, by a further expense of language.

The role of the Father in the Symbolic is to act as the fundamental guarantor of meaning, and without which psychosis is precipitated:

> It is the lack of the Name-of-the-Father in that place which, by the hole that it opens up in the signified, sets off the cascade of reshapings of the signifier from which the increasing disaster of the imaginary proceeds . . .
>
> (Lacan 1977: 217)

The disaster is located within the Imaginary because it was here that the child first constructed its saving fantasies of coherence and plenitude, which then catastrophically collapse with the destruction of the certitude formerly invested in the ideal paternal figure. The project of revenge which this symbolic father (the Father-of-the-Symbolic) places on his subject son is another demand which can only further divide the Prince's psyche:

> Let not the royal bed of Denmark be
> A couch for luxury and damnèd incest.
> But howsoever thou pursuest this act,
> Taint not thy mind, nor let thy soul contrive
> Against thy mother aught . . .

> (I.v.82–7)

The Ghost does not specify the nature of the revenge to be taken, only that the son should not become corrupted with hatred against his mother; this recalls the convention of the impersonal avenger who is all the more just because he is not personally involved in retribution (Jenkins 1982: 457). But in this particular 'family romance' it is also surely an impossible demand, and one which Hamlet is quite incapable of fulfilling – so much so, that he has to remind himself not to commit matricide at III.ii.377–9. As a consequence he is stricken with a sense of dislocation in the world which reaches all the way back to his birth, and which becomes synonymous with the crime: 'The time is out of joint. O cursèd spite,/That ever I was born to set it right!' (I.v.196). Having established how Hamlet is riven by the demands of the Symbolic, we can now go on to paraphrase Lacan's view of his relations with Gertrude, Ophelia and Laertes.

Gertrude: Desire and the Other

We have seen how Lacan's 'return to Freud' emphasized that the workings of the psyche are only to be found in the enchaining of signifiers (24: 15), and he insisted that language should be understood as an endless process of meaning-creation through which we try to articulate a need which can never be met: 'I am an other than that which I think I am' (25: 32). Désir is the motive which animates this insatiable craving for fulfilled meaning and it is addressed to 'the Other' via language; it should not therefore be associated only with a narrowly sexual meaning. The Other may respond, but can never do so adequately, therefore reciprocally compounding the demand deficit in both subjects: désir is not a state or a motion but a space, and not a unified space but a split and contorted one. Need and demand are its co-ordinates, but they cannot be co-ordinated. It is a dimension in which the subject is always destined to travel too far or not far enough.

(Bowie 1991: 137)

Lacan chose to analyse *Hamlet* during the period when he was formulating his ideas about *désir*, and he settled on the play because for him it offered a compelling demonstration of the ways in which *désir* functions in a subject via the filiations of language (Lacan 1977: 281–325; Bowie 1991: 131).

Lacan situates the Prince inexorably within this schema because he considers that Hamlet is tensioned between three competing demands: that of his dead father, and those of the two female figures. According to Lacan, Gertrude motivates Hamlet's compulsive need which drives him through speech in search of a fulfilment he cannot achieve. The 'closet scene' in Act III, scene iv, presents the clearest demonstration of the formula that 'human *désir* is *désir* for the Other . . . completely abolishing the subject' (25: 23). Hamlet addresses his mother, but is in fact speaking beyond her, to his father, because he is attempting to fulfil the patriarchal demand of revenge. But this torsion which Gertrude exerts within the subjectivity of her son is heightened further by the figure of Ophelia. She is an 'essential articulation' (26–7: 8) in Hamlet's narrative who propels him, in spite of himself, towards his 'act', the confrontation with his ideal-other, Laertes, and which brings down his death. This description of the final duel as an 'act' aligns Lacan at this phase of his career in the late 1950s with Sartrean existentialism, because Hamlet will vindicate himself in the authenticity of his choice to fight and die, where 'To be' as an act of authentic choice also inevitably enjoins 'not to be'. But Lacan is also extending the function of death-as-definitive-choice away from this concept of an existential truth, and in the direction of death-as-fulfilment, delivered by the deep Oedipal narrative at work in the tragedy. (For Lacan's 'rather tortured relations with Sartre' see Macey 1988: 102–7.)

There is a further link with existentialism because for Lacan, both Hamlet and Gertude are unable 'to choose', that is, to make decisive commitment to adequate aims. Both of them are immobilized between the spectacle of 'an eminent, idealized, exalted object' – old Hamlet – and the 'degraded, despicable object' – Claudius (26–7: 8; 12; and see Lukacher 1986: 213ff.). Since all subjectivity is articulated only through the address to the Other, Hamlet is 'hooked' inexorably into Gertrude's fixated immobility: 'this permanent dimension touches the very nerve and sinew of Hamlet's will' (26–7: 9; 13). Lacan develops a particular argument to account for that central feature of the Prince's imputed psychology, his procrastination and delay. Hamlet prevaricates, argues Lacan, because his neurosis renders him 'constantly suspended in the time of the Other' (26–7: 14; 17). He hesitates to kill Claudius at prayer, not primarily (as Hamlet himself reasons) so 'that [Claudius']' soul may be as damned and black/As hell, whereto it goes' (III.iii.94–5), but because 'this is not the hour of the Other . . . Whatever Hamlet may do, he will do it only at the hour of the Other' (26–7: 14; 18).

Here we meet a problem which is perhaps created by translation, and by Lacan's use of puns as a feature of argument. The 'hour of the Other', *l'heure de l'Autre*, puns on the phrase *leurre de l'Autre*, the 'lure of the Other', and *leurre* is therefore allied with the central idea of *méconnaissance*, the misconstrual of self and other which for Lacan is intrinsic to human expressivity as articulated by the regimes of the Imaginary and the Symbolic (Lacan 1979: 281). A useful Shakespearian word which might be used as an approximate equivalent to *méconnaissance* is 'misprision', originally a legal term meaning 'wrongful capture' (*OED*), but appropriated by Shakespeare in *Love's Labour's Lost* (IV.iii.96) to mean 'The mistaking of one thing, word, etc., for another' (*OED*). The pun *l'heure/leurre* delivers the Prince by fatal attraction to the point of Laertes' foil.

Ophelia: the Imaginary Phallus

Gertrude is 'the Other', the *grand Autre*, or 'big A', while Ophelia becomes the 'little a' in Hamlet's schema of inhibited meaning. As Hamlet's 'little other object' Ophelia is the primary focus for the Prince's sadistic fantasies which reach their climax in his outrageous verbal assaults on her during Act III, scenes i and ii, 'that sarcastic style of cruel aggression which makes these scenes . . . the strangest in all of classical literature' (26–7: 18; 22). Lacan argues that this sadism must also be directed at the subject himself: 'For a sadistic fantasy to endure, the subject's interest in the person who suffers humiliation must obviously be due to the possibility of the subject's being submitted to the same humiliation himself' (26–7: 12; 16). On this description, the shocking violence of Hamlet's response to Ophelia is in part provoked by the violence which he has himself suffered through Claudius' murder and usurpation.

Lacan enthused about the figure of Ophelia, 'one of the most fascinating creations ever offered to the imagination' (24: 14); the drama of 'the feminine object' which first appeared in the figure of Helen of Troy 'is perhaps carried to its highest point in Ophelia's misfortune' (24: 14); through her is demonstrated 'the horror of femininity as such' (24: 15). In one way, Lacan radically simplifies what might be the nature of the relationship between Hamlet and Ophelia, because he argues that from the moment of Hamlet's visit to Ophelia's closet, reported by her in Act II, scene i, she has become 'completely null and dissolved as a love object' for the Prince (26–7: 17; 22). For most readers and playgoers, this is surely an interpretation which impoverishes the dramatic possibilities of the relationship, more usually seen as a cruel parody of courtship which has become distorted by Hamlet's hatred for Ophelia as 'woman'. Lacan also interprets Hamlet's rejection of Ophelia in terms of a denial of sexual desire and procreation, but he redescribes the rejection as a denial of the status of the phallus, which has an additional, crucial meaning for his psychoanalytic theory.

All subjects – female as well as male – desire possession of the phallus, because it is the supreme signifier: 'it is the signifier intended to designate as a whole the effects of the signified' (Lacan 1977: 285). The phallus is an ideal sign and is not to be confused with the shrinking piece of flesh, the penis, which is its vulnerable prototype. The phallus is an 'enigmatic, universal thing, more male than female, and perhaps for which the female herself can become the symbol' (25: 32). In assigning supreme status to the phallus as the guarantor of all meaning in the dimension of the Symbolic, Lacan was once more elaborating on central themes in Freud's psychoanalytic theory. For Freud the Oedipus and castration complexes were the means by which individuals become reconciled (in more or less satisfactory ways) to a mature gendered identity as heterosexual males and females. These complexes act as rites of passage which have to be negotiated in the course of childhood and adolescent development. But Lacan metaphoricizes the male organ as the ever-present arbitrator of all symbolic meaning: 'For children of both sexes, [the phallus] is the emblem, only trivially "masculine", in and through which human desire finds form' (Bowie 1991: 128). This is a characteristic shift from a model based in (Freudian) developmental psychology, to a pervasive and inescapable (Lacanian) regime which is enforced throughout our desire for meaning.

The difference between the two conceptions can be demonstrated by contrasting a pre-Lacanian production of *Hamlet* with the kind of account offered in his seminars. Laurence Olivier's film version of 1948 notoriously staged the 'closet scene' between the Prince and Gertrude as a form of Oedipal contest. Mother and son are represented as being dangerously close to each other in age, and the Prince's hatred and revulsion for Gertrude catastrophically modulates to an erotic fascination (which the mother provokes and returns) just before the Ghost's intervention. Olivier's production of the closet scene, from a classical Freudian perspective, seems to stage a parody of the 'primal scene' in which the child envisions its own engendering, but in this case the displaced father returns to witness his son usurping his wife, now widow.

By contrast, Lacan disseminates the Oedipal struggle throughout Hamlet's language and consciousness, converting the figure of Ophelia into a cipher for this supreme signifier. Ophelia is 'at once image and pathos' (26-7: 11; 15), and from Act II, scene i, she stands for what the subject has lost – the phallus. She becomes

> a vision of life ready to bloom, of life bearing all other lives, and it is as such that Hamlet positions her in order to reject her – 'wouldst thou be a breeder of sinners?' This image of vital fecundity demonstrates for us more clearly than anything else the equation I have already established: Girl = Phallus.
>
> (25: 35)

Lacan makes an outrageous and (presumably) not altogether serious claim through one of his whimsical puns when he remarks: 'I'm just surprised that nobody's pointed out that Ophelia is O phallos' (26-7: 16; 20). Shakespeare's punning bawdy is of course extensive and full of psychoanalytic potential (Partridge 1955; Rubenstein 1989). The title of Much Ado About Nothing, for example, probably puns on confusion between 'nothing' and 'noting', which were near homophones in the period. Both Beatrice and Benedick construct their love for each other through 'notings' or over-hearings, and the false accusation of Hero is also a 'noting' constructed on 'nothing' (Humphreys 1981: 4). And beneath all of these playings upon misconstruction in Much Ado About Nothing there is also surely the sexual innuendo of 'nothing' as the female genitals, about which the 'ado' is raised. Yet, contrary to Lacan's reading of the name Ophelia, Shakespeare nowhere uses the word 'phallus' for what he most often designates as 'thing' – a usage to which Lacan was alert (26-7: 43). More usually the etymology of 'Ophelia' is linked to apheleia, or 'innocence'. The first recorded use for 'phallus' in English is however not far away: 'two Phalli, or Priapi (huge Images of the priuie part of a man) Purchas 1613' (*OED*). Here we meet one of the most debated areas of Lacan's contribution to psychoanalytic and cultural theory: how adequately does he theorize female sexuality and the nature of women's identity? There are a number of feminist-inspired critiques and appropriations of Lacan's theory (Grosz 1990; Bowie 1991), and here there is only space to point to an obvious opportunity which the original staging conventions might offer to a Lacanian perspective. Because all female roles in the English commercial theatre were played by youths until the late 1650s, the representation of 'woman' was rendered through a convention practised nowhere else in Europe. As Orgel (1989: 8) puts this: 'why were women more upsetting than boys to the English?'.

Laertes: Duelling in the Mirror

Lacan's discussion circles around central issues 'by means of a series of concentric strokes' (26–7: 37; 47), making successive descriptions which – depending on your point of view – either enrich his profound analysis, or make even hazier an already confused farrago. His account of the duel and tragic denouement is particularly layered, because this must be conclusive, and summarize his findings. But the mode of production of his *séminaire* was never conclusive, the nature of the research was necessarily one of delay and deferral as he staged the drama of his audience's *désir* for a complete – and in his terms – delusory knowledge: 'The most corrupting of comforts is intellectual comfort' (Bowie 1991: 3). There seem, however, to be at least three different emphases which he makes in analysing the tragic finale. First, Hamlet is driven towards the duel because the hour (*l'heure*) of his destruction is also a *leurre*, the kind of misprision or mis-taking which is endemic to human identity. Second, as a remnant of the notion of existential choice, the duel also promises to be an act which will deliver authenticity. Third, the challenge formalizes Hamlet's encounter with his ego ideal whom he must destroy in order to surpass: 'at this point Laertes is for Hamlet his double' (26–7: 25; 31).

Just as Gertrude occupies the place of the Other, and Ophelia acts as the substitutive, lesser other behind which is the presence of the veiled phallus, Laertes is also granted one of the major roles in Lacan's theory: he embodies Hamlet's mirror stage. The *stade du miroir* is Lacan's single most distinctive addition to Freudian psychoanalytic terminology. Lacan defines it as a stage in development occurring in every child between 6 and 18 months when the infant first realizes its singular, bounded identity, which stops at the body surface, and which can be seen as an other, for example by reflection in a mirror. Before this discovery, the child had felt itself either to be boundless, undifferentiated from the objects which it desired and which it hated or feared, or else it had been at the mercy of distinct, seemingly independent body parts [*membres*] which it could not control. The discovery of a personal autonomy at the mirror stage puts the child into a new, apparently more confident relation with its self, and with all other objects and persons. The mirror stage affords the child the ability to project an ideal self-image, but fatally, the self-image that is formed is necessarily another misprision, a notion of the self which cannot be coincident with the psyche and body which offers it to the world: 'It is an experience that leads us to oppose any philosophy directly issuing from the Cogito' (Lacan 1977: 1) – that is to say, from a fully conscious, resolving identity.

Lacan quotes Hamlet's description of Laertes in Act V, scene ii, 'an absolute gentleman, full of most excellent differences' (only present in the Second Quarto; see Hibbard 1987: 366), as evidence of the Prince's agonistic relation to his ideal-other: 'The playwright situates the basis of aggressivity in this paroxysm of absorption in the imaginary register, formally expressed as a mirror relationship, a mirrored reaction' (26–7: 25; 31). Just as the notion of the phallus as supreme signifier generalizes what had been a transitional phase in Freud, so the *stade du miroir* is a single period of development, but also the inescapable stage where all subjectivities must perpetually theatricalize themselves (Pye 1988; Lukacher 1989: 873). In staging his compulsive encounter with Laertes, the ideal-other, the subject which is Hamlet is driven to destruction through the need to fulfil the command from the voice-of-the-father.

Having seen how Lacan casts the major roles of his theoretical pantheon as the personnel of Shakespeare's tragedy, we can now explore some possible applications of this repertoire.

'[W]e are Pictures' (IV.v.82)

There are many conflicting approaches to the study of Shakespeare, but one of the sharpest contrasts is that between, on the one hand, text-based interpretation of the plays, and on the other, responses to the text in performance. Even today, most theoretically inspired interpretations of Shakespeare are made without any reference to playgoing, or to the existence of production history. Of all critical-theoretical approaches to literature, the psychoanalytic consideration of drama ought to be one of the most useful for comparing and contrasting our text-based readings of a work with the often starkly different responses which we feel in the theatre, or when watching a recorded version of a play. A practical application of a Lacanian approach to *Hamlet* might therefore be found in comparing the experience of watching the play in performance with the intense intersubjectivity of the analytic relationship itself.

Lacan's provocative reading of *Hamlet* is only a reading. In his second seminar he effectively removed the play from his French audience's comprehension by saying that they could have no idea what the drama represented in English: 'it is unplayable in French' (24: 23). And in the third seminar he despaired of understanding audience responses to performance: 'Let's leave aside spectators, who [unlike readers] are unfathomable' (25: 14). It may be that the complete fixation of Lacan's theory on the workings of language to the exclusion of all non-linguistic phenomena actually blinded him to the embodied, sensual dimension of drama in performance. This certainly seems to be the implication in his only extended discussion of the play on-stage, which is in fact a theory of performance.

Lacan asserts that the unconscious defined as 'the discourse of the Other' is perfectly illustrated in the audience's *rapport* with the actors and production as they watch the play. The dimension added by the actors 'is strictly analogous to that by which we ourselves are implicated [*intéressés*] in our own unconscious[, b]ecause our *rapport* with the unconscious is woven from our Imaginary, I would say from our *rapport* with our own body' (25: 17). Lacan goes on to say that it might seem as if he is unaware of the body as such, because his theory is one of 'disembodied analysis' [*l'analyse incorporelle*] since it is the signifier which is the focus of his teaching:

> It is with our own limbs – for the imaginary is precisely this – that we make the alphabet of this discourse which is unconscious, each of us in diverse ways, since we don't make use of the same elements. Similarly, the actor lends his limbs [*membres*], his presence, not simply as a puppet, but with his unconscious well and truly realized [*bel et bien réel*], that is to say the *rapport* of his limbs with a particular history which is his very own [*avec une certaine histoire qui est la sienne*].
>
> (25: 18)

For Lacan, the difference between a good and a bad actor is measured by the degree to which their unconscious is compatible with the 'role' which they are undertaking (*ce prêt de sa marionnette*).

Lacan's view of performance can be contrasted with the theory and practice of the surrealist dramatist Antonin Artaud, who also viewed language as a distorting carapace, and for whom a true performance evaded the linguistic by having recourse to primordial, embodied meaning. Artaud aspired to a theatre without texts where sensual effects would bypass discursive meaning, and the audience would irrationally 'contract' the players' intentions as if they were a disease (Roach 1985: 222–4). On the other hand, for Lacan, the role-in-the-text is so powerfully determining that he makes the extraordinary statement that *every* performance of *Hamlet* in English succeeds, as if the actor has only to inhabit the garment of the text for its power to be manifested: 'when an English actor plays Hamlet, he plays the part well. They all play it well' (24: 23). This is because the role articulates the place of desire in the body so effectively that no one can give a bad performance, every Hamlet conveys his effects to the spectators via the unconscious as the language of the Other. More sceptical playgoers might take issue with this argument by saying that they have never seen an entirely satisfactory performance of *Hamlet*, because the role offers so many options which no one actor can ever convey.

At the centre of the psychotherapeutic process of analysis is the experience of the transference, which is the intense dependency formed by the patient on the figure of the analyst in the course of treatment. The transference consists of a structure of fantasy and projection which the patient builds around the analyst, and which becomes a central means for the resolution of disorder (Laplanche and Pontalis 1973: 455–62). One of Lacan's clinical achievements is said to have been the focusing of analytic attention on the transference as the articulation of illness through intersubjectivity, that is, through the pragmatic reciprocities of a specific relationship (Bowie 1991: 200). The transference recapitulates essential features of the individual's difficulties which were formed in childhood development, and which have produced disabling neurosis, and together the analyst and analysand work through the damaging prehistory which is represented in the form of the transference (Lacan 1979: 123–260).

What might we gain in performance discussion if we were able to formulate our responses to specific productions in terms of a kind of transference? Attending a live performance involves the vigorous construction of fantasy within each member of the audience which is directed towards the players individually and the production as a whole. In a well-conducted discussion of a specific performance, this would involve drawing out the contrasts between different responses to the same role or detail of action. Rigorous performance criticism is even now a strangely underdeveloped branch of drama studies, and Lacanian criticism might be valuable in contributing to the accurate registration of our responses to specific productions. Discussion often begins at the level of 'I really liked Hamlet's leather trousers', which is a response not to be despised, because primary processes are obviously at work through the use of costume and the modelling of scenes. Clearly a post-performance seminar discussion of *Hamlet* is far removed from an extensive psychotherapeutic treatment, but we might be encouraged to think about the nature of our attachment to performances, and the reasons why we differ over interpretations, if we give more attention to the kind of rhetoric we use to express our affective responses.

'Something even Deeper Demands our Attention' (26–7: 29; 36)

If we now itemize four serious errors which Lacan makes out of ignorance or because he chooses to overlook facts, we will be in a position to assess what remains of his psychoanalytic interpretation of the play. Other writers have focused on Lacan's discussion of Ophelia and Gertrude (Elaine Showalter, 'Representing Ophelia: Women, Madness, and the Responsibilities of Feminist Criticism', in Parker and Hartman 1985), so it might be helpful to follow here his arguments about the function of the Ghost in the tragedy. It will also be useful to consider Lacan's analysis of the Prince's fatal duel with Laertes, because this is linked by Lacan to his father-loss at the level of an unconscious motivation. Here Lacan is, of course, condemned to follow the interpretation of *Hamlet* established by Freud, for whom the Prince delays because he cannot 'take vengeance on the man who . . . shows him the repressed wishes of his own childhood realized' (Freud 1953–72, 4: 265; Lacan 24: 9–10). But if we attend to historical context, period assumptions, and the logic of the text as a performance, Lacan's depth-psychological argument appears to be seriously compromised by at least four major misreadings:

First, Lacan's psychoanalytic perspective does not allow him to recognize the political dimension which is present in the question of the succession to the throne of Denmark: he mentions it in passing, but as a detail not worth analytical attention (24: 14). At the beginning of his second seminar, Lacan briefly situated the play in 'the transition between two epochs', those of Elizabeth I and James VI and I, which were 'of a quite different character' (24: 18–19). He does not, however, apply this context in any detailed way to the logic of the play's development. Cultural criticism inspired by psychoanalysis is often accused of failing to take account of immediate, pragmatic circumstances such as economic and political contexts, but more conventionally based approaches can also overlook the oddity of the politics in the Danish Court. It has been argued that the early modern English audiences would unfavourably compare the situation where Claudius has 'Popped in between th'election and [Hamlet's] hopes' (V.ii.66), which was allowed by the Danish system of elective monarchy, with the English practice of primogenture and the son's inalienable claim to his father's position (Edwards 1985: 42). That is to say, the English audience's prejudice for its native arrangement would be confirmed by the palpable injustice of Claudius succeeding instead of Hamlet. Anxiety about political continuity and the state of the nation was acute during the latter part of 1601, the probable period of the play's composition and first performances. The Court was widely perceived to be corrupt and there was popular discontent against the levels of taxation; Queen Elizabeth was 68, and in February 1601 the Earl of Essex – whom Lacan confidently describes as Elizabeth's *amant* (24: 18) – had staged his ineffectual rebellion (Somerset 1992: 538–52). Surrounded by these agitations, the early performances of *Hamlet* could have gained an urgent political dimension which can only now be supplied by an effort of historical imagination, or else in production, by directorial and design emphases which create parallels with contemporary concerns.

Second, because Lacan must insist that the appearance of the Ghost is only the effect of a psychosis of mourning, marking a profound rupture in Hamlet's Symbolic, his interpretation of the play has to ignore even such a crucial issue as the doubt over the Ghost's status. The dramatic logic of the play requires the possibility of the early modern belief that the Ghost might well be a devilish imposture rather than a genuine revenant. If this is the case then its message cannot be trusted, and Hamlet has to prevaricate about his revenge until the play-within-the-play has given him undeniable proof of Claudius' guilt. Critics of the Romantic period powerfully established the view of Hamlet as a psyche stricken with indecision; Hazlitt described him as 'the prince of philosophical speculators; and because he cannot have his revenge perfect, according to the most refined idea his wish can form, he declines it altogether' (Bate 1992: 325). But this psychologistic reading, which is so congenial to twentieth-century attitudes, has directed attention away from the radical doubt about the nature of the Ghost, as surely as we have also forgotten the immediate political issue of succession in the play. Lacan is therefore another true heir of post-Enlightenment, Romantic attitudes who must deny the reality of the supernatural for an early modern audience, but in doing this he also denies himself the opportunity of analysing how theology is intimately at work in the Renaissance psyche and ethical value.

Third, Lacan argues that Hamlet cannot freely speak about his father because he is suffering the alienation of himself through loss of the phallus as signifier. Lacan considers that Hamlet 'actually chokes and is strangulated' (26–7: 41) at I.ii.187, when in reply to Horatio he says, 'He was a man. Take him for all in all', as if this is all he can find to say in praise of the dead king and father. But we know from other instances that this is a use of 'man' which is recalling the Latin *vir*, connoting *virtus*, where to be 'manly' is to be supremely 'virtuous'. Horatio, as a 'scholar' (I.i.42) and 'fellow-student' (I.ii.177) might be expected to know this. Far from 'choking up' here, Hamlet is granting supreme, gendered praise to his father as a Man of Virtue, just as Antony, in his elegy for Brutus in the final moments of *Julius Caesar*, praises him by saying '. . . Nature might stand up/And say to all the world "This was a man."' (V.v.75). There are, then, arguments to be made about this construction of Virtue as a gendered type, but Lacan is in no position to make them, since he does not see the allusion.

Finally, because his theory commits him to a notion of unconscious compulsion in Hamlet's agreement to the duel with Laertes, Lacan cannot entertain the possibility that Hamlet is aware of some plotting and trickery between Claudius and Laertes. Yet Hamlet's poignant exchange with Horatio via informal, trusting prose immediately before the duel certainly allows for this possibility in performance: the play ends, as it began, with heart-sickness, when Hamlet confides 'thou wouldst not think how ill all's here about my heart' (V.ii.159), recalling Francisco's 'I am sick at heart' (I.i.9). In accepting that 'The readiness is all' (V.ii.169) the Prince condenses a number of powerful Stoic and Christian commonplaces which encouraged a consciously resolved fortitude in the face of adversity and danger (Wind 1967: 97–112). Lacan cannot allow the possibility of a consciously chosen heroism as a primary motive for the Prince at this point, because it would be in plain contradiction with his reading of a deep, unconscious compulsion working through the Prince's Imaginary. Lacan cannot afford to admit that the Prince is knowingly accepting a risk, rather than being the subject of 'the reverse side of a message which is not even his own' (26–7: 8; 12). But if only Lacan would be more Freudian at this point, he might have made a poignant connection between Hamlet's resignation which is also a resilience, and Freud's literary essay *Vergänglichkeit*, 'On Transience', written in November 1915, which argues for a level appreciation of earthly beauties *even though* they are transient: 'Transience value is scarcity value in time' (Freud 1953–74, 14: 305).

In Conclusion

The experience of trying to think through Lacan's categories to reveal new constructions within the intersubjectivities of *Hamlet* can be frustrating, but also tantalizing. Here are three tentative conclusions.

First, coming to terms with classical Freudian psychoanalytic theory and its subsequent development is in itself very demanding. But following its history brings the reader into contact with so many arguments which have been central to the modern period that the proper study of Freud and Freudians is highly rewarding.

Second, Lacan's particular emphasis on the rhetorical structure of psychical experience does seem to contribute to new ways of thinking about early modern literature, and about *Hamlet* in particular. Whether this is because his theories are true, or because they are analogous to early modern attitudes to language and self, is hard to determine: 'one finds in the authors of this period, alongside extravagant ignorance, things so penetrating, so staggering, which anticipate the speculations of the latest criticism' (25: 35).

Finally, every reader has to make up his or her own mind about the nature and contribution of the idea of unconscious experience in Freud and Lacan, as in literature and life. I have tried to refute central arguments which Lacan makes about the operation of unconscious motivation in *Hamlet* because I think that his proofs are poorly based in historical detail. But the notion that the unconscious may be at work in the gendered identities and the sexualites of the play, as between Hamlet, Gertrude and Ophelia, is much more persuasive, though perhaps only because for our own period this is a nearly inescapable conclusion. At its best, adopting the amateur Lacanian perspective can be like thinking about the Renaissance in the abstracted terms of Walter Benjamin's *The Origin of German Tragedy* (1977) or with the help of an essay such as Edgar Wind's 'Amor as a God of Death' (in Wind 1967: 152–70) because they heighten the sense of emotive, affective materials obscurely at work in the enigmatic forms of early modern culture. If psychoanalytic approaches can also be genuinely contextual, then they may still offer new readings, new performances.

Acknowledgements

My thanks to Nigel Wood for his helpful editorial work, and to Cathy Davies, Lisa Empson, Roz Minsky and Rick Rylance for their comments; thanks to Dr Felicia Gordon for help with my tenuous grip on Lacan's original language. All remaining misinterpretations are, of course, my own.

SUPPLEMENT

NIGEL WOOD: Lacan's theory prevented him from developing an adequate account of drama in performance, in part because the spectators' responses are 'unfathomable' (above p. 25). But isn't this true of any theory of performance since the only definitive feature of drama study is the text itself, in so far as it can be accurately established by editorial scholarship?

NIGEL WHEALE: None of the elements in the study of Shakespeare is really 'definitive': a performance is a tangible spectacle for as long as it lasts, but preserving our accurate responses to the evening is very difficult. Attending the same play later in the season can produce quite different reactions, either because we are noticing different details, or else because the production itself has changed in the course of the run, as the actors continue to shape their parts, or as the director introduces different emphases. A recorded version of *Hamlet* on film or video sets the play within another elaborate series of conventions of editing, framing and *mise-en-scène*, dictated by the media, which again reconfigure the text and our reception of it. Finally, the text of the play itself cannot be definitive, because of the early printing history which preserves three quite different forms of *Hamlet*, no one of which can claim ultimate authority: 'Everyone who wants to understand *Hamlet*, as reader, as actor, or director, needs to understand the nature of the play's textual problems, and needs to have his or her own view of them, however tentative' (Edwards 1985: 8).

The study of the plays in performance has recently been described as the new 'holy grail of Shakespeare studies' (Dillon 1994: 86), and it is a very welcome new approach. But the most productive criticism in future will probably combine awareness of textual history, cultural contexts and performance history. And if psychoanalytic considerations can make us more alert to the ways in which we are involved in the play, as text or performance, then that also will be valuable.

WOOD: Doesn't Lacan's attempt to include the entire 'symbolic register' within his analysis of a subject, for example of Hamlet, actually require us to construct a complete Elizo-Jacobean 'Symbolic' which would be an analysis of the integral mentality of the period?

WHEALE: The strict Lacanian response to this must be that it is impossible, because when we try and reconstruct a past 'mentality' in this way, all we are doing is projecting elements of our own Imaginary by way of our own inescapable Symbolic. To this extent Lacanian analytic concepts can never really be forensic instruments for historical research, because his apparatus is so committed to the ways in which the subject is utterly enmeshed in the linguistic/psychic economy of the unseizable present. Imagining past worlds will only ever be exactly that: past imagination. Therefore the value of Lacan's emphases is that they might indicate to us the kinds of emotional investment which we make in former periods, classical texts.

There is, however, a good deal of very careful and interesting work done by other kinds of critical scholarship which can add to a more conventional understanding of early modern attitudes to subjectivity, personality, reason and insanity; see, for example, the work discussed by Neely (1991).

WOOD: Does Lacan supersede Freud?

WHEALE: There are so many reasons for being sceptical about the truth of Freud's psychoanalytic findings and practice, that it is not actually helpful to think of progress as such being made in psychoanalytic theory. Lacan's analytic writing is no more and no less susceptible of proof than Freud's original work on which he elaborates. His career was a sustained dialogue with Freud's writing, in part conducted as a campaign to reclaim Freud from Freudianism, and therefore the most useful kind of reading of Lacan is one which simultaneously tests both interlocutors in the dialogue, modifying what we think of either in the light of the other.

As students of literature and as playgoers, actors or directors, we are exploring one very influential contemporary mythology as a way of articulating new responses to a play which there are very good reasons for associating with this twentieth-century myth. As amateurs practising what Freud termed 'wild psychoanalysis', we should feel free to modify or reject any aspect of the critical approach when it fails to take proper account of the play, as argued here in relation to political contexts and theatrical conventions: 'What Freud showed us were hitherto unnoticed facts, hitherto unrevealed motives, hitherto unrelated facets of our life. And in doing so his achievement broke all preconceived conceptual schemes – including his own' (MacIntyre 1971: 37).

Endpiece

NIGEL WOOD

T.S. Eliot regarded *Hamlet* in his essay on the play (Eliot 1975) as 'most certainly an artistic failure'. 'Puzzling' and 'disquieting' as the work is, this ambiguity is no rhetorical ploy, a way of finding a hidden direction out from apparent indirection, but rather evidence of how 'workmanship and thought' were 'in an unstable position' for Shakespeare at the time of composition. This prevents there occurring that full sense of tragic inevitability, where there is a 'complete adequacy of the external to the [writer's initial] emotion'. This, the baggy and, Eliot believed, misjudged text cannot deliver: 'Hamlet (the man) is dominated by an emotion which is inexpressible, because it is in *excess* of the facts as they appear' (Eliot 1975: 47–9). To appropriate Eliot's points only a little, it might be fruitful to consider how limited a full artistic success might be in these terms, where one's understanding of such an original 'emotion' might be transparently rendered by carefully calculated artistic form, that is, where there would be little or no superabundance of effect or meaning to exceed 'the facts as they appear'. For Samuel Johnson, in his note on the play in his 1765 edition, its 'variety' might be its 'particular excellence': 'The incidents are so numerous, that the argument of the play would make a long tale'. He also felt uncomfortable at the 'rudeness' with which Hamlet treated Ophelia, 'which seems to be useless and wanton cruelty', and the 'little regard' paid both to 'poetical justice' and 'poetical probability' (Johnson 1986: 344–5). Again, are these disquieting details necessarily unartistic? Does art always consist of orderly arrangement?

In one very important sense this perverse questioning of an Aristotelian blueprint for tragedy is necessary: to cultivate an awareness of how breaches of decorum (satirical, ironic or simply experimental gestures) might indeed sacrifice universal comment for instantaneous effect, how Shakespeare's texts might have dared to refer to transient, contemporary states of affairs as well as offered up treasures for posterity. With this in mind, *Hamlet* is difficult to characterize not so much as a comment on the human condition as a fully fledged and/or unified comment at all. To boil it down to such transitiveness is to mistake discourses; in letters to your bank manager it pays to be unambiguous and to the point, whereas it is often quite the reverse with dramatic art.

The contributions to this volume do not only illustrate current interpretative concerns but also touch on the *status* of a dramatic text. For Peter Holland the study-bound attraction of a carefully delimited 'text', where the probabilities of intention and meaning can be securely charted from words on the page (which series of words? on which occasion?) is tempting yet is ultimately an illusory comfort. Similarly, Mark Thornton Burnett's emphasis on the trickster figure in the play and Peter Smith's Introduction both outline how unresolved are the reactions of both audience and fictive characters to the events of the narrative. Motivation is never a 'given' in the play. One can describe the plot quite accurately, and not mistake Hamlet's university for Hamburg, for example, yet still find the connotational values of these apparently consistent details curiously elusive. For Nigel Wheale, this search for an identity between signifier and signified might pose as an encounter with hard evidence, yet the establishing of one's choice of substantive information 'about' the play (and the ensuing logic of unifying factors thereafter) is a disguised transference of audience/readerly desire. Hamlet believes himself a fully developed Subject, yet, as Lacan's work demonstrates, the integrated ego is actually a construction of the Symbolic Order to which we surrender when we perceive meaning through language – for both fictive voices (on the stage, in a novel) and also in our own responses to fictions. Sharon Ouditt places the focus on the character of Gertrude, and out of her lack of authorized comment (or voice) proceeds to trace how the patriarchal structures of critical consensus (often taken as some baseline of common sense) operate on the play and thus on our sense of what it is about.

As this collection is assembled on pluralist principles, it might be as well to address some objections to what may seem to be an evasive and obscurantist procedure. After all, writers might be able to express themselves perfectly well without critical help. Why intervene in this basically straightforward process? Most memorably, Nuttall has drawn a provocative distinction between 'Opaque' and 'Transparent' criticism.

The former indicates a critical language that aims to separate 'critic and reader (or spectator)'. It operates 'outside the mechanisms of art and [takes] those mechanisms as its object', whereas the latter aims to dissolve this divide between the act of criticism and the pure enjoyment of literature: deploying terms that are 'internal, realist, operating within the "world" presented in the work'. Nuttall's preference is for more of this appreciation of 'mimetic enchantment' and a reinstatement of the proposition that fictive action may be designed to tap an audience's comprehension of the Real by a wholly justifiable process of inference. What is more, Transparent critics are apparently able to accomplish so much more than Opaque ones, in that they are not fooled by the trickery of art: 'They know perfectly well that all is done by artificial means. But at the same time they can perceive the magic as magic. They know that Ophelia is not a real woman but are willing to think of her as a possible woman' (Nuttall 1983: 80–2). Quite why Nuttall thinks that Opaque critics might not be able to turn their hand (if they chose) to a paragraph or two of prose with exclamation marks he does not go on fully to explain. Why Transparent critics should wish to ignore the artifice of, say, a fresh-faced boy actor as the original Ophelia, or imagine that the terms, 'King' or 'Prince', might effortlessly communicate regality or authority is probably beside Nuttall's point – but, unfortunately, it is not out of account in even the most rudimentary theoretical understanding of literary texts.

Realism interpreted as an impressive means of engaging an audience's full emotional involvement might be a valuable rhetorical ploy, and be consciously attempted in the nineteenth-century novel or *cinéma vérité*. To appreciate its strongest qualities is not also to accede to the claim that its virtues operate as some sort of gold standard, equally applicable to various genres or historical periods. It is also, I would propose, fatally inadequate in promoting an understanding of ironic, allusive or mythic forms. As Frye (1957) noted, realism is only one of a number of possible rhetorical effects: 'Realism, or the art of verisimilitude, evokes the response "How like that is to what we know!" When what is written is *like* what is known, we have an art of extended or implied simile' (Frye 1957: 136). This analogy with the known might bring in its wake a certain engagement, but also a familiarity that is in itself spurious.

Ever since Erich Auerbach's *Mimesis* (written in 1946), the Renaissance past has appeared an increasingly foreign country, with its tolerance of mixed modes and styles, and its comprehension of theatrical effects that would simply not be viable in the changed contexts in which we instinctively understand the dramatic nowadays, 'what we know' (see esp. Auerbach 1953: 554–6). For a taste of what Elizabethan theatrical conditions actually entailed, the most succinct and sensitive accounts may be found in Thomson (1992: 114–41) and Gurr (1992: 2–4, 190–3); see also Brown (1966), Dessen (1976; 1984), Saunders (1960), Blackstone and Louis (1995). As such, they are nearer the elision of the literary, the spontaneous *and* the realistic as described by Brecht in his seminal 'The Popular and the Realistic' (Brecht 1964: 108–12), where 'sensuous' and 'realistic' theatre are in practice quite opposed.

An example: how does *Hamlet* end? Conceivably, if one were put to the description of the plot, one's account would have to come to a full stop: 'Go, bid the soldiers shoot' (V.ii.356); or the Folio's stage direction, 'Exeunt marching: after the which, a Peale of Ordenance are shot off'; or the simple 'Exeunt' of Q2, or none at all for Q1. Hamlet, here, is given the soldier's burial at which the preceding action rarely hints. The still and moving dialogue between Horatio and Hamlet can be rudely interrupted by the 'warlike noise' of Fortinbras' approach (V.ii.302). He may have Hamlet's 'dying voice' (V.ii.309), yet this verbal sanction cannot erase the visual and stylistic shock Fortinbras' approach marks. Horatio hopes for 'flights of angels' to 'sing' Hamlet 'to [his] rest', and he may well enquire, 'Why does the drum come hither?' (V.ii.313–14), yet what the audience actually sees is Hamlet accommodated to a warrior's image, where 'The soldiers' music and the rites of war' end up speaking 'loudly for him' (V.ii.352–3). In this bald and hardly exhaustive account I could have opted for an arrangement of these particulars that suggested some unified intention fulfilled inexorably in the fruition of the closing scene, a trip for Hamlet through purgatorial madness to a mature recognition that there is 'a special providence [even] in the fall of a sparrow' (V.ii.166–7). Certainly, one might agree with Brian Vickers that Shakespeare transformed source narrative materials to lend them dramatic focus, according to some shared aesthetic principles. I see no abiding problem about the solving, for example, of the theatrical problem provided by both Saxo Grammaticus and Belleforest that depicted the conflagration of Feng's court at the play's denouement. The stage-fight with Laertes and the succession of 'purposes mistook/Fallen on the inventors' heads' (V.ii.337–8) that leads to a charnel-house court does indeed multiply the tragic ironies.

With *Love's Labour's Lost* as a clear exception that proves the rule, Vickers (1993: 149) proceeds to declare that 'Shakespeare clearly had a concept of final unity. All his comedies end with weddings, sometimes multiple, having overcome any number of obstacles'. If by 'final unity' is meant a moment of closure where the *plot* is brought to a conclusive stop, then there is surely little room for argument, either, for there are very few plots I could quote where, even if there were an apparent lack of finality, such 'unity' could be demonstrated by claiming that that was indeed what the author required, and, retrospectively, I could rationalize the earlier events and pat them into shape. Here would have to lie the 'author', and Vickers (1993: 151) celebrates this critical item in more expansive terms later:

> In *Hamlet* and *King Lear* Shakespeare reshaped his source material to give a tragic ending, and in both cases he did so by a remark-able demonstration of an author's shaping power, which Current Literary Theory would be wholly unable to describe.

Here is such an obvious confusion between a description of plot and an account of a play's symbolic action that I cannot but conclude that Vickers is trying this on, deliberately. Having decided that an 'Author' exists, he is at pains to trace the designing hand throughout, and it is convenient to lump together all theory as some Spenserian allegorical beast for him to slay, by the simple addition of initial capital letters.

How coherent is the ending of *Hamlet*? I could describe it as *plot*, and, in Vickers's terms, believe I have slain the beast, but the example of the comedies is a questionable one, and points to the superficiality of the reading. One might point out that not all the comedies *end* with weddings. *A Midsummer Night's Dream* concludes with the world of fairy, which blesses the human weddings, but places them in a context that hardly cocoons them or unproblematically endorses them. *Twelfth Night* ends with the less than reassuring song from Feste. *The Merchant of Venice*'s last lines are Graziano's which remind the audience far more about the threat to Belmontian 'unity' than they endorse it. Why did Shakespeare have the Messenger in *Much Ado About Nothing* enter quite so late (four lines from the end) to declare that Don John (the per-petrator of the threat to final unity) had been captured and needed justice? Vickers obviously believes that the mere provision of a Happy or Unhappy Ending actually exorcises earlier contrary signals.

No, the 'facts as they appear' are rarely a secure means of getting to know how *symbolic* works go about their business. To account for this level of complexity means that telling the story in comparison with earlier source stories simply will not do. As Eliot realized in 1919, there is much about the play that cannot be affixed to conscious intention: 'We should have, finally, to know something which is by hypothesis unknowable, for we assume it to be an experience which . . . exceeded the facts. We should have to understand things which Shakespeare did not understand himself' (Eliot 1975: 49) – or else why did he not just come out and express himself more clearly?

Notes

Introduction

1 Eliot had already poetically personified the impotence and anxiety of the period of the Great War when Prufrock uttered his anti-heroic 'No! I am not Prince Hamlet, nor was meant to be . . .' (Eliot 1974: 17).

2 The version Evelyn saw was that adapted by Sir William D'Avenant in which Thomas Betterton played the Prince. Pepys mentions this production approvingly in his diary for 24 August, 27 November and 5 December 1661. In 1660, D'Avenant had been granted playing rights by Charles II (Pepys 1970, 2: 221).

3 The 1993 edition of *Shakespeare Survey* edited by Stanley Wells was specifically dedicated to '*Hamlet* and its Afterlife'.

4 See Batsleer *et al.* (1985), Bergonzi (1991), Wilson and Dutton (1992) and Evans (1993).

5 One wonders whether ideology would be as readily available to these critics, as a stick with which to beat theory, were it not for the theoretical work of Karl Marx, Walter Benjamin, Louis Althusser, Raymond Williams, Fredric Jameson, and so on.

6 For what follows I am indebted to Catherine Burgass's unpublished work to be presented as her PhD thesis (University of Leicester).

7 See also Nigel Wood's response in *Times Literary Supplement*, 1 October 1993: 15.

8 The authorship of *The Revenger's Tragedy* has been disputed since the end of the nineteenth century (Gibbons 1967: xi–xiii). One of the hypothetical sources of Shakespeare's *Hamlet*, the so-called *Ur-Hamlet*,

is usually thought to have been written by Kyd (see Hibbard 1987: 12–13).

9 Shakespeare uses *loose* to mean 'to offer for sex' in *The Merry Wives of Windsor*, II.i.167.

10 See Cook (1991: 151–233). Ernest Jones is interesting here: 'In psycho-analysis this idea, common in infancy, is known by the somewhat portentous title of the "combined parent concept". It dates from the phantasy of the parents in coitus, i.e. as one flesh' (Jones 1949: 99).

11 'Shakespeare's *Hamlet*, the *Hamlet* of the King's Men, was much nearer in its theatrical practice to that revenge tradition than the literary object was that we receive now and in our turn play with, in our RSCs or our national theatres' (Loughrey 1992: 129).

12 Keir Elam provides a detailed grid which maps out the first 79 lines of *Hamlet*. The grid is constructed across 18 columns and occupies 16 pages (Elam 1980: 192–207).

13 See de Grazia (1991).

14 Comparison is most conveniently achieved by the use of parallel texts. Any student of the textual history of *Hamlet* should be aware of the invaluable *Three-Text Hamlet* (Bertram and Kliman 1991). All line references in my discussion of the texts are to this volume.

15 References to F are to Hibbard's Oxford edition and, in line numbers, to *The Three-Text Hamlet*. For an explanation of TLN (through line numbers) and the numbering of passages extra to F, see Bertram and Kliman (1991: 8).

16 Hibbard amends F's 'O, o, o, o. *Dyes*' to '*He gives a long sigh and dies*' (V.ii.312).

17 Of course, we cannot eliminate Q2 or F as performance texts simply because they would take longer than two hours. *Romeo and Juliet* itself, at least in the modern theatre, often lasts over three hours. Since 1899, directors have produced 'conflated *Hamlets*' (i.e., the whole of F plus extra passages from Q2). These productions usually last over four hours and include recently, Peter Hall, 1976 (National Theatre) and 1994 (Peter Hall Co. tour); Richard Eyre, 1989 (National Theatre) and Adrian Noble, 1994 (Royal Shakespeare Company).

18 In Lyubimov's 1989 production the duel scene had Hamlet and Laertes facing downstage. They never touched swords, but the throwing of their weapons into the stage indicated contact with their opponent. The two of them swapped sides, removing their jumpers as they did so. This allowed exchange of swords as the weapons stayed on the same sides of the stage while the protagonists swapped, but as this movement was quite unprompt-ed and as one was concentrating on the removal of the clothes (for which there was no apparent reason either), it was too easy to miss the fact that Hamlet was now in possession of the unbaited sword. For those new to the play, this moment was particularly abstruse.

19 Holderness and Loughrey (1992: 8) are sceptical about the theory of memorial reconstruction: 'it is considerably more controversial than is generally recognised'. However, Janette Dillon notes that

> the parade of assertions about the theatrical nature of Q1, cited by Holderness and Loughrey to lend weight to the supposed link between this quarto and "the playhouse," are the direct product of earlier editors' belief in memorial reconstruction.
>
> (Dillon 1994: 80)

1 Hamlet as Trickster

1 On these aspects, see also Douglas (1966: 79); C.G. Jung, 'On the Psychology of the Trickster Figure', in Radin (1956: 207); Pelton (1980: 228); and Spinks (1991: 183).

2 On emblems in *Hamlet* in general, see John Manning, '*Symbols* and *Emblemata* in *Hamlet*', in Burnett and Manning (1994: 11–18). It might also be worth noting that the trickster of the Winnebago people of central Wisconsin and eastern Nebraska blackens his face to avoid being recognized by his enemies. See Radin (1956: 31).

3 Nardo (1991: 23) writes:

> When asked the play's title, Hamlet answers, '*The Mousetrap*. Marry, how? Tropically', with a pun on 'trapically' (III.ii.223). The humour of the pun conceals the truth that the play is both a trope, a figurative expression such as metaphor, and a trap. Indeed, Hamlet can turn a play into a trap precisely because it is a trope.

By extension, the play-within-the-play is as much a trick as it is a trap or a trope.

4 For a more specific Shakespearian instance, see *The Taming of the Shrew*, where Petruchio, criticizing the cap offered to Katharina by the Haberdasher, describes it as 'A knack, a toy, a trick, a baby's cap' (IV.iii.67).

5 Ophelia is here invoking a long history of false steward types from metrical romances and earlier drama (Burnett 1995).

6 On Richard Tarlton, see Billington (1984: 24, 29, 35, 40, 42–3, 44, 49).

7 Richard Hillman has some stimulating (although very brief) comments on Polonius as a 'rival trickster' in his section on the play. See Hillman (1992: 183).

8 For a specific identification of the trickster as a 'Foolish One', see the example of the Winnebago Trickster who is unaware that he eats his own intestines (Radin 1956: 18).

9 For a short analysis of the pairing of 'the Fool and Death' in the graveyard scene, see Hillman (1992: 184).

10 In related versions of the myth, Hermes steals Hektor's body, rather like Hamlet who conceals Polonius' body by the stairs leading to the castle's lobby (William G. Doty, 'A Lifetime of Trouble-Making: Hermes as Trickster', in Hynes and Doty 1993: 57). Other classical episodes show Hermes as a thief, a musician and an opponent of political tyranny. See Grimal (1986: 209–10).

11 There is obviously not the space here to rehearse these changes in detail, but initial remarks would concentrate on women in some urban centres who enjoyed a high degree of social mobility, had increasing standards of literacy and, when involved in crafts and trades, may have been able to ascend to relatively important positions in the livery companies. In political spheres, at least in the later seventeenth century, women in the metropolis played a dominant role in radical sectarian movements. For recent studies, see Corfield and Keene (1990), Houlbrooke (1984) and Prior (1985).

12 For a preliminary reading of the trickster's social functions in an Elizabethan and Jacobean context, see Dynes (1993: 366, 370–1).

2 *Hamlet*: Text in Performance

1 A revised and extended version of the book appeared in 1968 and in paperback in 1972. All quotations are from a reprint of the 1968 edition with a new introduction and bibliography by Graham Holderness (Williams 1991). Throughout this essay my thinking on Williams has been immeasurably helped by the work of my erstwhile research student, Drew Milne (see Milne 1992: 12–35).

2 It would be unwise to build an argument on an accident of omission, but O'Connor's fine bibliography of Williams, in Eagleton, (1989: 184–227), fails to note the 1972 paperback edition of *Drama in Performance*.

3 For a political reading of the theatrical production of Chekhov see Holland (1987).

4 Originally given as Williams' inaugural lecture as Professor of Drama in Cambridge, it was first published in 1974 and reprinted, in a slightly abbreviated form, in Williams (1984: 11–21).

5 In 'A Note on This Edition' of *Wild Strawberries*, Bergman (1986: 5) wrote: 'since this script was prepared before shooting began, it contains sequences and dialogue which do not appear in the final film'.

6 Bergman (1986: 9) wrote: 'I myself have never had any ambition to be an author. I do not want to write novels, short stories, essays, biographies, or even plays for the theatre. I only want to make films' in 'Bergman discusses film-making'.

7 In quoting title-pages I have freely adjusted capitalization, italicization and lineation.

8 In F there is only one English Ambassador.

9 The most reliable guide to the copy for Q2 is Hibbard (1987: 89–104).

10 See, for example, Carlson (1985), Issacharoff and Jones (1988), Worthen (1989), Dawson (1991) and Patrice Pavis, 'From Page to Stage: A Difficult Birth', in Pavis (1992: 24–47).

11 See also Berger's (1989) revision of his theory, and Hodgdon's (1985) response to an earlier formulation by Berger.

12 See, for example, Patrice Pavis, 'Reflections on the Notation of Theatrical Performance' in Pavis (1982: 109–30).

13 Comparison of the three texts has been greatly eased by Bertram and Kliman (1991).

14 For a more extended summary of this process, see, for example, Wells and Taylor (1987: 1–68).

15 On this stage in the process, see Bradley (1992).

16 See also Grady (1991: 57–63) and de Grazia and Stallybrass (1993).

17 See also Howard-Hill (1988; 1989).

18 Compare William Empson's comment in his provocative essay on *Hamlet* that 'the play varied a good deal on the night according to the reactions of the immediate audience' ('*Hamlet*' in Empson 1986: 94); the essay was first published as '*Hamlet* When New' (Empson 1953).

19 Compare also the prefatory comment to the Beaumont and Fletcher Folio: 'When these *Comedies* and *Tragedies* were presented on the Stage, the *Actours* omitted some *Scenes* and Passages (with the *Authour's* consent) as occasion led them' (Beaumont and Fletcher 1647: sig. A4r); see also Levin (1986).

20 I have explored this problem of title-page definition of texts further in Holland (1979), especially pp. 100–17.

21 See also Cloud (1982); Stephen Urkowitz, '"Well-sayd olde Mole": Burying Three *Hamlet*s in Modern Editions', in Ziegler (1986: 37–70); Urkowitz, 'Good News about "Bad" Quartos', in Charney (1988: 189–206); Urkowitz, 'Five Women Eleven Ways: Changing Images of Shakespearean Characterization in the Earliest Texts' in Habicht *et al.* (1988: 292–304). The two most significant contributions to the Q1 debate are Clayton's (1992) collection of essays and Holderness and Loughrey's (1992) edition of the text); but see also Dillon (1994) for a fine critique of the excesses of Holderness and Loughrey's introduction.

22 Hibbard (1987: 88) argued in his edition that Q1 'stems from the text behind F' but in 'The Chronology of the Three Substantive Texts of Shakespeare's *Hamlet*' (in Clayton 1992: 79–89) he shifted to argue that it stemmed from an acting version that preceded that represented by F.

23 See, for example, the discussion of the Orange Tree production in 1985 and the Swansea production in 1982 in Bryan Loughrey, 'Q1 in Recent Performance: An Interview' in Clayton (1992: 123–36). The Orange Tree production was reviewed by Shrimpton (1987), and the 1992 Medieval Players production by Holland (1994).

24 Taylor comments that 'the lute is unlikely to have been added in a provincial tour, or by a reporter' (Wells and Taylor 1987: 408) but I do not understand why it was not quite likely to have been added in such a way.

3 Explaining Woman's Frailty

1 Fuss is referring to Modleski's essay 'Feminism and the Power of Interpretation: Critical Readings' (de Lauretis 1986), in which Modleski argues for the empowering of 'real' women readers. Fuss takes issue with Modleski's democratizing impulse on the grounds that she does not account for the material differences between women of different races, class backgounds or sexual orientations. Modleski is trying to assert feminist criticism as something that is *for women*; a tool in the female resistance to patriarchy, rather than simply existing as one theoretical approach among many. The debate is explained in Landry and MacLean (1993: 149–50).

2 Showalter's essay, 'Toward a Feminist Poetics' was originally printed in Jacobus (1979); it is reprinted in Showalter (1986).

3 The best-known practitioners of the feminist critique are Kate Millett (see Millett 1970) and Germaine Greer (see Greer 1970). For an American perspective see also Fetterley (1978).

4 The term 'herstory' became part of feminist linguistic currency towards the beginning of the 'second wave'. It is normally used to emphasize that 'women's lives, deeds and participation in human affairs have been neglected or undervalued in standard histories' (see Miller and Swift 1976: 135).

5 Rose cites Freud's 'The Dissolution of the Oedipus Complex' (Freud 1953–74, 19: 173–9) and 'Some Psychical Consequences of the Anatomical Distinction between the Sexes' (Freud 1953–74, 19: 243–58). See also Mitchell (1974), esp. Chapters 6–8.

6 Boose (1987) goes into this further. She points up a division, commencing in or around 1982, between, on the one hand, approaches characterized by psychoanalysis, gender, the family, with emphasis on the microcosmic, and, on the other, new historicist approaches concentrating on what is implicitly masculine, Court politics, the macrocosmic. The problem with new historicism for feminists appears to be that it erases gender and femininity as analytical foci or contextual forces. In a Woolfian analogy, she further characterizes feminism as born 'outside' the 'manor of literary fathers' and thus detached and philosophically free to constitute itself, while new historicism she sees as the 'son and heir', born 'inside the academy and inside Renaissance studies' and therefore 'doomed by the obligation to repeat the oppressive struggle for power' (Boose 1987: 738).

7 In terms of method this may appear indistinguishable from new historicism; the political inflection is given by the specific concentration on the *female* subject.

8 See, for example Belsey (1985); and Eaton 'Defacing the Feminine in Renaissance Tragedy', in Wayne (1991).

4 Jacques Lacan and the Psychoanalytic Reading of *Hamlet*

1 Quotations from Lacan's first four seminars on Hamlet are referenced to the French text taken from the journal *Ornicar?*, giving the volume number followed by page number. Translations for these are my own. Lacan quoted from an unspecified English text and the French translation by Pierre le Tourneur (1737–88), which he considered to be 'the best available version' (24: 16). Le Tourneur's *Shakespeare, traduit de l'anglois, dédié au Roi* appeared in 20 volumes from 1776 to 1783, and was the first relatively complete translation, 'often inaccurate and inadequate . . . frequently grandiloquent and bombastic' (Cushing 1908: 240).
2 Quotations form Lacan's fifth, sixth and seventh seminars on Hamlet are referenced first to the French text, and then to the page number in James Hulbert's translation in *Yale French Studies* (Lacan 1977a, volumes 55/56), except where I have altered his version.

References

Unless otherwise stated, place of publication is London.

Adelman, Janet (1992) *Suffocating Mothers: Fantasies of Maternal Origin in Shakespeare's Plays, Hamlet to The Tempest.*

Agnew, Jean-Christophe (1986) *Worlds Apart: The Market and the Theatre in Anglo-American Thought.* Cambridge.

Archer, Ian W. (1991) *The Pursuit of Stability: Social Relations in Elizabethan London.* Cambridge.

Atwood, Margaret (1993) 'Gertrude Talks Back', in *Good Bones*: 15–18.

Auerbach, Eric (1953) *Mimesis: The Representation of Reality in Western Literature*, trans. Willard R. Trask. Princeton, NJ.

Axton, Marie and Williams, Raymond (eds) (1978) *English Drama: Forms and Development.* Cambridge.

Babcock-Abrahams, Barbara, (1975) '"A Tolerated Margin of Mess": The Trickster and His Tales Reconsidered', *Journal of the Folklore Institute*, 11: 147–86.

Bakhtin, Mikhail (1981) *The Dialogical Imagination: Four Essays by M.M. Bakhtin*, ed. Michael Holquist and trans. Caryl Emerson and Michael Holquist. Austin, TX.

Barish, Jonas (1988) 'Shakespeare in the Study, Shakespeare on the Stage', *Theatre Journal*, 40: 33–47.

Bate, Jonathan (ed.) (1992) *The Romantics on Shakespeare.* Harmondsworth.

Batsleer, Janet, Davies, Tony, O'Rourke, Rebecca and Weedon, Chris (eds) (1985) *Rewriting English: Cultural Politics of Gender and Class.*

Bayley, John (1994) 'The Rise of Theory – A Symposium', *Times Literary Supplement*, 15 July: 12–13.

Beaumont, Francis and Fletcher, John (1647) *Comedies and Tragedies*.

Beauvoir, Simone de (1972) *The Second Sex*. Harmondsworth (1st edn 1949).

Belsey, Catherine (1985) *The Subject of Tragedy*.

Benjamin, Walter (1973) *Illuminations*, ed. Hannah Arendt, trans. Harry Zohn.

Benjamin, Walter (1977) *The Origin of German Tragic Drama*, trans. John Osborne.

Bennett, Tony (1979) *Formalism and Marxism*.

Bentley, G.E. (1971) *The Profession of Dramatist in Shakespeare's Time, 1590–1640*. Princeton, NJ.

Berger Jr, Harry (1987) 'Textual Dramaturgy: Representing the Limits of Theatre in *Richard II*', *Theatre Journal*, 39: 135–55.

Berger Jr, Harry (1989) *Imaginary Audition: Shakespeare on Stage and Page*. Berkeley, CA.

Bergman, Ingmar (1986) *Wild Strawberries*, trans. Lars Malmström and David Kushner.

Bergonzi, Bernard (1991) *Exploding English: Criticism, Theory, Culture*. Oxford.

Berry, Philippa (1989) *Of Chastity and Power: Elizabethan Literature and the Unmarried Queen*.

Bertram, Paul and Kliman, Bernice W. (eds) (1991) *The Three-Text Hamlet*. New York.

Billington, Sandra (1984) *A Social History of the Fool*. Brighton.

Blackstone, Mary A. and Louis, Cameron (1995) 'Towards "A Full and Understanding Auditory": New Evidence of Playgoers at the First Globe Theatre', *Modern Language Review*, 90: 556–71.

Boas, Frederick S. (1953) *Christopher Marlowe: A Bibliographical and Critical Study*. Oxford.

Boccaccio, Giovanni (1963) *De claris mulieribus*, trans. G.A. Guarino. New Brunswick, NJ.

Bond, Edward (1981) *Restoration*.

Bond, Edward (1982) *Restoration and The Cat*.

Boose, Linda E. (1987) 'The Family in Shakespeare Studies – or – Studies in the Family of Shakespeareans – or – The Politics of Politics', *Renaissance Quarterly*, 40: 707–42.

Bowie, Malcolm (1991) *Lacan*.

Bradbrook, M.C. (1932) *Elizabethan Stage Conditions: a Study of their Place in the Interpretation of Shakespeare's Plays*. Cambridge.

Bradley, A.C. (1974) *Shakespearean Tragedy*, 2nd edn.

Bradley, David (1992) *From Text to Performance in the Elizabethan Theatre*. Cambridge.

Brecht, Bertolt (1964) *Brecht on the Theatre*, ed. John Willett.

Brenton, Howard (1976) *Weapons of Happiness*.

Bristol, Michael (1985) *Carnival and Theater: Plebeian Culture and the Structure of Authority in Renaissance England*. New York.

Brown, John Russell (1966) *Shakespeare's Plays in Performance*.

Brown, John Russell (1992a) 'Multiplicity of Meaning in the Last Moments of *Hamlet*', *Connotations*, 2: 16–33.

Brown, John Russell (1992b) 'Connotations of Hamlet's Final Silence', *Connotations*, 2: 271–4.

Burnett, Mark (1995) 'Ophelia's "false steward" Contextualized', *Review of English Studies*, n.s. 49: 48–56.

Burnett, Mark Thornton and Manning, John (eds) (1994) *New Essays on 'Hamlet'*. New York.

Callaghan, Dympna, Helms, Lorraine and Singh, Jyotsna (eds) *The Weyward Sisters: Shakespeare and Feminist Politics*. Oxford.

Carlson, Marvin (1985) 'Theatrical Performance: Illustration, Translation, Fulfilment, or Supplement?', *Theatre Journal*, 37: 5–11.

Charney, Maurice (ed.) (1988) *'Bad' Shakespeare*.

Charney, Maurice (1992) 'The Rest is Not Silence: a Reply to John Russell Brown', *Connotations*, 2: 186–9.

Chatman, Seymour (ed.) (1971) *Literary Style: A Symposium*. Oxford.

Chodorow, Nancy (1978) *The Reproduction of Mothering*. Berkeley, CA.

Clayton, Thomas (ed.) (1992) *The 'Hamlet' First Published (Q1, 1603)*. Newark, DE.

Cloud, Random [Randall McCleod] (1982) 'The Marriage of Good and Bad Quartos', *Shakespeare Quarterly*, 33: 421–31.

Coleridge, S.T. (1962) *Shakespearean Criticism*, ed. T.M. Raysor, 2 vols.

Conklin, Paul S. (1947) *A History of Hamlet Criticism 1601–1821*.

Cook, Ann Jennalie (1991) *Making a Match: Courtship in Shakespeare and His Society*. Princeton, NJ.

Corfield, Penelope J. and Keene, Derek (eds) (1990) *Work in Towns 850–1850*.

Creigh, Geoffrey and Belfield, Jane (eds) (1987) *'The Cobler of Caunterburie' and 'Tarltons Newes Out of Purgatorie'*. Leiden.

Cushing, Mary Gertrude (1908) *Pierre Le Tourneur*. New York.

Davison, Peter (1983) *Hamlet: Text and Performance*.

Dawson, Anthony B. (1991) 'The Impasse over the Stage', *English Literary Renaissance*, 21: 309–27.

Dessen, Alan C. (1976) *Elizebethan Drama and the Viewer's Eye*. Chapel Hill, NC.

Dessen, Alan C. (1984) *Elizebethan Stage Conventions and Modern Interpreters*. Cambridge.

Dillon, Janette (1994) 'Is There a Performance in This Text?', *Shakespeare Quarterly*, 45: 74–86.

Dinnerstein, Dorothy (1976) *The Rocking of the Cradle and the Ruling of the World*.

Dollimore, Jonathan and Sinfield, Alan (eds) (1985) *Political Shakespeare: New Essays in Cultural Materialism*. Manchester.

Douglas, Mary (1966) *Purity and Danger: An Analysis of Concepts of Pollution and Taboo*.

Drakakis, John (ed.) (1985) *Alternative Shakespeares*.

Dusinberre, Juliet, (1975) *Shakespeare and the Nature of Women.*

Dutton, Richard (1983) *Ben Jonson: To the First Folio.* Cambridge.

Dynes, William R. (1993) 'The Trickster-Figure in Jacobean City Comedy', *Studies in English Literature,* 33: 365–84.

Eagleton, Terry (ed.) (1989) *Raymond Williams: Critical Perspectives.* Oxford.

Edwards, Philip (ed.) (1985) *Hamlet.* Cambridge.

Elam, Keir (1980) *The Semiotics of Theatre and Drama.*

Eliot, T.S. (1920) *The Sacred Wood: Essays on Poetry and Criticism.*

Eliot, T.S. (1951) *Selected Essays,* 3rd edn.

Eliot, T.S. (1974) *Collected Poems 1909–1962.*

Eliot, T.S. (1975) *Selected Prose of T.S. Eliot,* ed. Frank Kermode.

Elsky, Martin (1989) *Authorizing Words: Speech, Writing and Print in the English Renaissance.* Ithaca, NY.

Empson, William (1953) '*Hamlet* When New', *Sewanee Review,* 61: 15–42, 185–205.

Empson, William (1986) *Essays on Shakespeare.* Cambridge.

Erickson, Peter (1991) *Rewriting Shakespeare, Rewriting Ourselves.* Berkeley, CA.

Evans, Colin (1993) *English People: The Experience of Teaching and Learning in British Universities.*

Evans-Pritchard, E.E. (ed.) (1967) *The Zande Trickster.* Oxford.

Evelyn, John (1955) *Diary,* ed. E.S. de Beer, 6 vols. Oxford.

Fetterley, Judith (1978) *The Resisting Reader.* Bloomington, IN.

Foakes, R.A. (1993) *Hamlet versus Lear: Cultural Politics and Shakespeare's Art.* Cambridge.

Foakes, R.A. and Rickert, T.T. (eds) (1961) *Henslowe's Diary.* Cambridge.

Freud, Sigmund (1953–74) *The Standard Edition of the Complete Psychological Works,* ed. J. Strachey, 24 vols.

Frye, Northrop (1957) *The Anatomy of Criticism.* Princeton, NJ.

Fuss, Diana (1989) *Essentially Speaking: Feminism, Nature and Difference.*

Gellner, E.C. (1993) *The Psychoanalytic Movement: the Cunning of Unreason* (1st edn 1965).

Gibbons, Brian (ed.) (1967) *The Revenger's Tragedy.*

Gorfain, Phyllis (1991) 'Towards a Theory of Play and the Carnivalesque in *Hamlet*', *Hamlet Studies,* 13: 25–49.

Grady, Hugh (1991) *The Modernist Shakespeare: Critical Texts in a Modern World.* Oxford.

de Grazia, Margreta (1988) 'The Essential Shakespeare and the Material Book', *Textual Practice,* 2: 69–87.

de Grazia, Margreta (1991) *Shakespeare Verbatim: The Reproduction of Authenticity and the 1790 Apparatus.* Oxford.

de Grazia, Margreta and Stallybrass, Peter (1993) 'The Materiality of the Shakespearean Text', *Shakespeare Quarterly,* 44: 255–83.

Greer, Germaine (1970) *The Female Eunuch.*

Grimal, Pierre (1986) *A Dictionary of Classical Mythology.* Oxford.

Grosz, Elizabeth (1990) *Jacques Lacan: A Feminist Introduction.*

Gurr, Andrew (1987) *Playgoing in Shakespeare's London.* Cambridge.

Gurr, Andrew (1992) *The Shakespearean Stage, 1574–1642.* Cambridge (1st edn 1970).

Habicht, Werner, Palmer, D.J. and Pringle, Roger (eds) (1988) *Images of Shakespeare.* Newark, DE.

Halliwell-Phillipps, J.O. (1879) *Memoranda on the Tragedy of Hamlet.*

Harrison, Alan (1989) *The Irish Trickster.* Sheffield.

Harrison, Tony (1987) *Selected Poems,* 2nd edn. Harmondsworth.

Hawkes, Terence (1986) *That Shakespeherian Rag: Essays on a Critical Process.*

Hawkes, Terence (1992) *Meaning by Shakespeare.*

Henderson, Katherine Usher and McManus, Barbara F. (eds) (1985) *Half Humankind: Context and Texts of the Controversy about Woman in England, 1540–1640.* Urbana, IL, and Chicago.

Hibbard, G.R. (ed.) (1987) *Hamlet.* Oxford.

Hillman, Richard (1992) *Shakespearean Subversions: The Trickster and the Play-text.*

Hodgdon, Barbara (1985) 'Parallel Practices, or the *Un*-necessary Difference', *Kenyon Review,* 7: 57–65.

Holderness, Graham (1987) *Hamlet.* Milton Keynes.

Holderness, Graham and Loughrey, Bryan (eds) (1992) *The Tragicall Historie of Hamlet Prince of Denmarke.* Hemel Hempstead.

Holland, Peter (1979) *The Ornament of Action: Text and Performance in Restoration Comedy.* Cambridge.

Holland, Peter (1987) 'The Director and the Playwright: Control over the Means of Production', *New Theatre Quarterly* 3: 207–17.

Holland, Peter (1994) 'Shakespeare Performances in England, 1992', *Shakespeare Survey,* 46: 159–89.

Holstein, Michael E. (1976) '"Actions that a Man Might Play": Dirty Tricks at Elsinore and the Politics of Play', *Philological Quarterly,* 55: 323–39.

Honigmann, E.A.J. (1976) 'Re-enter the Stage Direction: Shakespeare and Some Contemporaries', *Shakespeare Survey,* 29: 117–25.

Houlbrooke, Ralph A. (1984) *The English Family 1450–1700.*

Howard-Hill, T.H. (1988) 'Playwrights' Intentions and the Editing of Plays', *TEXT,* 4: 269–78.

Howard-Hill, T.H. (1989) 'Modern Textual Theories and the Editing of Plays', *The Library,* 6th series, 11: 89–115.

Hoy, Cyrus (ed.) (1991) *Hamlet: an Authoritative Text, Intellectual Backgrounds, Extracts from the Sources and Essays in Criticism.* New York.

Humphreys, Arthur (1981) 'Introduction', in *Much Ado About Nothing,* ed. Humphreys.

Hynes, William J. and Doty, William G. (eds) (1993) *Mythical Trickster Figures: Contours, Contexts, and Criticisms.*

Ioppolo, Grace (1991) *Revising Shakespeare.* Cambridge, MA.

Irigaray, Luce (1985) *This Sex Which is Not One*. Ithaca, NY.

Isler, Alan (1995) *The Prince of West End Avenue*.

Issacharoff, Michael and Jones, Robin F. (eds) (1988) *Performing Texts*. Philadelphia, PA.

Jacobus, Mary (ed.) (1979) *Women Writing and Writing about Women*.

Jardine, Lisa (1989) *Still Harping on Daughters: Women and Drama in the Age of Shakespeare*. Hemel Hempstead (1st edn 1983).

Jenkins, Harold (1960) 'Playhouse Interpolations in the Folio Text of *Hamlet*', *Studies in Bibliography*, 13: 31–47.

Jenkins, Harold (ed.) (1982) *Hamlet*.

Johnson, Samuel (1986) *Selections from Johnson on Shakespeare*, ed. Bertrand H. Bronson with Jean M. O'Meara. New Haven, CT.

Jones, Ernest (1949) *Hamlet and Oedipus*.

Keene, Donald (ed.) (1970) *Twenty Plays of the No Theatre*. New York.

Kerrigan, William (1994) *Hamlet's Perfection*.

Kinney, Arthur F. (ed.) (1990) *Rogues, Vagabonds, & Sturdy Beggars*. Amherst, MA.

Lacan, Jacques (1977) *Écrits: A Selection*, trans. Alan Sheridan.

Lacan, Jacques (1979) *The Four Fundamental Concepts of Psycho-analysis*, trans. Alan Sheridan and ed. Jacques-Alain Miller. Harmondsworth.

Landry, Donna and MacLean, Gerald (eds) (1993) *Materialist Feminisms*. Oxford.

Laplanche, Jean and J.-B. Pontalis (1973) *The Language of Psycho-Analysis*.

Laroque, François (1991) *Shakespeare's Festive World: Elizabethan Seasonal Entertainment and the Professional Stage*, trans. Janet Lloyd. Cambridge.

de Lauretis, Teresa (ed.) (1986) *Feminist Studies/Critical Studies*. Bloomington, IN.

Lenz, Carolyn, Swift, Ruth, Greene, Gayle and Neely, Carol Thomas (eds) (1983) *The Woman's Part: Feminist Criticism of Shakespeare*.

Levin, Richard (1986) 'Performance-Critics vs Close Readers in the Study of English Renaissance Drama', *Modern Language Review*, 81: 545–59.

Loughrey, Bryan (1992) 'Q1 in Recent Performance: An Interview', in Thomas Clayton (ed.), *The Hamlet First Published (Q1, 1603)*: 123–36.

Lukacher, Ned (1986) *Primal Scenes: Literature, Philosophy, Psychoanalysis*.

Lukacher, Ned (1989) 'Anamorphic Stuff: Shakespeare, Catharsis, and Lacan', *South Atlantic Quarterly*, 88: 863–98.

Lyly, John (1902) *The Complete Works of John Lyly*, ed. R. Warwick Bond, 3 vols. Oxford.

MacCabe, Colin (1979) *James Joyce and the Revolution of the Word*.

Macey, David (1988) *Lacan in Contexts*.

McGann, Jerome J. (1988) *The Beauty of Inflections: Literary Investigations in Historical Method and Theory*. Oxford.

McGann, Jerome J. (1991) *The Textual Condition*. Princeton, NJ.

MacIntyre, Alasdair (1971) *Against the Self-images of the Age: essays on Ideology and Philosophy*.

Maclean, Ian (1992) *Interpretation and Meaning in the Renaissance: the Case of Law*. Cambridge.

Mehl, Dieter (1992) 'Hamlet's Last Moments: A Note on John Russell Brown', *Connotations*, 2: 182–5.

Miller, Casey and Swift, Kate (1976) *Words and Women: New Language in New Times*. New York.

Millett, Kate (1970) *Sexual Politics*.

Milne, Andrew Greg (1992) 'A Critique of the Philosophy of Modern Theatre', Ph.D. thesis, University of Cambridge, pp. 12–35.

Mitchell, Juliet (1974) *Psychoanalysis and Feminism*. Harmondsworth.

Morgan, W. John and Preston, Peter (eds) (1993) *Raymond Williams: Politics, Education, Letters*.

Mullaney, Stephen (1988) *The Place of the Stage: License, Play and Power in Renaissance England*. Chicago.

Murphy, Arthur (1801) *The Life of David Garrick*.

Nardo, Anna K. (1991) *The Ludic Self in Seventeenth-Century English Literature*. Albany, NY.

Neely, Carol Thomas (1991) '"Documents in Madness": Reading Madness and Gender in Shakespeare's Tragedies and Early Modern Culture', *Shakespeare Quarterly*, 42: 315–38.

Nuttall, A.D. (1983) *A New Mimesis: Shakespeare and the Representation of Reality*.

O'Connor, Alan (1989) *Raymond Williams: Writing, Culture, Politics*. Oxford.

Oliver, J. (ed.) (1984) *The Taming of the Shrew*. Oxford.

Orgel, Stephen (1981) 'What is a Text?', *Research Opportunities in Renaissance Drama*, 26: 3–6.

Orgel, Stephen (1988) 'The Authentic Shakespeare', *Representations*, 21: 1–25.

Orgel, Stephen (1989) 'Nobody's Perfect: or Why Did the English Stage Take Boys for Women?', *South Atlantic Quarterly*, 88: 7–30.

Osofsky, Gilbert (ed.) (1969) *Puttin' On Ole Massa: The Slave Narratives of Henry Bibb, William Wells Brown and Solomon Northrup*. New York.

O'Toole, John (1992) *The Process of Drama: Negotiating Art and Meaning*.

Parker, Patricia and Hartman, Geoffrey (eds) (1985) *Shakespeare and the Question of Theory*.

Partridge, Eric (1955) *Shakespeare's Bawdy: A Literary and Psychological Essay and a Comprehensive Glossary*.

Pavis, Patrice (1982) *Languages of the Stage*. New York.

Pavis, Patrice (1992) *Theatre at the Crossroads of Culture*.

Pelton, Robert D. (1980) *The Trickster in West Africa: A Study of Mythic Irony and Sacred Delight*.

Pepys, Samuel (1970) *Diary*, ed. Robert Lathan and William Matthews, 11 vols.

Prior, Mary (ed.) (1985) *Women in English Society 1500–1800*.

Pye, Christopher (1988) 'The Betrayal of the Gaze: Theatricality and Power in Shakespeare's *Richard II'*, *English Literary History*, 55: 575–98.

Radin, Paul (ed.) (1956) *The Trickster: A Study in American Indian Mythology*.

Roach, Joseph R. (1985) *The Player's Passion: Studies in the Science of Acting*. Newark, DE.

Rose, Jacqueline (1982) *Feminine Sexualities: Jaques Lacan and the École Freudienne*, trans. and ed. with Juliet Mitchell.

Rose, Jacqueline (1986) *Sexuality and the Field of Vision*.

Rose, Jacqueline (1991) *The Haunting of Sylvia Plath*.

Rose, Jacqueline (1993) *Why War? Psychoanalysis, Politics and the Return to Melanie Klein*. Oxford.

Rosenberg, Marvin (1992) *The Masks of Hamlet*.

Roudinesco, Elizabeth (1990) *Jacques Lacan & Co.: A History of Psychoanalysis in France, 1925–1985*, trans. Jeffrey Mehlman.

Rubenstein, Frankie (1989) *A Dictionary of Shakespeare's Sexual Puns and their Significance*.

Rushdie, Salman (1990) *Haroun and the Sea of Stories*.

Sartre, Jean-Paul (1973) *Politics and Literature*, trans. J.A. Underwood and John Calder.

Saunders, J.W. (1960) 'Staging at the Globe, 1599–1613', *Shakespeare Quarterly*, 11: 401–25.

Schwartz, Murray M. and Kahn, Coppélia (eds) (1980) *Representing Shakespeare: New Psychoanalytic Essays*.

Scott, James C. (1990) *Domination and the Arts of Resistance: Hidden Transcripts*.

Shakespeare, William (1603) *The tragicall historie of Hamlet prince of Denmarke*.

Shaw, George Bernard (1932) *Our Theatre in the Nineties*, 3 vols.

Shrimpton, Nicholas (1987) 'Shakespeare Performances in London and Stratford-Upon-Avon, 1984–5', *Shakespeare Survey*, 39: 191–206.

Singer, André and Street, Brian V. (eds) (1972) *Zande Themes: Essays Presented to Sir Edward Evans-Pritchard*. Oxford.

Showalter, Elaine (ed.) (1986) *The New Feminist Criticism*.

Sokol, B.J. (ed.) (1993) *'The Undiscovered Country': New Essays on Psychoanalysis and Shakespeare*.

Somerset, Anne (1992) *Elizabeth I*.

Summers, Joseph H. (ed.) (1980) *The Literary Freud: Mechanisms of Defense and the Poetic Will*.

Spender, Dale (1980) *Manmade Language*.

Spinks, C.W. (1991) *Semiosis, Marginal Signs and Trickster: A Dagger of the Mind*.

Stone, Lawrence (1977) *The Family, Sex and Marriage in England, 1500–1800*. Harmondsworth.

Stoppard, Tom (1968) *Rosencrantz and Guildenstern Are Dead*.

Timms, Edward and Collier, Peter (eds) (1988) *Visions and Blueprints*. Manchester.

Thomson, Peter (1992) *Shakespeare's Theatre*, 2nd edn (1st edn 1983).

Treblicot, Joyce (ed.) (1983) *Mothering: Essays in Feminist Theory*. Totowa, NJ.

Vickers, Brian (1993) *Appropriating Shakespeare: Contemporary Critical Quarrels.*
Voloshinov, V.N. (1987) *Freudianism: A Critical Sketch*, trans. I.R. Titunik and
ed. I.R. Titunik and Neal H. Bruss. Bloomington and Indianapolis, IN.
Waldock, A.J.A. (1931) *Hamlet: A Study in Critical Method.* Cambridge.
Warren, John (1993) *Elizabeth I: Religion and Foreign Affairs.*
Waswo, Richard (1987) *Language and Meaning in the Renaissance.* Princeton,
NJ.
Wayne, Valerie (ed.) (1991) *The Matter of Difference: Materialist Feminist
Criticism of Shakespeare.* Hemel Hempstead.
Weitz, Morris (1965) *Hamlet and the Philosophy of Literary Criticism.*
Wells, Stanley and Taylor, Gary (eds) (1986) *William Shakespeare: The Com-
plete Works.* Oxford.
Wells, Stanley and Taylor, Gary (eds) (1987) *William Shakespeare: A Textual
Companion.* Oxford.
Wells, Stanley and Taylor, Gary (eds) (1988) *William Shakespeare: The Com-
plete Works*, Compact Edition. Oxford.
White, Richard Grant (1854) *Shakespeare's Scholar.* New York.
Williams, Gordon (1994) *A Dictionary of Sexual Language and Imagery in
Shakespearean and Stuart Literature*, 3 vols.
Williams, Paul V.A. (ed.) (1979) *The Fool and the Trickster: Studies in Honour
of Enid Welsford.* Cambridge.
Williams, Raymond (1952) *Drama from Ibsen to Eliot.*
Williams, Raymond (1965) *The Long Revolution.* Harmondsworth.
Williams, Raymond (1968) *Drama from Ibsen to Brecht.* Harmondsworth.
Williams, Raymond (1974) *Television, Technology and Cultural Form.*
Williams, Raymond (1979a) *Modern Tragedy.*
Williams, Raymond (1979b) *Politics and Letters.*
Williams, Raymond (1984) *Writing in Society.*
Williams, Raymond (1991) *Drama in Performance.* Milton Keynes.
Williams, Raymond and Orrom, Michael (1954) *Preface to Film.*
Williamson, Claude, C.H. (ed.) (1950) *Readings on the Character of Hamlet
1661–1947.*
Wilson, J. Dover (1934) *The Manuscript of Shakespeare's 'Hamlet'.* Cambridge.
Wilson, J. Dover (1935) *What Happens in Hamlet.* Cambridge.
Wilson, R. Rawdon (1990) *In Palamedes's Shadow: Explorations in Play, Game,
& Narrative Theory.* Boston, MA.
Wilson, Richard and Dutton, Richard (eds) (1992) *New Historicism and
Renaissance Drama.*
Wind, Edgar (1967) *Pagan Mysteries in the Renaissance.* Harmondsworth.
Worthen, W.B. (1989) 'Deeper Meanings and Theatrical Technique:
The Rhetoric of Performance Criticism', *Shakespeare Quarterly*, 40: 441–55.
Wright, George T. (1981) 'Hendiadys and *Hamlet*', *Publications of the Modern
Language Association of America*, 96: 168–93.
Wrightson, Keith (1982) *English Society 1580–1680.*
Ziegler, Georgianna (ed.) (1986) *Shakespeare Study Today.* New York.

Further Reading

1 Hamlet as Trickster

Barbara Babcock-Abrahams, '"A Tolerated Margin of Mess": The Trickster and His Tales Reconsidered', *Journal of the Folklore Institute*, 11: 147–86 (1975).
  This is the starting-point for any discussion of the trickster. The article combines a wide range of material with diverse approaches to the figure.

William J. Hynes and William G. Doty (eds), *Mythical Trickster Figures: Contours, Contexts and Criticisms* (Tuscaloosa and London, 1993).
  Generally this is a very fine anthology, which looks at (but does not always clearly analyse) the incarnations of the trickster in various cultural systems.

Richard Hillman, *Shakespearean Subversions: The Trickster and the Play-text* (London and New York, 1992).
  Hillman shows with what profit anthropological theory can be applied to the Shakespearian text. He offers a very useful overview of the field, but his discussion of *Hamlet* leaves large areas unexplored.

Paul Radin (ed.), *The Trickster: A Study in American Indian Mythology* (London, 1956).
  Radin's study was one of the first in the field. It has the virtue of concentrating on the trickster in one of his mythic incarnations, and also includes a now standard essay by Jung on the subject.

James C. Scott, *Domination and the Arts of Resistance: Hidden Transcripts* (New Haven, CT, and London, 1990).

An excellent synthesis, which theorizes the modes of resistance exploited by underprivileged groups and interests.

2 *Hamlet*: Text in Performance

Raymond Williams, *Drama in Performance* ed., with a new introduction and bibliography, by Graham Holderness (Milton Keynes, 1991).
In spite of the reservations explored in the chapter, this is still the necessary starting-point for all work on the relationship of text to performance.

Michael Issacharoff and Robin F. Jones (eds), *Performing Texts* (Philadelphia, 1988).
A fine collection of essays exploring the nature of text in the theatre, setting out the terms of much recent thinking on the subject.

Harry Berger, Jr, *Imaginary Audition: Shakespeare on Stage and Page* (Berkeley, CA, 1989).
A densely argued attempt to define the connection between the act of reading and the imagination of performance, separating such work from the account of actual performances (i.e. theatre history).

Stanley Wells and Gary Taylor, 'General Introduction' in *William Shakespeare: A Textual Companion* (Oxford, 1987), pp. 1–68.
The best introduction to the history of the transmission of the texts of Shakespeare.

Margreta de Grazia, 'The Essential Shakespeare and the Material Book', *Textual Practice* 2: 69–87 (1988), and Margreta de Grazia and Peter Stallybrass, 'The Materiality of the Shakespearean Text', *Shakespeare Quarterly* 44: 255–83 (1993).
Two articles focusing on the nature of modern textual bibliography and the nature of the Shakespeare text; both are provocative and informative.

Thomas Clayton (ed.), *The 'Hamlet' First Published (Q1, 1603)* (Newark, DE, 1992).
An excellent collection of essays about *Hamlet* Q1, looking at it from a wide variety of perspectives, many of which can be applied to the other two early *Hamlet* texts or to a range of other drama-texts.

3 Explaining Woman's Frailty

Janet Adelman, *Suffocating Mothers: Fantasies of Maternal Origin in Shakespeare's Plays, Hamlet to The Tempest* (New York and London, 1992).
Psychoanalytical approach which takes *Hamlet* as the starting-point for a reading of mothers in Shakespeare's plays. Concentrates on the material of

infantile fantasy and sees the maternal body as the locus of power and dread, crucial to the formation of masculine identity and to that of sexual relationships.

Juliet Dusinberre, *Shakespeare and the Nature of Women* (London and Basingstoke, 1975).

Early feminist intervention in Shakespeare studies, focusing on the largely unrecognized feminism of Shakespeare's time in the context of Renaissance humanism and changing ideas of marriage and education in Protestant England. Her conclusions have since been disputed, but the study contains much detailed historical material.

Donna Landry and Gerald MacLean (eds), *Materialist Feminisms* (Oxford, 1993).

Useful review of recent debates between Marxism and feminism in Britain and the United States, and of the effects of those debates on literary and cultural theory. Provides a context for the material discussed in this chapter.

Carolyn Swift, Ruth Lenz, Gayle Greene and Carol Thomas Neely (eds), *The Woman's Part: Feminist Criticism of Shakespeare* (Urbana, IL, and London, 1980; reprinted in 1983).

Early collection of feminist essays on Shakespeare (including Rebecca Smith's piece on Gertrude). The Introduction outlines the feminist context and early influences, the relationship of the feminism emerging from the 1970s to the new criticism, and an emergent, if not explicit, interest in psychoanalysis.

Ania Loomba, *Gender, Race, Renaissance Drama* (Manchester and New York, 1989).

This book contains little direct reference to *Hamlet*, but Chapter 4, 'Women's Division of Experience', continues the debate on the 'discontinuities' of the female subject using post-colonial as well as feminist theory.

Valerie Wayne (ed.), *The Matter of Difference: Materialist Feminist Criticism of Shakespeare* (Hemel Hempstead, 1991).

Very useful collection of essays, with helpful introduction, which explains the particular slant in materialist feminism that the editor acknowledges, and comments on the 'fluidity' between materialist-feminist and other feminist approaches.

4 Jacques Lacan and the Psychoanalytic Reading of *Hamlet*

The selection of Lacan's work translated by Alan Sheridan, *Écrits* (London, 1977), is a convenient place to begin, and in particular 'The Function and Field of Speech and Language in Psychoanalysis', a declaration of principles which Lacan made in 1953. Malcolm Bowie's *Lacan* (1991), is the best single-volume general account, lucid, discriminating and highly informed in both

Freud and cultural contexts for Lacan. Freud can be studied through Jean Laplanche and J.-B. Pontalis, *The Language of Psycho-Analysis* (London, trans. Donald Nicholson-Smith 1973), which is referenced to Freud's *Collected Works* and helpfully traces the development of the key concepts. B.J. Sokol's *'The Undiscover'd Country': New Essays on Psychoanalysis and Shakespeare* (London, 1993) has a comprehensive listing of critical discussions of Shakespeare inspired by psychoanalysis, and a selection of articles, of which the best by far is Ruth Nevo's 'The Perils of Pericles' (pp. 150–78). A sustained critique of 'psychocriticism' is Chapter 5 of Brian Vickers's *Appropriating Shakespeare: Contemporary Critical Quarrels* (New Haven, CT, 1993), a comprehensive rebuttal of all theory-derived readings of Shakespeare; Vickers argues specifically against Nevo's reading of *Pericles*. A discussion of audience response in terms of the transference effect is Helen Golding's '"The Story of the Night Told Over": D.W. Winnicott's Theory of Play and *A Midsummer Night's Dream*', in Gary Waller (ed.) *Shakespeare's Comedies* (Harlow, 1991). A critical description which, among other insights, makes a convincing case for the presence of 'Freudian' materials in Shakespeare is Jonathan Bate's Introduction to his new Arden edition of *Titus Andronicus* (London, 1995).

Index

Adelman, Janet, 106
Agnew, Jean-Christophe, 49, 51
Archer, Ian W., 49
Aristotle, 133
Atwood, Margaret, 4
Auerbach, Erich, 135–6

Babcock-Abrahams, Barbara, 30–1, 36
Bakhtin, Mikhail, 25–6
Barish, Jonas, 71
Barthes, Roland, 15, 112
Bayley, John, 6
Beaumont, Francis, 142 n19
Beauvoir, Simone de, 83–4
Beckett, Samuel, 87
Belsey, Catherine, 100–1, 144 n8
Benjamin, Walter, 80, 130
Bennett, Tony, 13
Bentley, G.E., 55
Berger, Harry, 73, 142 n11
Bergman, Ingmar, 63, 141 ns 5, 6
Bergonzi, Bernard, 138 n4
Berry, Philippa, 84
Betterton, Thomas, 138 n2
Billington, Sandra, 41–2, 140 n6
Blackstone, Mary A., 136
Bond, Edward, 71–2

Boose, Lynda E., 85, 143 n6
Bowie, Malcolm, 113, 119, 121, 123, 126
Bradbrook, M.C., 59–60
Bradley, A.C., 1, 17, 92
Bradley, David, 142 n15
Branagh, Kenneth, 81–2
Brecht, Bertold, 81, 136
Brenton, Howard, 72
Bristol, Michael, 25
Brown, John Russell, 66–70, 136
Browne, Ned, 26–8, 35, 37–8, 42, 51
Burgass, Catherine, 138 n6
Burnett, Mark Thornton, 24, 47–8, 134, 140 n5
Burton, Richard, 14
Byron, George Gordon, Lord, 3

Carlson, Marvin, 142 n10
carnival, 26
Charney, Maurice, 68
Chekhov, Anton, 58
Chodorow, Nancy, 90
Clayton, Thomas, 142 n21
Cloud, Random, 142 n21
Coleridge, Samuel Taylor, 8–9, 71
Condell, Henry, 16, 75

Congreve, William, 81
Conklin, Paul S., 3
Cook, Ann Jennalic, 139 n10
Corfield, Penelope J.,141 n11
Crane, Ralph, 74
Cushing, Mary Gertrude, 144 n1

Davenant, Sir William, 64–5, 138 n2
Davidson, Ellis, 29
Dawson, Anthony B., 142 n10
Dessen, Alan, 136
Dillane, Stephen, 82
Dillon, Janette, 79, 131, 140 n19, 142 n21
Dinnerstein, Dorothy, 90
Dollimore, Jonathan, 5
Doty, William C., 141 n10
Douglas, Mary, 140 n1
Drakakis, John, 5, 94
Dusinberre, Juliet, 100
Dutton, Richard, 16, 138 n4
Dynes, William R., 141 n12

Eagleton, Terry, 141 n2
Eaton, Sarah, 101, 103, 144 n8
Edwards, Philip, 20–1, 76, 128, 131
Elam, Keir, 139 n12
Eliot, T.S., 1, 94–8, 105–6, 133, 137, 138 n1
Elizabeth I, 46–7, 101–2, 104, 128
Elsky, Martin, 24
Empson, William, 142 n18
Erickson, Peter, 84
Essex, Earl of, 128
Evans, Colin, 138 n4
Evelyn, John, 2, 138 n2
Eyre, Richard, 139 n17

feminism, 83–107
Fetterley, Judith, 143 n3
Fineman, Joel, 33
Fletcher, John, 73
Foakes, R.A., 3, 5–7, 20
Foucault, Michel, 112
French, Marilyn, 86
Freud, Sigmund, 97, 108–11, 113–14, 118, 122, 127, 130, 132, 143 n5
Frye, Northrop, 135

Furness, Horace Howard, 15, 66
Fuss, Diana, 86, 143 n1

Garrick, David, 64–6, 81
Gellner, Ernest, 111
Gibson, Mel, 3
Gielgud, John, 14
Gorfain, Phyllis, 39, 50
Grady, Hugh, 4, 142 n16
Grant, Richard E., 4
Gray, H.D., 20
Grazia, Margreta de, 75–6, 139 n13, 142 n16
Greenblatt, Stephen, 61
Greene, Robert, 26–8
Greer, Germaine, 143 n3
Grimal, Pierre, 141 n10
Grosz, Elizabeth, 123
Guiness, Peter, 22
Gurr, Andrew, 42, 55, 136

Hall, Peter, 82, 139 n17
Halliwell-Phillips, J.O., 23
Harman, Thomas, 43
Hartman, Geoffrey, 5
Hawkes, Terence, 13–15, 77
Hazlitt, William, 128
Helms, Lorraine, 84
Heminges, John, 16, 75
Henslowe, Philip, 73
heteroglossia, 26
Hibbard, G.R., 1–2, 15, 17, 19–20, 66–8, 78, 82, 139 n16, 142 ns 9, 22
Hillman, Richard, 140 ns 7,9
Hodgdon, Barbara, 142 n11
Holderness, Graham, 4, 20, 59, 140 n19, 141 n1, 142 n21
Holland, Peter, 55–6, 134, 141 n3, 142 ns 20, 23
Holstein, Michael D., 34
Honigmann, E.A.J., 67
Houlbrooke, Ralph, 141 n11
Howard-Hill, T.H., 142 n17
Howell, James, 103
Hulbert, James, 144 n2
Humphreys, Arthur, 122
Hynes, William J., 29–30
Hytner, Nicholas, 82

Ibsen, Henrik, 58
Irigaray, Luce, 83–4
Isler, Alan, 4
Issacharoff, Michael, 142 n10

Jardine, Lisa, 84–7, 91
Jenkins, Harold, 15, 19, 66, 68, 73, 118
Johnson, Samuel, 15, 64, 133
Jones, Ernest, 4, 98, 139 n10
Jones, Robin F., 142 n10
Jonson, Ben, 15–16, 18, 74, 77, 81
Jung, C.G., 140 n1

Kahn, Coppélia, 99
Keene, Derek, 141 n11
Keene, Donald, 78
Kerrigan, William, 5–6, 8, 20
Kozintsev, Grigori, 88
Kyd, Thomas, 9, 74, 139 n8

Lacan, Jacques, 108–32, 134
Landry, Donna, 143 n1
Laroque, François, 41
Loughrey, Brian, 20, 22, 139 n11, 140
    n19, 142 ns 21,23
Louis, Cameron, 136
Lukacher, Ned, 119, 124
Lyly, John, 49
Lyubimov, Yuri, 17, 139 n18

MacCabe, Colin, 109
Macey, David, 112, 119
McGann, Jerome, 15, 56
Macintyre, Alasdair, 111, 132
Maclean, Gerald, 143 n1
Maclean, Ian, 24–5
McLuskie, Kate, 85
Malone, Edmond, 15
Manning, John, 140 n2
Marlow, Christopher, 47, 77
Mehl, Dieter, 67–9
Middleton, Thomas, 9
Millett, Kate, 143 n3
Milne, Drew, 141 n1
Mitchell, Juliet, 143 n5
Modleski, Tania, 86, 143 n1
Mullaney, Stephen, 25

Nardo, Anna K., 40, 140 n3

Neely, Carol Thomas, 99, 132
Nemirovitch-Danchenko, Vladimir, 58
Nevo, Ruth, 110–11
new historicism, 53–4
Noble, Adrian, 82, 139 n17
Nuttall, A.D., 134–5

O'Connor, Alan, 57, 59, 141 n2
Olivier, Laurence, 13, 82, 88–9, 121–2
Orgel, Stephen, 56, 64, 77, 123
Orrom, Michael, 61
Osovsky, Gilbert, 30
O'Toole, John, 56
Ouditt, Sharon, 83–4, 134

Parker, Patricia, 5
Partridge, Eric, 122
Pavis, Patrice, 142 ns 10,12
Pelton, Robert D., 30, 33, 38, 140 n1
Pepys, Samuel, 138 n2
performance study, 55–82, 126–7, 131–2
Poel, William, 21
Pope, Alexander, 15
Prior, Mary, 141 n11
psychoanalytic criticism, 106–32
Pye, Christopher, 124

Quin, James, 64

Radin, Paul, 29, 33–5, 38, 43, 140 ns 1, 2
Ramsey, Margaret, 72
Richardson, Tony, 88
Rid, Samuel, 43
Roach, Joseph R., 126
Robinson, Bruce, 3
Rose, Jacqueline, 87, 94–9, 105–6, 143
    n5
Rosenberg, Marvin, 2, 21, 67
Roudinesco, Elizabeth, 112
Rowe, Nicholas, 66
Rubinstein, Frankie, 122
Ruddick, Sarah, 90
Rushdie, Salman, 4

Sartre, Jean-Paul, 116
Saunders, J.W., 136
Saussure, Ferdinand de, 109
Schlegel, Friedrich, 2–3
Scott, James C., 30–1, 38–9, 54

Shakespeare, William
  Antony and Cleopatra, 16, 60
  As You Like It, 16
  Henry VIII, 73
  Julius Caesar, 129
  Love's Labour's Lost, 120, 136
  Macbeth, 16, 64–7
  Merchant of Venice, The, 137
  Merry Wives of Windsor, The, 139
    n9
  Midsummer Night's Dream, A, 137
  Pericles, 110
  Richard II, 16, 19
  Richard III, 115
  Romeo and Juliet, 16, 139 n17
  Taming of the Shrew, The, 140 n4
  Twelfth Night, 137
  Two Noble Kinsmen, The, 73
Shaw, George Bernard, 80
Showalter, Elaine, 83–5, 88, 90–1, 127,
  143 n2
Shrimpton, Nicholas, 142 n23
Sinfield, Alan, 5
Smith, Peter, 134
Smith, Rebecca, 87–94, 104–5
Somerset, Anne, 128
Sophocles, 114
Spender, Dale, 90
Spinks, C.W., 33, 140 n1
Stallybrass, Peter, 142, n16
Stanislavsky, Konstantin, 58
Stone, Lawrence, 84
Stoppard, Tom, 3
Street, Brian V., 30–1, 35–6
Swetnam, Joseph, 48

Tarlton, Richard, 40, 140 n6

Taylor, Gary, 21, 66, 68, 74–6, 78, 82,
  142 n14, 143 n24
Theobald, Lewis, 15, 64
Thomson, Peter, 136
Tourneur, Cyril, 9
Tourneur, Pierre le, 144 n1

Urkowitz, Stephen, 142 n21

Vickers, Brian, 6–7, 111, 136–7
Volshinov, V.N., 111
Voltaire, Arouet, François-Marie, 2

Waldock, A.J.A., 3
Wallis, Mick, 57, 59
Walters, Sam, 22
Warburton, William, 64
Warren, John, 46
Waswo, Richard, 24, 51
Wayne, Valerie, 99, 105
Webster, John, 77, 104
Weitz, Morris, 3
Wells, Stanley, 21, 66, 68, 78, 82, 138
  n3, 142 n14
Wheale, Nigel, 134
Williams, Gordon, 11
Williams, Raymond, 56–64
Wilson, J. Dover, 1, 76
Wilson, Richard, 138 n4
Wind, Edgar, 129–30
Winnicott, D.W., 98
Wood, Nigel, 138 n7
Woolf, Virginia, 106, 143 n6
Worthen, W.B., 142 n10
Wrightson, Keith, 49

Zeffirelli, Franco, 3, 13